OXFORD WORLD'S CLASSICS

THE COMPLEAT ANGLER

IZAAK WALTON (1593–1683), ironmonger, biographer, and angler, was born at Stafford, lived much of his life in London (where he was a parishioner of John Donne) but spent the last twenty years at Winchester, where he is buried in the cathedral. In his *Lives*, as in *The Compleat Angler*, Walton shows his concern with the contemplative rather than the active life, and chooses to show his subjects striving, in their differing ways, to lead the Christian life. Fishing was 'allowed to Clergymen, as being . . . a recreation that invites them to contemplation and quietness', something which in the turmoil of the middle years of the seventeenth century Walton, like Marvell, must have found as hard to achieve as it was desirable. He was well-read, with a taste that he was not ashamed to admit old-fashioned, and in the year of his death he edited a poem which must have been written in his youth, by a connection of his second wife, John Chalkhill.

CHARLES COTTON (1630–87), country gentleman, poet, and translator of Montaigne, was born at Beresford Hall, Derbyshire, by the River Dove, where he built the Fishing House for himself and Walton. Author of *The Compleat Gamester*, 1674, and *The Planter's Manual*, 1675; in 1676, at Walton's invitation, he added the second part to *The Compleat Angler*.

JOHN BUXTON, Reader Emeritus in English Literature at Oxford and for more than thirty years Fellow of New College, has edited *Poems* of Charles Cotton, 1958. Among his books are *Elizabethan Taste*, 1963, *A Tradition of Poetry*, 1967 (including an essay on Cotton), and works on the countryside. He is General Editor, with Norman Davis, of the *Oxford History of English Literature*.

JOHN BUCHAN (1875–1940), first Baron Tweedsmuir, was born in Perth and educated at Glasgow and Oxford Universities. Statesman, biographer, and novelist he is best known for his adventure stories, which include *Prester John*, 1910, *The Thirty-Nine Steps*, 1915, and *Huntingtower*, 1922.

OXFORD WORLD'S CLASSICS

*For almost 100 years Oxford World's Classics have brought
readers closer to the world's great literature. Now with over 700
titles—from the 4,000-year-old myths of Mesopotamia to the
twentieth century's greatest novels—the series makes available
lesser-known as well as celebrated writing.*

*The pocket-sized hardbacks of the early years contained
introductions by Virginia Woolf, T. S. Eliot, Graham Greene,
and other literary figures which enriched the experience of reading.
Today the series is recognized for its fine scholarship and
reliability in texts that span world literature, drama and poetry,
religion, philosophy and politics. Each edition includes perceptive
commentary and essential background information to meet the
changing needs of readers.*

OXFORD WORLD'S CLASSICS

IZAAK WALTON AND
CHARLES COTTON

The Compleat Angler

Edited with Notes by
JOHN BUXTON

With an Introduction by
JOHN BUCHAN

OXFORD
UNIVERSITY PRESS

OXFORD
UNIVERSITY PRESS

Great Clarendon Street, Oxford OX2 6DP

Oxford University Press is a department of the University of Oxford.
It furthers the University's objective of excellence in research, scholarship,
and education by publishing worldwide in

Oxford New York

Athens Auckland Bangkok Bogotá Buenos Aires Calcutta
Cape Town Chennai Dar es Salaam Delhi Florence Hong Kong Istanbul
Karachi Kuala Lumpur Madrid Melbourne Mexico City Mumbai
Nairobi Paris São Paulo Shanghai Singapore Taipei Tokyo Toronto Warsaw

with associated companies in Berlin Ibadan

Oxford is a registered trade mark of Oxford University Press
in the UK and in certain other countries

Published in the United States
by Oxford University Press Inc., New York

First published by Oxford University Press 1935
First issued, with new editorial matter, as a World's Classics paperback 1982
Reissued as an Oxford World's Classics paperback 2000

British Library Cataloguing in Publication Data

Data available

Library of Congress Cataloging in Publication Data

Walton, Izaak, 1593–1683.
The Compleat angler.—(Oxford world's classics)
1. Fishing—Early works to 1800.
I. Cotton, Charles, 1630–1687. II. Buxton, John.
III. Title. SH433.A1982 999.1'2
81–16984AACR2

ISBN 0–19–283786–9

1 3 5 7 9 10 8 6 4 2

Printed in Great Britain by
Cox & Wyman Ltd.
Reading, Berkshire

CONTENTS

INTRODUCTION

I

IZAAK WALTON

IZAAK WALTON was born in the parish of St. Mary, at Stafford, on August 9th, 1593, apparently at a small house in the East Gate Street of the town. His father was a certain Jervis Walton, who, according to Sir Harris Nicolas, was the son of one George Walton, bailiff, of Yoxall, who claimed kin with the Waltons of Hanbury. The boy was in all likelihood sent to the Grammar School of Stafford, where he was taught the rudiments of a sound, if unconventional, education.

The early life of the young Walton has been made the subject of curious speculation and much cumbrous ingenuity. Sir Harris Nicolas discovered that he was bound apprentice to a certain kinsman, Henry Walton, a Whitechapel haberdasher; and the will of Samuel Walton of St. Mary's Cray in Kent proves the existence of this haberdasher, though it does not prove any connexion with the young Izaak. The only ascertained facts are that on November 12th, 1618, Walton, described as 'late apprentice to Mr. Thomas Grinsell', was made a member of the Ironmongers' Company; and that in his marriage licence with Rachel Floud, dated December 27th, 1626, he is described as of the 'Citie of London, Ironmonger'. So it would seem that the 'linen-draper in Fleet Street' theory must be relinquished, a thing bitter to the mind of the connoisseur in picturesque trades.

His first dwellings, if we may trust Sir John Hawkins and the parish books of St. Dunstan's, were in Fleet Street and in Chancery Lane, 'about the seventh house on the left-hand side'. He filled all the ordinary municipal offices as constable, juryman, grand-juryman, sidesman, and vestryman. He seems to have prospered in his trade, and to have speedily become a man of some social consequence. His marriage with Rachel Floud allied him with the episcopal family of the Cranmers, and we find him early in life an intimate friend of Dr. John Donne, John Hales of Eton, Dr. Henry King, and 'that under-valuer of money, Sir Henry Wotton'. On the 10th of July 1640, his wife died, and six years later he took as his second wife a Somersetshire lady, Anne Ken, a half-sister of the famous Bishop. She bore him one daughter and two sons, and, dying in 1662, was buried in Worcester Cathedral, where her husband's quaint and beautiful epitaph still preserves her memory.

In all the troubled years between 1644 and the Restoration, Walton seems to have remained in London, except for such occasional visits to the country as he could snatch from a busy life. In 1651 we find the peaceful and meditative angler engaged in an incursion into high politics. One of the King's jewels, known as the 'lesser George', was saved from Cromwell's hands by a certain Colonel Blague, who passed it from Mr. George Barlow to Mr. Robert Milward and thence into the 'trusty hands of Mr. Izaak Walton'. Blague meanwhile lay prisoner in the Tower, but on his escape he received the jewel and conveyed it safe to the King's hands. Clearly Walton was known as a staunch loyalist, and, clearly, too, he was still in favour with the other side; in all ages it is the quiet, unpractical men who are the points of contact between parties.

From 1650 to 1661 Walton seems to have lived in Clerkenwell, but in December of 1662 he obtained from Gilbert Sheldon, Bishop of London, a forty years' lease of a new building, adjoining the house called the 'Cross Keys' in Paternoster Row. The house was burnt down in the Great Fire, but already Walton seems to have begun that life of visiting which characterized his last years, 'mostly in the families of the eminent clergymen of England, of whom he was much beloved'. He had apartments reserved for him in the houses of Dr. Morley, Bishop of Winchester, and Dr. Ward, Bishop of Salisbury. He spent the Christmas of 1678 at Farnham Castle, and it was under Morley's roof at Chelsea that in all likelihood several of the 'Lives' were written. In 1683 we find him again at Farnham, and on August 9th of the same year, being ninety years of age, he made his will. The document shows him a man of considerable property, with a wide circle of friends, a true bookman bequeathing his treasures considerately. On the 15th of December in the same year he died at the Prebendal House of his son-in-law, Dr. Hawkins. He is buried in the Cathedral, in a place in the south transept called Prior Silkstead's Chapel, and a large marble slab in the floor bears his epitaph.

Few long lives have been so free from conspicuous misfortune. He had sorrow in his own family, and to one of his peculiar temperament the Royalist reverses must have come as real afflictions. But in the main he lived his easy life of books and angling undisturbed. He attained to considerable prosperity. A humble tradesman at the start, he seems to have climbed to

the circle of gentle birth, and in a decree of the Court
of Judicature in 1670 he is described as 'Izaak Walton,
gentleman'. His friends were in the main of one
ecclesiastical and political party, and one mental type.
Leigh Hunt in a famous essay has analysed this
quietistic temperament with a somewhat unusual
acuteness; but it is wiser to grant its charm, while
we admit its limitations. The strong rude wind of
the outer world rarely disturbed those peaceful dove-
cots; gentle meditation, mild and sincere devotion,
innocent pleasures—such was the order of their days.
Hence the 'Lives' are models of perfect biography.
Herbert, Donne, Hooker, Sanderson, all with this
old-world, Jacobean flavour, churchmen all, members of the church quiescent, devout, learned, each
with a quaint turn of wit, they lived and died as
cloistered in their virtues as any Trappist; and if
Mr. Donne in his hot youth lost his heart and loved
like a Cavalier, why, it is the part of his biographer
to justify and pardon. It is rarely that we find a man
so well agreed with his intimates, so whole-heartedly
in love with his friends. Such intimacies Walton
found early in life, and in all the days of storm they
were never broken. A man of letters pure and simple,
the main incidents in his career are the dates of his
book, and any attempt at biography is a monotonous
chronicle.

CHARLES COTTON

Into the circle of gentle quietists Cotton comes
like a swashbuckling and adventurous Cavalier into
a Quaker's meeting. At first, we confess, the conjunction of Walton and Cotton is a thing to surprise.
A bold and taking gentleman, who wrote not always

for edification, the scion of a great house, the intimate
of Somers, full of the traditions which produced a
Suckling, a Lovelace, a Claverhouse, and a Montrose,
he seems a little out of place in an atmosphere of
pious and lettered middle age. It is not till we find
in the Derbyshire squire a genuine honesty of heart,
a love of books, and some considerable talent of his
own, and in the London citizen some feeling for other
sport than that of drowsy meadows, that the contra-
diction is solved. It is probable too, that, as Lowell
hinted, Walton, like Johnson, dearly loved a gentleman of blood; more, Cotton was the soundest of
churchmen and royalists, and the owner of good
trouting water; and, above all, he had known his
father. But the paradox of this conjunction has given
a chance for many homilies; and a certain exquisite
and maidenly editor has hoped 'that Walton's serious
occupations and intercourse with pious men of learning kept him happily away from companions where
loose writings would be named, and that, ignorant of
Cotton's vicious folly, he judged him rather by the
truly beautiful sentiments breathed through the
"Stanzes Irreguliers"'.

Clarendon has drawn the elder Cotton in his
stately manner. 'He had all those qualities which in
youth raise men to the reputation of being fine
gentlemen; such a pleasantness and gaiety of humour,
such a sweetness and gentleness of nature, and such
a civility and delightfulness in conversation, that no
man, in court or out of it, appeared a more accom-
plished person; all these extraordinary qualifications
being supported by as extraordinary a clearness of
courage and fearlessness of spirit, of which he gave
too often manifestation.' He was a friend of Herrick,

Carew, Lovelace, Selden, and Davenant, and by his
marriage with Olive Stanhope allied himself with the
old Derbyshire houses of Cockayne, Port, and Stanhope. It is probable, though we have no proof, that
the young Cotton went, like his father, to Cambridge,
and left without a degree. At some time in his life
he must have been a hard student, for besides considerable classical attainments he had a most unusual
acquaintance with French and Italian. He married in
1656 his cousin Isabella, daughter of Sir Thomas
Hutchinson of Owthorp, and the following year Sir
Peter Lely in his famous portrait set down the dress
and features of this young gentleman of twenty-
seven. He is in armour, with a full-bottomed wig
falling down to his steel cuirass, and a white cravat
at his throat, a handsome open-air young man, with
very honest eyes. In 1658 his father died, and he
succeeded to his estates—an impoverished heritage
it would appear, for he had twice to petition Parliament to break the entail in part, and current scandal
shows him often in hiding from his creditors. His
sole occupation was literature and the care of his
land, and he seems to have made his Dovedale abode
at once a quiet country retreat for himself and a
hospitable house for his friends. 'The pleasantness
of the river, mountains, and meadows about it,' says
Walton with grateful recollections, 'cannot be described, unless Sir Philip Sidney and Mr. Cotton's
father were alive to do it again.'

In 1675 he married a second time, his second wife
being Mary, daughter of Sir William Russell, and
widow of the Earl of Ardglass. The lady survived
him, for he died of a fever some time in the February
of 1687, only four years after the death of Walton.

His son, Beresford Cotton, seems to have espoused the Whig cause, for we find him commanding a company in a regiment of foot raised by the Earl of Derby for the service of King William.

II

The bibliography of Walton is the true form which the chronicle of his life should take, and no author has been more fortunate in his pious bibliographers. Thomas Westwood in his *Chronicle of the Compleat Angler* has provided all that one can need, and Mr. R. B. Marston has made an enthusiastic study of angling literature. The first edition was published in 1653, in the most troubled years of the early Commonwealth. Its full title was *The Compleat Angler, or the Contemplative Man's Recreation: Being a Discourse of Fish and Fishing not unworthy the perusal of most anglers: "Simon Peter said, 'I go a-fishing;' and they said, 'We also will go with thee.' "—* John xxi. 3. (*London: Printed by T. Maxey, for Rich. Marriot, in St. Dunstan's Churchyard, Fleet Street,* 1653.) The name of the author does not occur on the title-page, but in *The Perfect Diurnall* (Monday, May 9th to Monday, May 16th, 1653) we find the following advertisement:

'*The Compleat Angler, or the Contemplative Man's Recreation, being a discourse of Fish and Fishing, not unworthy the perusal of most Anglers, of* 18 *pence price. Written by Iz. Wa. Also the known Play of the Spanish Gipsie, never till now published: Both printed for Richard Marriot, to be sold at his shop in Saint Dunstan's Churchyard, Fleet Street.*' Of this first edition the earliest printed copies contain a small printer's error—*contention* for *contentment*—in the last line but one of the *Farewell to the Vanities of the World* ascribed to Dr. Donne. The second edition, which is if possible a greater rarity, appeared two years later, in 1655. This is practically the first edition of the book as we know it. The work was all but re-written, its size was increased by more than one-third, and the interlocutors, who were formerly two (Piscator and Viator) are now three—Piscator, Venator, and Auceps. The erring Viator appears to our joy in the Second Part. The book was garnished with fine illustrations, and Mr. Marston has shown good reason for believing that the engravings were copied from the revised and enlarged German trans-lation by Dr. Conrad Forer of Gesner's great work, *Latein erstmals beschrichen*, printed at Frankfort in 1598. The third edition was issued in 1661, but before many copies had been sold the sale of the book was transferred from Richard Marriot to Simon Gape (near the Inner Temple Gate in Fleet Street), by whom the remainder of the impression was sent forth, with a fresh title-page, dated 1664. In this edition the chapter on the Laws of Angling appears for the first time. The fourth edition, which is a mere reprint of the second, was printed by R. Marriot in 1668. The last edition published in Walton's life-time was the fifth edition of 1676. Sir Harris Nicolas falls foul of the changes made in this edition: 'the garrulity and sentiments', he says, 'of an octogenarian are very apparent, and the subdued colouring of religious feeling . . . is so much heightened as to become almost obtrusive.' Here Charles Cotton's 'Instructions How to Angle for a Trout or Grayling in a Clear Stream' appear for the first time. To certain copies of this edition there was also added

Colonel Richard Venables's *The Experienc'd Angler, or Angling Improved*; and in a letter to the author, who was a distinguished Parliamentarian soldier and Commander-in-Chief of the Ulster Forces, Walton declares 'since my reading of thy book, I cannot look upon some notes of my own gathering, but methinks I do *puerilia tractare*'. When the third part was included the book was called *The Universal Angler*, but Venables's contribution dropped out in later editions.

In 1750, 1759, and 1772, Moses Browne, on the advice of Dr. Johnson, published three editions of the *Angler*. Browne takes scandalous liberties with the text, and in general represents the worst editorial tradition. Sir John Hawkins in 1760 prepared a much more valuable reprint. His edition is still the main fount of our biographical material as far as the authors are concerned, for he drew upon the researches of the famous antiquarian Oldys, the Norroy King-of-Arms. The editions of John Major in 1823 and 1824 are models of workmanship, but otherwise unimportant. But the great edition was that of Sir Harris Nicolas, which appeared in two imperial volumes in 1836, a book handsome in appearance and full of the results of the patient labour of years. Dr. Bethune's American edition is learned, dull, and marred by a consistent priggishness, but it is of great value to the student of Walton and the lover of fair books; while Mr. R. B. Marston's 'Lea and Dove' edition of 1888 is one of the most genuinely attractive ever issued. Of smaller reprints and foreign translations it is needless to speak; but Mr. John Lane's edition of 1897 deserves mention, if only for the beauty of Mr. E. H. New's illustrations.

The other literary works of Walton may be briefly noticed. They consist of his famous *Lives*, and a few poems, prefaces, and letters. He edited and prefaced with an elegy of his own the 1633 edition of Donne's Poems, and in 1638 he prefixed commendatory verses to *The Merchants' Map of Commerce*. In 1640 he issued a *Life of Dr. Donne* as a preface to a volume of his sermons, a Life which Dr. Johnson thought the best ever written. In 1643 he wrote some lines on the death of his friend William Cartwright, the poet; and in 1646 he seems to have contributed the address 'To the Reader' to Francis Quarles's *Shepherd's Eclogues*. In 1651 he edited the *Reliquiae Wottonianae*, and prefixed his famous Life of the author. In 1652 he seems to have written the usual address to the reader for Sir John Skeffington's *Heroe of Lorenzo*. At the Restoration he showed his joy in 'An humble Eclog, To my Ingenuous Friend, Mr. Browne, on his various and excellent Poems'. In 1665 appeared the *Life of Hooker*, prefaced by a letter from Dr. King, the Bishop of Chichester, in which 'Honest Izaak' is first used of the author. In 1670 appeared the *Life of Mr. George Herbert*, to my mind the finest of the five. The *Life of Robert Sanderson, Bishop of Lincoln*, was published in 1678, written when Walton was already far on in the vale of years. ' 'Tis now too late to wish that my life may be like his; for I am in the eighty-fifth year of my age; but I humbly beseech Almighty God that my death may; and do as earnestly beg of every reader to say Amen.' He may have written the pamphlet called 'Love and Truth', published in 1680, but many of the chief Waltonian experts have decided against his authorship. In 1683 appeared *Thealma*

*and Clearchus, a Pastoral History, in smooth and easie
verse,* written long ago, so Walton says, by 'John
Chalkhill, Esq., an Acquaint and Friend of Edmund
Spenser'. Many will have it that this 'Jo. Chalkhill'
is a fiction, and that Walton really wrote the verses,
or, at least, as Mr. Lowell maintains, 'tinkered his
friend's composition'.

In his own day, and in later times, Walton has
been the mark for a eulogy which has scarcely been
given to any other Englishman short of the very
greatest. To Drayton he was his 'honest old friend'.
To Cotton he was a 'second father', a master in
angling:

> But, my dear friend, 'tis so, that you and I,
> By a condition of mortality,
> With all this great, and more proud world, must die.

> In which estate, I ask no more of fame,
> Nor other monument of honour's claim,
> Than that of your true friend to advance my name.

Of numerous poetical epistles addressed to Walton,
we may notice the verses to 'Iz. Wa.' published as
early as 1619 in the *Love of Amos and Laura, by S. P.*,
which some have attributed to Samuel Purchas, the
author of *The Pilgrimage*. Indeed in his own day the
single dissentient voice in the chorus of praise was
that of Richard Franck, the Cromwellian soldier, who,
having a taste for rough and moorland waters, had
little patience with Walton's gentle pastoral. In the
next century Johnson led the way in appreciation by
saying that 'he considered the preservation and
elucidation of Walton a pious work'; and he turned
certain of the verses into tolerable Latin. So, too,
Charles Lamb:—'Among all your quaint readings

did you ever light upon Walton's *Compleat Angler*?
. . . it breathes the very spirit of innocence, purity,
and simplicity of heart; . . . it would sweeten a man's
temper at any time to read it.' Sir Walter Scott, in
his edition of Franck, wished that 'Walton, who had
so true an eye for nature . . . had made this northern
tour instead of Franck, and had detailed in the beautiful simplicity of his Arcadian language his observations on the scenery and manners of Scotland'.
Wordsworth has written two sonnets on 'Walton,
sage benign'. To Byron, who was no fisher and not
even a well-wisher, he is merely the 'quaint old cruel
coxcomb'; and to Leigh Hunt, himself the most
effeminate of men, he is something of the old woman.
Among later appreciations we need only mention Mr.
Lang's graceful epistle in the *Letters to Dead Authors*,
and Mr. Lowell's acute and interesting essay.

Cotton's second part, as I have said, was added
to the fifth edition, and ever since the two parts have
been issued together. Cotton's letter, which accom-
panied his work, is as modest as can be. He lays no
claim to the grace and wisdom of his master; but
chance has placed much sport in his way, especially
of the north-country kind, and the reader may find
certain of his hints of use. He is the practical angler,
writing without airs or postures for plain men by
the riverside. His other literary works cover many
fields. He wrote verses with a certain rude vigour
and melody, sometimes attaining to something like
poetry, as in *The Retirement* and *The Contentation*,
and again sinking to sheer doggerel in *The Angler's
Ballad*. In 1649 he wrote an elegy upon the death of
Henry, Lord Hastings; and in 1654, in the spirit of
the true loyalist, he attacked Waller for his panegyric

upon the Protector. He wrote many burlesques, the most notable being *Scarronides or Virgil Travestie* in 1664, a Voyage to Ireland in burlesque in 1671, and the *Burlesque upon Burlesque: or the Scoffer Scoff'd* in 1675. He translated Du Vaix's *Moral Philosophy of the Stoics*, Gerard's *History of the Life of the Duke of Espernon*, Corneille's *Les Horaces*, the *Commentaries of Blaise de Montluc, Marshal of France*, the *Fair One of Tunis*, a novel from the French, the *Memoirs of the Sieur de Pontis*, and—the work by which he is best known—the *Essays of Montaigne*. In addition he wrote a *Planter's Manual*, and he may possibly be the author of the *Compleat Gamester*. Cotton has not, like Walton, been the beloved of all later writers; but he has had his share of praise. His cousin, Sir Aston Cockayne, in a dedicatory poem, believes that his 'lines are great and strong, the *nihil ultra* of the English tongue'; and Mr. Lowell, a more unprejudiced witness, declares that 'Cotton was a man of genius, whose life was cleanlier than his muse always cared to be. If he wrote the *Virgil Travestie*, he also wrote verses which the difficult Wordsworth could praise, and a poem of gravely noble mood addressed to Walton on his "Lives", in which he shows a knowledge of what goodness is that no bad man could have acquired. Let one line of it at least shine in my page, not as a sample, but for its own dear sake—

For in a virtuous act all good men share.'

III

The *Angler* has been so praised for centuries that a modern writer must refrain from eulogy and seek

only the bare phrases of justice. It is worth noting
that the book is in its purpose a treatise or practical
guide, and not an idyll; and it is on such an avowed
purpose that Franck made his criticisms. To us of
to-day the quaint learning from Gesner and Dubravius and the 'divine Du Bartas', the fantastic speculation, the equally fantastic piety, have the charm of
echoes from an elder world. But it is easy to look
on the work merely as a quaint medley, and forget
that in its own day it was a most valuable treatise on
the practice of the art, and that still it is not wholly
superseded. The advocacy of 'fence months', some of
the rules for baits, the whole account of chub-fishing,
the theory of the 'Fordidge Trout', are as modern
as the work of Mr. Stewart. When we turn to Cotton
we find a still more modern exponent. His account
of clear-worm fishing, written two centuries before
Stewart, would be hard to improve on, and his
description of flies for long remained the standard
authority. I confess that I can never judge that second
part of the *Angler* with anything like impartiality.
As a small boy, it was long before I could be made to
read Walton, but I early knew Cotton by heart. The
whole atmosphere, the swift bright waters, the hills,
the northern air, came more kindly to the fancy of
one who knew of coarse fish only by hearsay, and
of chalk-stream trout not at all.

I am not sure if Walton ever deserved the fine
name of sportsman in its truer sense. The adventurous Franck assuredly deserved it, with his journey
to the wild dark lochs and rivers of Scotland, and his
fishings in the 'glittering and resolute streams of
Tweed'. Cotton, with his love of hills and wild
waters, may claim it; but a name which implies a

joy in fierce activity, an adventurous love of peril, a glory in hardship and excitement, is out of place in connexion with the idyllic angler who loved to fish quietly by 'lilied lowland waters'. Walton, indeed, marks the beginning of true angling literature, for he was the first to give the sport a halo of letters which it has never lost. With all his modest intention he is a past master of the little country idyll. Cotton can sketch you a fine scene, and tell of the cooking of the trout with gusto, but it is Walton who draws the unforgettable pictures of riverside inns, of gipsy singing and milkmaids' choruses. The pastoral drama, really a lost art since Theocritus, in spite of Roman, Italian, and Elizabethan revivals, is here restored in all its fresh and courtly grace. It is this which has made the book immortal, for while Maudlin and Coridon sing their catches in the meadow the world will always have ears for their singing.

The mere tricks of writing are a perpetual joy to the lover of crisp English. The style is constantly praised for its naïve simplicity, but this gift of limpid speech may mean a painful and conscious art. In a sentence in the *Life of Herbert* he says beautifully of Donne's hymns, 'These hymns are now lost to us; but doubtless they were such as they two now sing in Heaven.' Yet in his copy of Eusebius, preserved at Salisbury, Walton has written down three attempts at this sentence, each much inferior to the present form. But whatever the means employed, the result remains a model of ease and charm. At its worst it is monotonous, the sentence falling away into shapelessness and a flat and ugly close. At its best, perhaps, it never rises to that strength of eloquence, that far-away, haunting beauty to which the best passages in Bunyan (an author in the same class) attain. Mr. Lowell has noted two aspects of the writing which go to constitute its charm. One is that he seems always to speak with the living voice, and it is the living voice that is wanted in a country book. 'This sweet persuasiveness of the naturally-cadenced voice is never wanting in Walton. It is indeed his distinction, and a very rare quality in writers, upon most of whom, if they ever happily forget themselves and fall into the tone of talk, the pen too soon comes sputtering in.' Again, he finds in Walton's failure in poetry, and his honest love for the art, some of the secrets of his prose—the deftness of phrase, the use of mellifluous words, the pleasant cadence of the sentences. 'I think', he says, 'that Walton's prose owes much of its charm to the poetic sentiment in him which was denied a refuge in verse, and that his practice in metres may have given to his happier periods a measure and a music they would otherwise have wanted.'

But the real value of the *Angler* seems to me to be not as an exercise in clear English, nor as a text-book to a great sport, but to lie in the something which the book contains beyond this obvious purpose. It is a transcript of old English country life, a study of the folk-heart, and two books only that I know can compare with it. One is Gilbert White's *Selborne*, a book done without art and in the most pedestrian manner, but a classic by virtue of its love for the open world and its genius for observation. The other is the *Pilgrim's Progress*, the text-book of a very grave and noble creed, and yet none the less an idyll of an elder English world. One cannot compare Walton and Bunyan, the gentle quietist with his ecclesiastical friends and his reverence for the powers that be, and the strong peasant with the world-sickness in his soul and the kingdom of God ever building itself in delectable fancies in his brain. Yet in Bunyan the scenery throughout is Bedfordshire, the 'delicate plain called Ease' is one of the Ouse meadows, the men are the peasants of an English country town, and the manner has the straightforward vigour, the tender kindliness, the graceful simplicity, which still delight the world in the *Angler*.

But more, the *Angler* is the study of one type, and that type is in large measure its creation. It unfolds the heart and soul of the angler—not necessarily the sportsman, but the *angler*—a man who loves books as well as his art, who sees nature through the glass of culture, the townsman and the gentleman. In the next century we witness the degradation of the type, when the fisherman is part of the poetic properties of a landscape, an absurd masquerading figure, as in Gay. And in later times the type has tended to merge in the sportsman, or be debased into the literary humbug who talks cant about nature and bespatters the noblest of subjects with his vulgar praise. In the age of Walton it was still possible to find it pure, and in all times there have been the few who could unite sport and culture. Your good sportsman may be often an idler; but the good angler, who loves the country with a more intimate affection, is frequently the hard-worked and capable man of the world, who, in using the talents which God gave him, has still room for other interests in his soul. No book on angling since Walton has so delighted us as Sir Edward Grey's volume on *Fly-fishing*, because in it the true angler's attitude to the world is most clearly portrayed. To men with some heritage of gipsy blood, life must be a dull business if it is confined to urban streets and the routine of affairs; yet to a man, given brain and will, there is his work before him which he cannot shirk. Hence comes the angler —the sportsman, I love to think, who can feel all the old primeval excitement of his sport, and yet the man of culture to whom nature is more than a chalk-stream or a salmon-river, who has ears for Coridon's song as well as the plash of trout below the willows.

JOHN BUCHAN.

EDITOR'S FOREWORD

The Compleat Angler is first of all a book of instruction about how to catch and cook fish, and the condition of most surviving copies of the early editions shows that it was so used. They look as if they had spent some time in a fisherman's creel along with his sandwiches and his bait, if not with his catch. The form of the title was suggested by Henry Peacham's *The Compleat Gentleman*, 1622, and suited a practical manual. But Walton knew that his book had another interest: he gave it the subtitle, *The Contemplative Man's Recreation*, and thereby claimed for it a place in the pastoral tradition. And indeed it is *The Contemplative Man's Recreation* rather than *The Compleat Angler* that has claims to be, as the most often reprinted book in the language (after the Bible and the Book of Common Prayer), the best loved and most popular book we have.

In his opening chapter Walton refers to the debate that 'hath risen . . . whether the happiness of man in this world doth consist more in contemplation or action'. When he wrote he had lived through years of civil strife during which he had observed the misery imposed by men dedicated to the active life, which had culminated in the martyrdom of King Charles and the setting up of the Puritan Commonwealth. His book was presumably completed by the early months of 1650 when Thomas Weaver and Edward Powel wrote their verses of commendation, though it was not published until 1653. Now this

debate between the life of action and the life of contemplation is represented in the division of literature
into the heroic and pastoral modes which was
generally accepted in Walton's time. Sir Francis
Bacon, whose work Walton often quotes, had defined
the two complementary modes with characteristic
precision by means of a reference to the story of Cain
and Abel. In this, he said, 'we see an image of the
two estates, the contemplative state and the active
state, figured . . . in the two simplest and most
primitive trades of life; that of the shepherd,
(who . . . is a lively image of a contemplative life,)
and that of the husbandman: where we see again the
favour and election of God went to the shepherd.'
The greatest poems of Walton's lifetime, *The Faerie
Queene* and *Paradise Lost*, were heroic poems, but
neither Spenser nor Milton disdained pastoral. And
when Walton was a young man in London, apprenticed to a member of the Ironmongers' Company,
a group of poets who regarded Michael Drayton as
their pattern, and of whom William Browne of
Tavistock was the leader, wrote poetry in the
tradition of pastoral poetry of the 1590s and far
removed from the 'metaphysical' tradition which
was coming into fashion. Walton was a year older
than Browne and, though he knew Donne and was
to write his life, his own taste in poetry was, as his
quotations show, for what he acknowledged to be
'old-fashioned poetry, but choicely good, – I think
much better than the strong lines that are now in
fashion'. 'Strong lines' was the phrase then used for
the poetry of Donne and his followers. Francis
Quarles, another of Walton's generation, used the
phrase in the preface to *Argalus and Parthenia*, 1629

(a versification of an episode in Sidney's *Arcadia* which remained extraordinarily popular for a hundred years), where he said, 'I have not affected to set thy understanding on the rack, by the tyranny of strong lines, which are the mere itch of wit.' Drayton had said much the same and Walton, who called Drayton his 'old friend', would surely have agreed.

Associated with William Browne were other poets: George Wither, William Ferrar (brother of Nicholas, who founded the Anglican community at Little Gidding), and Christopher Brooke. Brooke must have seemed a notable recruit, for he was the friend of Donne who had given away Ann More at their clandestine marriage, and had been imprisoned for his pains. These were the poets who were setting a new trend when Walton was first in London, in his early twenties and at his most impressionable. Wither, who later declined to Puritan propaganda but who in the years 1613–16 was a true poet, wrote dialogue poems in which his friends Browne, Ferrar, and Brooke are interlocutors. Dialogue poems had been part of the pastoral tradition from Theocritus on, and perhaps these were as important in suggesting the dialogue form to Walton as was the recently discovered *The Arte of Angling*, 1577, which Walton had certainly seen.

The Compleat Angler, then, should be considered in the literary context of the revival of pastoral poetry when Walton was young. His taste was for poetry in an older tradition than that which had become fashionable, and his preference was for the pastoral life of contemplation. Fishing was 'allowed to Clergymen, as being . . . a recreation that invites them to contemplation and quietness', in contrast to hunting, which was forbidden them. And he ends his book with a quotation from St. Paul's First Epistle to the Thessalonians: 'Study to be quiet.'

The book has yet another aspect, noted by Walton himself as 'a picture of my own disposition'. Much of its charm certainly derives from this. As we read we find ourselves in the company of a man who loves the English countryside, who is well-read in English poetry, and who is ready to share his skill in the sport for which he has such enthusiasm with anyone who cares to listen. He is not insistent: he never suggests that anyone who does not choose to catch fish is beneath contempt; he knows others may prefer hunting or hawking. But if we care to go with him we shall learn much, not only of fishing, but of the English countryside, and of a countryside which, after three centuries of urban intrusion, seems somewhat idealized. Yet it is still recognizably English even though one meets, without surprise, a shepherd named Coridon who plays his pipes to an English milkmaid and her cousin Betty, for, in spite of Puritans and politics, Arcadia is never far away. So does Walton create for us the image of what we look forward to when we go for a picnic on a fine spring day in the countryside; and that, surely, is the reason for the book's unrivalled charm, for its success with many who have never thought of trying to catch a fish.

Walton was a Royalist, who detested the Puritans – 'Schismaticks' he calls them – and the authors of the verses of commendation suggest a company of like-minded men meeting together in private in London. James Duport was, at the time, Regius Professor of

Greek at Cambridge and 'the main instrument by which literature was upheld' there during the Civil War and Interregnum; later he was Master of Magdalene College. Thomas Weaver, a minor canon of Christ Church, Oxford, published *Songs and Poems of Love and Drollery* in 1654 and found himself arraigned on a capital charge of treason for a ballad called 'Zeal overheated', but he was acquitted. Christopher Harvey was more cautious and waited till the Restoration before publishing anti-Puritan tracts. In such company the young Charles Cotton would have been welcome and at ease.

In 1676 Walton invited Cotton to supplement his book with instructions about fishing for trout and grayling in a clear stream such as the Dove, on whose banks Cotton had his house, Beresford Hall, and where two years before he had built the little Fishing House (which still stands) adorned with their initials in cipher. Cotton was thirty-seven years younger than Walton, a contemporary of Dryden – their first published verses appeared in the same book, *Lachrymae Musarum* (1649) – not of Browne. To him the countryside was not for holidays but for every day, and he had the generous nature to wish to share his pleasure and understanding with others, to advise them on planting and pruning fruit trees, on how to play a variety of games from chess to billiards, from ombre (soon to be exquisitely described by Pope) to cockfighting, and on sports, riding, archery and, of course, the sport which he enjoyed most of all in the beautiful river by which he had the happiness to live. To him the High Peak was not a National Park to be preserved for the recreation of townsmen; it was his home, and he was especially pleased when visitors complimented him on it. He wrote his longest poem on *The Wonders of the Peake*.

He was brought up in a household where books and learning were regarded as being as much a part of a gentleman's inheritance as skill in field sports or an understanding of how to manage an estate. He was an excellent French scholar, and his translation of Montaigne is far closer to the original than Florio's, for Cotton had much more in common with Montaigne than the irascible Italian lexicographer. Among other translations from French was one of Corneille's *Horace*.

He made poetry out of the life of a country gentleman, on easy terms with his servants who 'knew his certain hours', as he said, and would have a meal ready for him when he came in. He would converse with his steward with interest and knowledge,

> Gravely inquiring how ewes are a score,
> How the hay harvest and the corn was got,
> And if or no there's like to be a rot.

He could turn a humorous eye on himself and on the friends whom he delighted to entertain at Beresford Hall. As a poet he has a unique quality which makes him stand apart from all his contemporaries, and prevents comparison with them; but he was much admired by Wordsworth, Coleridge, and Lamb, and still has much to give which we find nowhere else. He said of himself that he was 'an old-fashioned country squire'; the description could not be bettered. And the second part which he added to *The Compleat Angler* supplements but does not distort the book: it is perfectly in harmony but distinct, and adds to the excellence of the whole.

ACKNOWLEDGMENTS

I wish to thank Dr. Jonquil Bevan and Miss Sandra
Raphael for information and advice.

CHRONOLOGY

1593   (9 Aug.) Izaak Walton born, Stafford.

*c.*1611   Walton apprenticed to Thomas Grinsell of the Ironmongers' Company.

1614   Walton in possession of half a shop in Fleet Street.

1618   (12 Nov.) Walton made free of the Ironmongers' Company.

1630   (28 April) Charles Cotton born at Beresford Hall, Derbyshire.

1631   John Donne gives Walton a bloodstone seal.

1633   Walton contributes an Elegy upon the Author to Donne's *Poems.*

1636   (27 Dec.) Walton marries Rachel Floud.

1640   Walton's *Life* prefixed to Donne's *LXXX Sermons.* (2 Aug.) Death of Rachel Walton.

1646   Walton marries Anne Ken, half-sister of Bishop Ken.

1649   (30 Jan.) King Charles executed in Whitehall. Cotton contributes an elegy on Lord Hastings to *Lachrymae Musarum.*

1651   Walton's *Life of Sir Henry Wotton* published in *Reliquiae Wottonianae,* which he edited. After the Battle of Worcester (3 Sept.) Walton is entrusted with the lesser George jewel of King Charles II, which he delivers to Col. Blague in London.

1653   *The Compleat Angler,* first edition published.

1655   *The Compleat Angler,* second edition.

1656   Cotton marries Isabella Hutchinson, sister of

the Col. Hutchinson whose wife wrote the *Memoirs* of his *Life*.

1659 Cotton's elegy on Lovelace printed with *Lucasta*.

1661 *The Compleat Angler*, third edition.

1662 Walton takes up residence in the Bishop's Palace, Winchester, after the death of his second wife.

1664 Cotton's *Scarronides or the First Book of Virgil Travestie* published. (*Fourth Book*, 1665.)

1665 Walton's *Life of Mr. Richard Hooker* published.

1668 *The Compleat Angler*, fourth edition.

*c.*1670 Death of Isabella Cotton.

*c.*1674 Cotton marries Mary (née Russell) widow of the 2nd Earl of Ardglass.

1674 Cotton's *The Compleat Gamester* published. Cotton builds the Fishing House in Beresford Dale.

1675 Walton's *Life of Mr. George Herbert* published. Cotton's *The Planters Manual* published.

1676 Cotton's second part appeared for the first time with the fifth edition of *The Compleat Angler*.

1681 Cotton's *The Wonders of the Peake* published.

1683 Walton edits John Chalkhill's *Thealma and Clearchus*. (Oct.) Walton signs his will and seals it with the seal given him by Donne. (15 Dec.) Walton dies in Winchester and is buried in the cathedral (N. transept) where the black marble ledger carries an inscription by Bishop Ken.

1685 Cotton's translation of Montaigne's *Essays* published.

1687 (Feb.) Charles Cotton dies and is buried at St. James's, Piccadilly.

1689 Cotton's *Poems on several occasions* published.

The Compleat Angler
or the
Contemplative man's
Recreation.

The first part.

PART. I.

BEING A

DISCOURSE

OF

Rivers, Fish-ponds, Fish and Fishing.

Written by *IZAAK WALTON.*

The Fifth Edition much corrected and enlarged.

LONDON,

Printed for *Richard Marriott* . 1676.

FACSIMILE OF THE TITLE-PAGE TO THE FIFTH EDITION OF

PART I, 1676

TO
the Right worshipful
JOHN OFFLEY
OF
Madely Manor in the County of *Stafford*, Esq;

My most honoured Friend.

SIR,

I HAVE made so ill use of your former favours, as by them to be encouraged to intreat that they may be enlarged to the *Patronage* and *protection* of this Book; and I have put on a modest confidence, that I shall not be deny'd, because it is a Discourse of *Fish* and *Fishing*, which you know so well, and both love and practise so much.

You are assured (though there be ignorant men of another belief) that *Angling* is an *Art*; and you know that *Art* better than others; and that this is truth is demonstrated by the fruits of that pleasant labour which you enjoy when you purpose to give rest to your mind, and divest yourself of your more serious business, and (which is often) dedicate a day or two to this *Recreation*.

At which time, if *common Anglers* should attend you, and be eye witnesses of the success, not of your *fortune* but your *skill*, it would doubtless beget in them an emulation to be like you, and that emulation might beget an industrious diligence to be so; but

I know it is not attainable by common capacities. And there be now many men of great *wisdom, learning,* and *experience* which love and practise this *Art,* that know I speak the truth.

Sir, this pleasant curiosity of Fish and Fishing, (of which you are so great a Master) has been thought worthy the *Pens* and *Practices* of divers in other Nations, that have been reputed men of great *Learning* and *Wisdom,* and amongst those of this Nation, I remember Sir *Henry Wotton* (a dear lover of this Art) has told me that his intentions were to write a Discourse of the Art, and in praise of *Angling,* and doubtless he had done so, if death had not prevented him; the remembrance of which hath often made me sorry, for if he had lived to do it, then the unlearned *Angler* had seen some better Treatise of this Art, a Treatise that might have prov'd worthy his perusal, which (though some have undertaken) I could never yet see in English.

But mine may be thought as *weak,* and as *unworthy* of common view; and I do here freely confess, that I should rather excuse my self, than censure others, my own Discourse being liable to so many exceptions; against which you (Sir) might make this one, *That it can contribute nothing to your Knowledge.* And lest a longer epistle may diminish your pleasure, I shall make this no longer than to add this following Truth, *That I am really,*

SIR,

Your most affectionate Friend,
and most humble Servant,

IZ. WA.

To all Readers of this Discourse, but especially to the honest
ANGLER.

I think fit to tell thee these following truths, That I did neither undertake, nor write, nor publish, and much less own, this Discourse to please myself: and having been too easily drawn to do all to please others, as I propos'd not the gaining of credit by this undertaking, so I would not willingly lose any part of that to which I had a just title before I begun it, and do therefore desire and hope, if I deserve not commendations, yet I may obtain pardon.

And though this Discourse may be liable to some Exceptions, yet I cannot doubt but that most Readers may receive so much pleasure or profit by it, as may make it worthy the time of their perusal, if they be not too grave or too busie men. And this is all the confidence that I can put on concerning the merit of what is here offered to their consideration and censure; and if the last prove too severe, as I have a liberty, so I am resolv'd to use it, and neglect all sowre Censures.

And I wish the Reader also to take notice, that in writing of it I have made myself a recreation of a recreation; and that it might prove so to him, and not read dull and tediously, I have in several places mixt (not any scurrility, but) some innocent, harmless mirth; of which, if thou be a severe, sowre-complexion'd man, then I here disallow thee to be a competent judge; for Divines say, There are offences given, and offences not given but taken.

And I am the willinger to justifie the pleasant part of it, because though it is known I can be serious at seasonable times, yet the whole Discourse is, or rather was, a picture of my own disposition, especially in such days and times as I have laid aside business, and gone a fishing with honest Nat. *and* R. Roe; *but they are gone, and with them most of my pleasant hours, even as a shadow, that passeth away, and returns not.*

And next let me add this, that he that likes not the book, should like the excellent picture of the Trout, *and some of the other fish; which I may take a liberty to commend, because they concern not myself.*

Next let me tell the Reader, *that in that which is the more useful part of this* Discourse, *that is to say, the observations of the* nature *and* breeding, *and* seasons, *and* catching *of Fish, I am not so simple as not to know, that a captious Reader may find exceptions against something said of some of these; and therefore I must entreat him to consider, that experience teaches us to know, that several Countries alter the time, and I think almost the manner, of fishes breeding, but doubtless of their being in season; as may appear by three rivers in* Monmouthshire, *namely* Severn, Wie, *and* Usk, *where* Cambden (Brit. *f. 633*) *observes, that in the river* Wie, *Salmon are in season from* September *to* April; *and we are certain, that in* Thames *and* Trent, *and in most other Rivers, they be in season the six hotter months.*

Now for the Art *of* catching *fish, that is to say, how to make a man that was none, to be an Angler by a book? he that undertakes it shall undertake a harder task, than* Mr. Hales (*a most valiant and excellent Fencer*), *who in a printed book called,* A private School of Defence *undertook to teach that art or science, and was laugh'd at for his labour. Not but that many useful things might*

be learnt by that book, but he was laugh'd at, because
that art was not to be taught by words, but practice: and
so must Angling. And note also, that in this Discourse
I do not undertake to say all that is known, or may be
said of it, but I undertake to acquaint the Reader with
many things that are not usually known to every Angler;
and I shall leave gleanings and observations enough to
be made out of the experience of all that love and practise
this recreation, to which I shall encourage them. For
Angling may be said to be so much like the Mathematicks,
that it can ne'r be fully learnt; at least not so fully, but
that there will still be more new experiments left for the
tryal of other men that succeed us.

But I think all that love this game may here learn
something that may be worth their money, if they be not
poor and needy men: and in case they be, I then wish
them to forbear to buy it; for I write not to get money,
but for pleasure, and this Discourse boasts of no more,
for I hate to promise much, and deceive the Reader.

And however it proves to him, yet I am sure I have
found a high content in the search and conference of what
is here offered to the Reader's view and censure. I wish
him as much in the perusal of it, and so I might here take
my leave, but will stay a little and tell him, that whereas
it is said by many, that in flye-fishing for a Trout, the
Angler must observe his 12 several flies for the twelve
months of the year, I say, he that follows that rule, shall
be as sure to catch fish, and be as wise, as he that makes
Hay by the fair days in an Almanack, and no surer; for
those very flies that use to appear about and on the water
in one month of the year, may the following year come
almost a month sooner or later, as the same year proves
colder or hotter: and yet in the following Discourse I
have set down the twelve flies that are in reputation with

many *Anglers*, and they may serve to give him some *observations concerning them. And he may note that there are in* Wales, *and other Countries, peculiar* flies, *proper to the particular place or Country; and doubtless, unless a man makes a* flie *to counterfeit that very* flie *in that place, he is like to lose his labour, or much of it; but for the generality, three or four* flies *neat and rightly made, and not too big, serve for a* Trout *in most rivers, all the Summer. And for winter* flie-fishing *it is as useful as an Almanack out of date. And of these* (*because as no man is born an artist, so no man is born an Angler*) *I thought fit to give thee this notice.*

When I have told the Reader, that in this fifth Impression there are many enlargements, gathered both by my own observation, and the communication with friends, I shall stay him no longer than to wish him a rainy evening to read this following Discourse; *and that* (*if he be an honest Angler*) the East wind may never blow when he goes a Fishing.

I. W.

To my dear Brother Mr. Izaak Walton, upon his Compleat Angler.

Erasmus in his learned Colloquies
Has mixt some toys, that by varieties
He might entice all readers: for in him
Each *child* may wade, or tallest *giant* swim.
And such is this Discourse: there's none so low,
Or highly learn'd, to whom hence may not flow
Pleasure and information: both which are
Taught us with so much art, that I might swear
Safely, the choicest Critick cannot tell,
Whether your matchless judgment most excell
In *Angling* or its *praise*: where commendation
First charms, then makes an *art* a *recreation*.
　'Twas so to me; who *saw* the chearful *Spring*
Pictur'd in every *meadow*, heard *birds* sing
Sonnets in every *grove*, saw *fishes* play
In the cool *crystal streams*, like *lambs* in *May*:
And they may play, till *Anglers* read this *book*;
But after, 'tis a wise *fish* 'scapes a *hook*.

Jo. Floud, Mr. of Arts.

To the Reader of the *Compleat Angler*.

FIRST mark the Title well; my Friend that gave it
Has made it good; this book deserves to have it.
For he that views it with judicious looks,
Shall find it full of *art*, *baits*, *lines*, and *hooks*.
　The *world* the *river* is; both you and I,
And all mankind, are either *fish* or *fry*:
If we pretend to reason, first or last
His baits will tempt us, and his hooks hold fast.

Pleasure or profit, either prose or rhime,
If not at first, will doubtless take's in time.
   Here sits in secret blest *Theology*,
Waited upon by grave *Philosophy*,
Both *natural* and *moral*, *History*,
Deck'd and adorn'd with flowers of *Poetry*,
The matter and expression striving which
Shall most excell in worth, yet not seem rich:
There is no danger in his *baits*; that *hook*
Will prove the safest, that is surest took.
   Nor are we caught alone, but (which is best)
We shall be wholesom, and be toothsom drest;
Drest to be fed, not to be fed upon:
And danger of a surfeit here is none.
The solid food of serious Contemplation
Is sauc'd, here, with such harmless recreation,
That an *ingenuous* and *religious* mind
Cannot inquire for more than it may find
Ready at once prepar'd, either t' excite
Or satisfie a curious appetite.
   More praise is due: for 'tis both positive
And truth, which once was interrogative,
And utter'd by the Poet then in jest,
'*Et piscatorem piscis amare potest.*'

                   Ch. Harvie, Mr. of Arts.

To my dear Friend, Mr. Iz. Walton, in praise of Angling, which we both love.

Down by this smooth streams wandering side,
Adorn'd & perfum'd with the pride
Of *Flora*'s Wardrobe, where the shrill
Aerial Quire express their skill,

First in alternate melody,
And, then, in chorus all agree.
Whilst the charm'd fish, as extasi'd
With sounds, to his own throat deni'd,
Scorns his dull Element, and springs
I' th' air, as if his Fins were wings.

'Tis here that pleasures sweet and high
Prostrate to our embraces lye:
Such as to Body, Soul, or Fame
Create no sickness, sin, or shame:
Roses not fenc'd with pricks grow here,
No sting to th' Hony-bag is near.
But (what's perhaps their prejudice)
They difficulty want and price.

An obvious rod, a twist of hair,
With hook hid in an insect, are
Engines of sport, would fit the wish
O' th' Epicure, and fill his dish.

In this clear stream let fall a *Grub*;
And straight take up a *Dace* or *Chub*.
Ith' mud your worm provokes a *Snig*,
Which being fast, if it prove big
The *Gotham* folly will be found
Discreet, e're ta'ne she must be drown'd.
The *Tench* (Physician of the Brook)
In yon dead hole expects your hook;
Which having first your pastime been,
Serves then for meat or medicine.
Ambush'd behind that root doth stay
A *Pike*, to catch, and be a prey.
The treacherous Quill in this slow stream
Betrays the hunger of a *Bream*.
And at that nimbler Ford, (no doubt)
Your false flie cheats a speckled *Trout*.

When you these creatures wisely chuse
To practise on, which to your use
Owe their creation, and when
Fish from your arts do rescue men;
To plot, delude, and circumvent,
Ensnare and spoil, is innocent.
Here by these crystal streams you may
Preserve a Conscience clear as they;
And when by sullen thoughts you find
Your harassed, not busied, mind
In sable melancholy clad,
Distemper'd, serious, turning sad;
Hence fetch your cure, cast in your bait,
All anxious thoughts and cares will straight
Fly with such speed, they'l seem to be
Possest with the *Hydrophobie*.
The waters calmness in your breast,
And smoothness on your brow shall rest.
    Away with sports of charge and noise,
And give me cheap and silent joys,
Such as *Actaeons* game pursue,
Their fate oft makes the tale seem true.
The sick or sullen *Hawk*, to day,
Flyes not; tomorrow, quite away.
Patience and Purse to Cards and Dice
Too oft are made a sacrifice:
The Daughters dower, th' inheritance
O' th' son, depend on one mad chance.
The harms and mischiefs which th' abuse
Of wine doth every day produce,
Make good the Doctrine of the *Turks*,
That in each grape a devil lurks.
And by yon fading sapless tree,
Bout which the *Ivy* twin'd you see,

His fate's foretold, who fondly places
His bliss in woman's soft embraces.
All pleasures, but the Angler's, bring
I' th' tail repentance like a sting.
    Then on these banks let me sit down,
Free from the toilsom Sword and Gown,
And pity those that do affect
To conquer Nations and protect.
My Reed affords such true content,
Delights so sweet and innocent,
As seldom fall unto the lot
Of Scepters, though they'r *justly got*.

1649.   *Tho. Weaver*, Mr. of Arts.

To the Readers of my most ingenuous Friends Book, The Compleat Angler.

He that both knew and writ the lives of men,
  Such as were once, but must not be agen:
Witness his matchless *Donne* and *Wotton*, by
  Whose aid he could their speculations try:
He that convers'd with *Angels*, such as were
  Ouldsworth and *Featly*, each a shining star
Shewing the way to *Bethlem*; each a Saint
  (Compar'd to whom our *Zelots* now but paint);
He that our pious and learn'd *Morley* knew,
  And from him suck'd *wit* and *devotion* too:
He that from these such excellencies fetch'd,
  That *He* could tell how high and far they reach'd;
What learning this, what graces th' other had;
  And in what several dress each soul was clad.

Reader, this HE, this *Fisherman*, comes forth,
And in these Fishers weeds would shroud his worth.

Now his mute Harp is on a Willow hung,
With which when finely toucht and fitly strung,
He could friends passions for these times allay;
Or chain his fellow-*Anglers* from their prey.
But now the musick of his pen is still,
And he sits by a brook watching a quill:
Where with a fixt eye, and a ready hand,
He studies first to hook, and then to land
Some *Trout*, or *Pearch*, or *Pike*; and having done,
Sits on a Bank, and tells how this was won,
And that escap'd his hook; which with a wile
Did eat the bait, and Fisherman beguile.
Thus, whilst some vex they from their lands are thrown,
He joys to think the waters are his own,
    And like the *Dutch*, he gladly can agree
    To live at peace now, and have *fishing* free.
April 3, 1650.   *Edv. Powel*, Mr. of Arts.

To my dear Brother, *Mr.* Iz. Walton, *on his* Compleat Angler.

This Book is so like you, and you like it,
For harmless Mirth, Expression, Art, and Wit,
That I protest ingenuously, 'tis true,
I love this Mirth, Art, Wit, the Book, and You.
                         Rob. Floud, C.

Clarissimo amicissimoq; Fratri, Domino *Isaaco Walton*, Artis Piscatoriae peritissimo.

Unicus est Medicus reliquorum piscis, & istis,
   Fas quibus est Medicum tangere, certa salus.

Hic typus est Salvatoris mirandus JESU,
 [b]*Litera mysterium quaelibet hujus habet.*
Hunc cupio, hunc capias (bone frater Arundinis) ἰχθύν;
 [q]*Solveret hic pro me debita, teque Deo.*
Piscis is est, & piscator (mihi credito) qualem
 Vel piscatorem piscis amare velit.

Henry Bayley, Artium Magister.

Ad Virum optimum, & Piscatorem peritissimum, *Isaacum Waltonum.*

MAGISTER *artis docte Piscatoriæ,*
Waltone, *salve! magne dux arundinis,*
Seu tu reductâ valle solus ambulas,
Praeterfluentes interim observans aquas,
Seu fortè puri stans in amnis margine,
Sive in tenaci gramine & ripâ sedens,
Fallis peritâ squameum pecus manu;
O te beatum! qui procul negotiis,
Foriq; & urbis pulvere & strepitu carens,
Extraq; turbam, ad lenè manantes aquas
Vagos honestâ fraude pisces decipis.
Dum cætera ergo paenè gens mortalium
Aut retia invicem sibi & technas struunt,
Donis, ut hamo, aut divites captant senes,
Gregi natantûm tu interim nectis dolos,
Voracem inescas advenam hamo lucium,

b	᾿Ιχθὺς	*Piscis.*
	Ι ᾿Ιησοῦς	*Jesus.*
	χ Χριστὸς	*Christus.*
	θ Θεοῦ	*Dei.*
	υ Υἱὸς	*Filius.*
	ς Σωτὴρ	*Salvator.*

q Matt. 17. 27, the last words of the Chapter.

Avidamvè percam parvulo alburno capis,
Aut verme ruffo, musculâ aut truttam levi,
Cautumvè cyprinum, & ferè indocilem capi
Calamoq; linoq; (ars at hunc superat tua)
Medicamvè tincam, gobium aut escâ trahis,
Gratum palato gobium, parvum licet,
Praedamvè, non aeque salubrem barbulum,
Etsi ampliorem, & mystace insignem gravi.
Hae sunt tibi artes, dum annus & tempus sinunt,
Et nulla transit absq; linea dies.
Nec sola praxis, sed theoria & tibi
Nota artis hujus; unde tu simul bonus
Piscator, idem & scriptor; & calami potens
Utriusq; necdum & ictus, & tamen sapis.
Ut hamiotam nempe tironem instruas,!
Stylo eleganti scribis en Halieutica
Oppianus alter, artis & methodum tuae, &
Praecepta promis rite piscatoria,
Varias & escas piscium, indolem, & genus.
Nec tradere artem sat putas piscariam,
(Virtutis est et haec tamen quaedam schola
Patientiamq; & temperantiam docet)
Documenta quin majora das, & regulas
Sublimioris artis, & perennia
Monimenta morum, vitae & exempla optima;
Dum tu profundum scribis HOOKERUM, *& pium*
DONNUM *ac disertum, sanctum et* HERBERTUM, *sacrum*
Vatem; hos videmus nam penicillo tuo
Graphicè, & peritâ, Isace, *depictos manu.*
Post fata factos hosce per te Virbios
O quae voluptas est legere in scriptis tuis!
Sic tu libris nos, lineis pisces capis,
Musisq; litterisq; dum incumbis, licet
Intentus hamo, interq; piscandum studes.

Aliud ad *Isaacum Waltonum*, virum & Piscatorem optimum.

Isace, Macte bâc arte piscatoriâ;
Hâc arte Petrus *Principi censum dedit;*
Hâc arte Princeps nec Petro *multò prior,*
Tranquillus ille, teste Tranquillo, Pater
Patriae, solebat recreare se lubens
Augustus, bamo instructus ac arundine.
Tu nunc, Amice, proximum clari et decus
Post Cæsarem bami, gentis ac Halieuticæ:
Euge O Professor artis baud ingloriæ,
Doctor Cathedræ, perlegens Piscariam!
Ne tu Magister, & ego discipulus tuus,
(Nam candidatum & me ferunt arundinis)
Socium bac in arte nobilem Nacti sumus.
Quid amplius, Waltone, *nam dici potest?*
Ipse hamiota *Dominus en orbis fuit.*

Jaco. Dup. D.D.

THE
COMPLEAT
ANGLER,

OR,

The Contemplative Man's Recreation.

PART I.

CHAP. I

A Conference betwixt an Angler, *a* Faulkner, *and a* Hunter, *each commending his recreation.*

> PISCATOR
> VENATOR
> AUCEPS

Pisc. You are well overtaken, Gentlemen! A good morning to you both; I have stretched my legs up *Tottenham-hill* to overtake you, hoping your business may occasion you towards *Ware* whither I am going this fine, fresh May morning.

Venat. Sir, I, for my part, shall almost answer your hopes, for my purpose is to drink my morning's draught at the *Thatcht House* in *Hodsden*; and I think not to rest till I come thither, where I have appointed a friend or two to meet me: but for this Gentleman that you see with me, I know not how far he intends his journey; he came so lately into my company, that I have scarce had time to ask him the question.

Auceps. Sir, I shall by your favour bear you company as far as *Theobalds*, and there leave you; for then I turn up to a friend's house, who mews a Hawk for me, which I now long to see.

Venat. Sir, we are all so happy as to have a fine, fresh, cool morning; and I hope we shall each be the happier in the others' company. And, Gentlemen, that I may not lose yours, I shall either abate or amend my pace to enjoy it, knowing that (as the Italians say) *Good company in a journey makes the way to seem the shorter*.

Auceps. It may do so, Sir, with the help of good discourse, which, methinks, we may promise from you, that both look and speak so chearfully: and for my part, I promise you, as an invitation to it, that I will be as free and openhearted as discretion will allow me to be with strangers.

Ven. And, Sir, I promise the like.

Pisc. I am right glad to hear your answers, and, in confidence you speak the truth, I shall put on a boldness to ask you, Sir, Whether business or pleasure caused you to be so early up, and walk so fast, for this other Gentleman hath declared that he is going to see a Hawk, that a friend mews for him.

Ven. Sir, mine is a mixture of both, a little business and more pleasure; for I intend this day to do all my business, and then bestow another day or two in hunting the *Otter*, which a friend, that I go to meet, tells me is much pleasanter than any other chase whatsoever: howsoever, I mean to try it; for to-morrow morning we shall meet a pack of Otter-dogs of *noble Mr. Sadler's*, upon *Amwell hill*, who will be there so early, that they intend to prevent the Sun-rising.

Pisc. Sir, my fortune has answered my desires, and my purpose is to bestow a day or two in helping to destroy some of those villanous vermin; for I hate them perfectly, because they love fish so well, or rather, because they destroy so much; indeed so much, that in my judgment all men that keep *Otter-dogs* ought to have pensions from the King, to encourage them to destroy the very breed of those base *Otters*, they do so much mischief.

Ven. But what say you to the Foxes of the Nation, would not you as willingly have them destroyed? for doubtless they do as much mischief as *Otters* do.

Pisc. Oh Sir, if they do, it is not so much to me and my fraternity, as those base Vermine the *Otters* do.

Auc. Why Sir, I pray, of what Fraternity are you, that you are so angry with the poor *Otters*?

Pisc. I am (Sir) a Brother of the *Angle*, and therefore an enemy to the *Otter*: for you are to note, that we Anglers all love one another, and therefore do I hate the *Otter* both for my own and for their sakes who are of my brotherhood.

Ven. And I am a lover of Hounds; I have followed many a pack of dogs many a mile, and heard many merry huntsmen make sport and scoff at Anglers.

Auc. And I profess myself a Faulkner, and have heard many grave, serious men pity them, 'tis such a heavy, contemptible, dull recreation.

Pis. You know, Gentlemen, 'tis an easie thing to

scoff at any Art or Recreation; a little *wit* mixed with ill nature, confidence, and *malice*, will do it; but though they often venture boldly, yet they are often caught, even in their own trap, according to that of *Lucian*, the father of the family of Scoffers.

> Lucian, *well skill'd in scoffing, this hath writ,*
> *Friend, that's your folly, which you think your wit:*
> *This you vent oft, void both of wit and fear,*
> *Meaning another, when yourself you jeer.*

If to this you add what *Solomon* says of Scoffers, that they are abomination to mankind. Let him that thinks fit scoff on, and be a Scoffer still; but I account them enemies to me, and to all that love vertue and Angling.

And for you that have heard many grave, serious men pity Anglers; let me tell you, Sir, there be many men that are by others taken to be serious and grave men, which we contemn and pity. Men that are taken to be grave, because Nature hath made them of a sowre complexion, money-getting-men, men that spend all their time, first in getting, and next, in anxious care to keep it; men that are condemned to be rich, and then always busie or discontented: for these poor-rich-men, we Anglers pity them perfectly, and stand in no need to borrow their thoughts to think our selves so happy. No, no, Sir, we enjoy a contentedness above the reach of such dispositions, and as the learned and ingenuous *Mountaigne* says,
In Apol. for like himself, freely, 'When my Cat and
Ra. Sebeud. 'I entertain each other with mutual apish 'tricks (as playing with a garter) who knows but 'that I make my Cat more sport than she makes 'me? Shall I conclude her to be simple, that has her

'time to begin or refuse to play as freely as I my self
'have? Nay, who knowes but that it is a defect of my
'not understanding her language (for doubtless Cats
'talk and reason with one another) that we agree no
'better: and who knows but that she pitties me for
'being no wiser than to play with her, and laughs
'and censures my follie, for making sport for her,
'when we two play together?'

Thus freely speaks *Mountaigne* concerning Cats,
and I hope I may take as great a liberty to blame any
man, and laugh at him too let him be never so grave,
that hath not heard what Anglers can say in the
justification of their Art and Recreation; which I may
again tell you is so full of pleasure, that we need not
borrow their thoughts, to think our selves happy.

Venat. Sir, you have almost amazed me, for
though I am no scoffer, yet I have, I pray let me
speak it without offence, alwayes looked upon Anglers
as more patient and more simple men, than I fear I
shall find you to be.

Pisc. Sir, I hope you will not judge my earnestness to be impatience: and for my *simplicity*, if by that
you mean a harmlessness, or that simplicity which
was usually found in the primitive Christians, who
were, as most Anglers are, quiet men, and followers of peace; men that were so simply-wise, as
not to sell their Consciences to buy riches, and with
them vexation and a fear to die, If you mean such
simple men as lived in those times when there were
fewer Lawyers? when men might have had a Lord-
ship safely conveyed to them in a piece of Parchment
no bigger than your hand, (though several sheets
will not do it safely in this wiser age); I say, Sir, if
you take us Anglers to be such simple men as I have

spoke of, then my self and those of my profession will be glad to be so understood: But if by simplicity you meant to express a general defect in those that profess and practise the excellent Art of Angling, I hope in time to disabuse you, and make the contrary appear so evidently, that if you will but have patience to hear me, I shall remove all the Anticipations that discourse, or time, or prejudice, have possess'd you with against that laudable and ancient art; for I know it is worthy the *knowledge* and *practise* of a wise man.

But (Gentlemen) though I be able to do this, I am not so unmannerly as to ingross all the discourse to my self; and, therefore, you two having declared your selves, the one to be a lover of *Hawks*, the other of *Hounds*, I shall be most glad to hear what you can say in the commendation of that recreation which each of you love and practise; and having heard what you can say, I shall be glad to exercise your attention with what I can say concerning my own Recreation & Art of Angling, and by this means, we shall make the way to seem the shorter: and if you like my motion, I would have Mr. *Faulkner* to begin.

Auc. Your motion is consented to with all my heart; and to testifie it, I will begin as you have desired me.

And first, for the Element that I use to trade in, which is the Air, an Element of more worth than weight, an Element that doubtless exceeds both the Earth and Water; for though I sometimes deal in both, yet the Air is most properly mine, I and my Hawks use that most, and it yields us most recreation; it stops not the high soaring of my noble, generous *Falcon*; in it she ascends to such an height, as the dull eyes of beasts and fish are not able to reach to; their bodies

are too gross for such high elevations; in the Air my
troops of Hawks soar up on high, and when they are
lost in the sight of men, then they attend upon and
converse with the gods; therefore I think my *Eagle*
is so justly styled, *Joves servant in Ordinary*: and that
very *Falcon*, that I am now going to see deserves no
meaner a title, for she usually in her flight endangers
her self, (like the son of *Dædalus*) to have her wings
scorch'd by the Suns heat, she flyes so near it, but her
mettle makes her careless of danger; for she then
heeds nothing, but makes her nimble Pinions cut the
fluid air, and so makes her high way over the steep-
est mountains and deepest rivers, and in her glorious
carere looks with contempt upon those high Steeples
and magnificent Palaces which we adore and wonder
at; from which height I can make her to descend by a
word from my mouth (which she both knows and
obeys), to accept of meat from my hand, to own me
for her Master, to go home with me, and be willing
the next day to afford me the like recreation.

And more; this element of air which I profess to
trade in, the worth of it is such, and it is of such
necessity, that no creature whatsoever, not only those
numerous creatures that feed on the face of the Earth,
but those various creatures that have their dwelling
within the waters, every creature that hath life in its
nostrils, stands in need of my Element. The waters
cannot preserve the Fish without Air, witness the
not breaking of Ice in an extream Frost; the reason is,
for that if the inspiring and expiring Organ of any
animal be stopt, it suddenly yields to Nature, and
dies. Thus necessary is air to the existence both of
Fish and Beasts, nay, even to Man himself; that Air,
or breath of life, with which God at first inspired

Mankind, he, if he wants it, dies presently, becomes a sad object to all that loved and beheld him, and in an instant turns to putrefaction.

Nay more, the very birds of the air, (those that be not Hawks) are both so many, and so useful and pleasant to mankind, that I must not let them pass without some observations. They both feed and refresh him; feed him with their choice bodies, and refresh him with their Heavenly voices. I will not undertake to mention the several kinds of Fowl by which this is done; and his curious palate pleased by day, and which with their very excrements afford him a soft lodging at night. These I will pass by, but not those little nimble Musicians of the air, that warble forth their curious Ditties, with which Nature hath furnished them to the shame of Art.

At first the *Lark*, when she means to rejoyce, to chear her self and those that hear her, she then quits the earth, and sings as she ascends higher into the air, and having ended her Heavenly imployment, grows then mute and sad to think she must descend to the dull earth, which she would not touch, but for necessity.

How do the *Black-bird* and *Thrassel* with their melodious voices bid welcome to the chearful Spring, and in their fixed Months warble forth such ditties as no art or instrument can reach to?

Nay, the smaller birds also do the like in their particular seasons, as namely the *Leverock*, the *Titlark*, the little *Linnet*, and the honest *Robin*, that loves mankind both alive and dead.

But the *Nightingale* (another of my Airy Creatures) breathes such sweet loud musick out of her little instrumental throat, that it might make mankind to think Miracles are not ceased. He that at midnight (when the very labourer sleeps securely) should hear (as I have very often) the clear airs, the sweet descants, the natural rising and falling, the doubling and redoubling of her voice, might well be lifted above earth, and say; 'Lord, what Musick hast thou provided for the Saints in Heaven, when thou affordest bad men such musick on Earth!'

And this makes me the less to wonder at the many *Aviaries* in *Italy*, or at the great charge of *Varro* his *Aviarie*, the ruines of which are yet to be seen in *Rome*, and is still so famous there, that it is reckoned for one of those Notables which men of forraign Nations either record, or lay up in their memories when they return from travel.

This for the birds of pleasure, of which very much more might be said. My next shall be of Birds of Political use; I think 'tis not to be doubted that Swallows have been taught to carry Letters betwixt two Armies. But 'tis certain that when the Turks besieged *Malta* or *Rhodes* (I now remember not which 'twas) *Pigeons* are then related to carry and recarry letters. And Mr. *G. Sandis*, in his Travels (*fol.* 269) relates it to be done betwixt *Aleppo* and *Babylon*. But if that be disbelieved, 'tis not to be doubted that the *Dove* was sent out of the Ark by *Noah*, to give him notice of Land, when to him all appeared to be Sea; and the *Dove* proved a faithful and comfortable messenger. And for the sacrifices of the Law, a pair of *Turtle Doves*, or young *Pigeons* were as well accepted as costly *Bulls* and *Rams*. And when God would feed the Prophet *Elijah* (1 *King*. 17), after a kind of miraculous manner he did it by *Ravens*, who brought him meat morning and evening. Lastly, the Holy Ghost when he descended visibly upon our Saviour, did it by assuming the shape of a *Dove*. And, to conclude this part of my discourse, pray remember these wonders were done by birds of the Air, the Element in which they and I take so much pleasure.

There is also a little contemptible winged Creature, an inhabitant of my Aerial Element, namely the laborious *Bee*, of whose *Prudence*, *Policy* and regular Government of their own Commonwealth I might say much, as also of their several kinds, and how useful their honey and wax is both for meat and Medicines to mankind; but I will leave them to their sweet labour, without the least disturbance, believing them to be all very busie at this very time amongst the herbs and flowers that we see nature puts forth this *May* morning.

And now to return to my Hawks from whom I have made too long a digression; you are to note, that they are usually distinguished into two kinds; namely, the long-winged and the short-winged Hawk: of the first kind, there be chiefly in use amongst us in this Nation,

> The *Gerfalcon* and *Jerkin*.
> The *Falcon* and *Tassel-gentel*.
> The *Laner* and *Laneret*.
> The *Bockerel* and *Bockeret*.
> The *Saker* and *Sacaret*.
> The *Marlin* and *Jack Marlin*.
> The *Hobby* and *Jack*.
> There is the *Stelletto* of *Spain*.
> The *Bloud* red *Rook* from *Turky*.
> The *Waskite* from *Virginia*.
> And there is of short-winged Hawks

The *Eagle* and *Iron*.

The *Goshawk* and *Tarcel*.

The *Sparhawk* and *Musket*.

The French *Pye* of two sorts.

These are reckoned Hawks of note and worth; but we have also of an inferiour rank.

The *Stanyel*, the *Ringtail*.

The *Raven*, the *Buzzard*.

The forked *Kite*, the bald *Buzzard*.

The *Hen-driver*, and others that I forbear to name.

Gentlemen, if I should enlarge my discourse to the observation of the *Eires*, the *Brancher*, the *Ramish Hawk*, the *Haggard*, and the two sorts of *Lentners*, and then treat of their several *Ayries*, their *Mewings*, rare order of casting, and the renovation of their *Feathers*: their reclaiming, dyeting, and then come to their rare stories of practice; I say, if I should enter into these, and many other observations that I could make, it would be much, very much pleasure to me: but lest I should break the rules of Civility with you, by taking up more than the proportion of time allotted to me, I will here break off, and entreat you, Mr. *Venator*, to say what you are able in the commendation of Hunting, to which you are so much affected, and if time will serve, I will beg your favour for a further enlargement of some of those several heads of which I have spoken. But no more at present.

Venat. Well Sir, and I will now take my turn, and will first begin with a commendation of the earth, as you have done most excellently of the Air, the Earth being that Element upon which I drive my pleasant, wholesom, hungry trade. The Earth is a solid, settled Element; an Element most universally beneficial

both to man and beast; to men who have their
several Recreations upon it, as Horse-races, Hunting,
sweet smells, pleasant walks: The Earth feeds man,
and all those several beasts that both feed him, and
afford him recreation: What pleasure doth man take
in hunting the stately *Stag*, the generous *Buck*, the
Wild Boar, the cunning *Otter*, the crafty *Fox*, and the
fearful *Hare?* And if I may descend to a lower Game?
what pleasure is it sometimes with Gins to betray
the very vermine of the earth? as namely, the *Fichat*,
the *Fulimart*, the *Ferret*, the *Pole-cat*, the *Mouldwarp*,
and the like creatures that live upon the face, and
within the bowels of the earth. How doth the earth
bring forth *herbs, flowers,* and *fruits*, both for *physick*
and the *pleasure* of mankind? and above all, to me at
least, the fruitful *Vine*, of which when I drink moder-
ately, it clears my brain, chears my heart, and
sharpens my wit. How could *Cleopatra* have feasted
Mark Antony with eight Wild Boars roasted whole
at one Supper, and other meat suitable, if the earth
had not been a bountiful mother? But to pass by the
mighty *Elephant*, which the earth breeds and nourish-
eth, and descend to the least of creatures, how doth
the earth afford us a doctrinal example in the little
Pismire, who in the Summer provides and lays up her
Winter provision, and teaches man to do the like? the
earth feeds and carries those horses that carry us. If
I would be prodigal of my time and your patience
what might not I say in commendations of the earth?
that puts limits to the proud and raging *Sea*, and by
that means preserves both man and beast that it
destroys them not, as we see it daily doth those that
venture upon the Sea, and are there ship-wrackt,
drowned, and left to feed Haddocks; when we that

are so wise as to keep our selves on *earth*, *walk*, and *talk*, and *live*, and *eat*, and *drink*, and go a *hunting*: of which recreation I will say a little, and then leave Mr. *Piscator* to the commendation of Angling.

Hunting is a game for Princes and noble persons; it hath been highly prized in all Ages; it was one of the qualifications that *Xenophon* bestowed on his *Cyrus*, that he was a hunter of wild beasts. Hunting trains up the younger nobility to the use of manly exercises in their riper age. What more manly exercise than *hunting the Wild Bore*, the *Stag*, the *Buck*, the *Fox*, or the *Hare?* How doth it preserve health, and increase strength and activity?

And for the Dogs that we use, who can commend their excellency to that height which they deserve? How perfect is the Hound at *smelling*, who never leaves or forsakes his first scent, but follows' it through so many changes and varieties of other scents, even over, and in the water, and into the earth? What musick doth a pack of Dogs then make to any man, whose heart and ears are so happy as to be set to the tune of such instruments? How will a right *Greyhound* fix his eye on the best *Buck* in a *herd*, single him out, and follow him, and him only through a whole herd of Rascal game, and still know and then kill him? For my Hounds I know the language of them, and they know the language and meaning of one another as perfectly as we know the voices of those with whom we discourse daily.

I might enlarge my self in the commendation of *Hunting*, and of the noble Hound especially, as also of the docibleness of *dogs* in general; and I might make many observations of Land-creatures, that for composition, order, figure, and constitution, approach nearest to the compleateness and understanding of man; especially of those creatures which *Moses* in the Law permitted to the Jews, (which have cloven Hoofs and chew the Cud) which I shall forbear to name, because I will not be so uncivil to Mr. *Piscator*, as not to allow him a time for the commendation of *Angling*, which he calls an Art; but doubtless 'tis an easie one: and Mr. *Auceps*, I doubt we shall hear a watry discourse of it, but I hope twill not be a long one.

Auc. And I hope so too, though I fear it will.

Pisc. Gentlemen let not prejudice prepossess you. I confess my discourse is like to prove suitable to my Recreation *calm* and *quiet*; we seldom take the name of God into our mouths, but it is either to praise him, or to pray to him: if others use it vainly in the midst of their recreations, so vainly as if they meant to conjure; I must tell you, it is neither our fault nor our custom; we protest against it. But, pray remember, I accuse no body; for as I would not make a *watry* discourse, so I would not put too much *vinegar* into it; nor would I raise the reputation of my own Art by the diminution or ruine of anothers. And so much for the Prologue to what I mean to say.

And now for the *Water*, the Element that I trade in. The *water* is the eldest daughter of the Creation, the Element upon which the Spirit of God did first move, the Element which God commanded to bring forth living creatures abundantly; and without which those that inhabit the Land, even all creatures that have breath in their nostrils must suddenly return to putrefaction. *Moses* the great Law-giver and chief Philosopher, skilled in all the learning of the Egyptians, who was called the friend of God, and knew the mind of the Almighty, names this element the first in the Creation: this is the element upon which the Spirit of God did first move, and is the chief ingredient in the Creation: many Philosophers have made it to comprehend all the other Elements, and most allow it the chiefest in the mixtion of all living creatures.

There be that profess to believe that all bodies are made of *water*, and may be reduced back again to water only: they endeavour to demonstrate it thus,

Take a *Willow* (or any like speedy growing plant) newly rooted in a box or barrel full of earth, weigh them altogether exactly when the tree begins to grow, and then weigh all together after the tree is increased from its first rooting, to weigh an hundred pound weight more than when it was first rooted and weighed; and you shall find this augment of the tree to be without the diminution of one dram weight of the earth. Hence they infer this increase of wood to be from water of rain, or from dew, and not to be from any other Element. And they affirm, they can reduce this wood back again to water; and they affirm also, the same may be done in any *animal* or *vegetable*. And this I take to be a fair testimony of the excellency of my Element of Water.

The *Water* is more productive than the *Earth*. Nay, the earth hath no fruitfulness without showers or dews; for all the *herbs*, and *flowers*, and *fruit* are produced and thrive by the water; and the very Minerals are fed by streams that run under ground, whose natural course carries them to the tops of many high mountains, as we see by several springs breaking forth on the tops of the highest hills; and this is also witnessed by the daily trial and testimony of several Miners.

Nay, the increase of those creatures that are bred
and fed in the water, are not only more and more
miraculous, but more advantagious to man, not only
for the lengthening of his life, but for the preventing
of sickness; for 'tis observed by the most learned
Physicians, that the casting off of Lent, and other
fish-daies, (which hath not only given the Lie to so
many learned, pious, wise Founders of Colledges, for
which we should be ashamed) hath doubtless been the
chief cause of those many putrid, shaking, intermitting Agues, unto which this Nation of ours is now
more subject than those wiser Countries that feed on
Herbs, Sallets, and plenty of Fish; of which it is
observed in Story, that the greatest part of the world
now do. And it may be fit to remember that *Moses*
(*Lev*. 11. 9, *Deut*. 14. 9) appointed Fish to be the chief
diet for the best Common-wealth that ever yet was.

And it is observable, not only that there are *fish*,
(as namely the *Whale*) three times as big as the
mighty Elephant; that is so fierce in battel, but that
the mightiest Feasts have been of fish. The *Romans*,
in the height of their glory have made fish the
mistress of all their entertainments; they have had
Musick to usher in their *Sturgeons*, *Lampreys*, and
Mullets, which they would purchase at rates rather to
be wondered at than believed. He that shall view the
Writings of *Macrobius* or *Varro*, may be confirmed
and informed of this, and of the incredible value of
their Fish and fish-ponds.

But, Gentlemen, I have almost lost my self, which
I confess I may easily do in this Philosophical Discourse; I met with most of it very lately (and I hope
happily) in a conference with a most learned Physician, Dr. *Wharton*, a dear Friend, that loves both me

and my Art of Angling. But however I will wade no deeper in these mysterious Arguments, but pass to such Observations as I can manage with more pleasure, and less fear of running into error. But I must not yet forsake the Waters, by whose help we have so many known advantages.

And first (to pass by the miraculous cures of our known *Baths*) how advantagious is the *Sea* for our daily Traffique; without which we could not now subsist? How does it not only furnish us with food and Physick for the bodies, but with such Observations for the mind as ingenious persons would not want?

How ignorant had we been of the beauty of *Florence*, of the *Monuments*, *Urns*, and *Rarities* that yet remain in, and near unto old and new *Rome*, (so many as it is said will take up a years time to view, and afford to each of them but a convenient consideration;) and therefore it is not to be wondred at, that so learned and devout a father as St. *Jerome*, after his wish to have seen Christ in the flesh, and to have heard St. *Paul* preach, makes his third wish, to *have seen Rome in her glory*; and that glory is not yet all lost, for what pleasure is it to see the Monuments of *Livy*, the choicest of the Historians; of *Tully*, the best of Orators; and to see the Bay-trees that now grow out of the very Tomb of *Virgil*? These to any that love Learning must be pleasing. But what pleasure is it to a devout Christian to see there the humble house in which St. *Paul* was content to dwell; and to view the many rich *Statues* that are there made in honour of his memory? nay, to see the very place in which St. *Peter* and he lie buried together? These are in and near to *Rome*. And how much more doth it please the pious curiosity of a Christian to see that place, on which the blessed Saviour of the world was pleased to humble himself, and to take our nature upon him, and to converse with men: to see Mount *Sion*, *Jerusalem*, and the very Sepulchre of our Lord Jesus? How may it beget and heighten the zeal of a Christian to see the Devotions that are daily paid to him at that place? Gentlemen, lest I forget my self, I will stop here, and remember you, that but for my Element of water the Inhabitants of this poor Island must remain ignorant that such things ever were, or that any of them have yet a being.

Gentlemen, I might both enlarge and lose myself in such like Arguments; I might tell you that Almighty God is said to have spoken to a *Fish*, but never to a *Beast*; that he hath made a *Whale* a Ship to carry and set his Prophet *Jonah* safe on the appointed shore. Of these I might speak, but I must in manners break off, for I see *Theobalds* house. I cry you mercy for being so long, and thank you for your patience.

Auceps. Sir, my pardon is easily granted you: I except against nothing that you have said; nevertheless, I must part with you at this Park-wall, for which I am very sorry; but I assure you, Mr. *Piscator*, I now part with you full of good thoughts, not only of your self, but your Recreation. And so Gentlemen, God keep you both.

Pisc. Well, now Mr. *Venator* you shall neither want time nor my attention to hear you enlarge your discourse concerning Hunting.

Venat. Not I Sir, I remember you said that *Angling* it self was of great Antiquity, and a perfect Art, and an Art not easily attained to; and you have so won upon me in your former discourse, that I am very desirous to hear what you can say further concerning those particulars.

Pisc. Sir, I did say so; and I doubt not but if you and I did converse together but a few hours, to leave you possesst with the same high and happy thoughts that now possess me of it; not only of the Antiquity of *Angling*, but that it deserves commendations, and that it is an Art, and an Art worthy the knowledg and practise of a wise man.

Venat. Pray, Sir, speak of them what you think fit, for we have yet five miles to the *Thatcht-House*, during which walk, I dare promise you, my patience, and diligent attention shall not be wanting. And if you shall make that to appear which you have undertaken, first, that it is an Art, and an art worth the learning, I shall beg that I may attend you a day or two a fishing, and that I may become your Scholar, and be instructed in the Art it self which you so much magnifie.

Pisc. O Sir, doubt not but that *Angling* is an Art; is it not an Art to deceive a *Trout* with an artificial Flie? a *Trout*! that is more sharp sighted than any Hawk you have nam'd, and more watchful and timorous than your high mettled *Marlin* is bold? and yet, I doubt not to catch a brace or two to morrow, for a friends breakfast: doubt not therefore, Sir, but that *Angling* is an Art, and an art worth your learning: the Question is rather, whether you be capable of learning it? for *Angling* is somewhat like *Poetry*, men are to be born so: I mean, with inclinations to it, though both may be heightened by discourse and practice, but he that hopes to be a good *Angler* must not only bring an inquiring, searching, observing wit; but he must bring a large measure of hope and patience, and a love and propensity to the Art it self; but having once got and practis'd it, then doubt not but *Angling* will prove to be so pleasant, that it will prove to be like Vertue, *a reward to it self*.

Venat. Sir, I am now become so full of expectation that I long much to have you proceed; and in the order that you propose.

Pisc. Then first, for the *antiquity* of *Angling*, of which I shall not say much, but onely this; Some say it is as ancient as *Deucalions* Flood: others that *Belus*, who was the first Inventer of Godly and vertuous Recreations, was the first Inventer of *Angling*: and some others say (for former times have had their disquisitions about the Antiquity of it) that *Seth*, one of the Sons of *Adam*, taught it to his Sons, and that by them it was derived to posterity: others say, that he left it engraven on those pillars which he erected, and trusted to preserve the knowledge of the *Mathematicks*, *Musick*, and the rest of that precious knowledge, and those useful *Arts* which by God's appointment or allowance and his noble industry were thereby preserved from perishing in *Noahs* flood.

These, Sir, have been the opinions of several men, that have possibly endeavored to make *Angling* more ancient than is needful, or may well be warranted; but for my part, I shall content my self in telling you that Angling is much more ancient than the Incarnation of our Saviour; for in the Prophet *Amos* mention is made of *fish-hooks*; and in the Book of *Job* (which was long before the days of *Amos* (for that book is said to be writ by *Moses*) mention is made also of fish-hooks, which must imply Anglers in those times.

But, my worthy friend, as I would rather prove my self a *Gentleman*, by being *learned* and *humble*,

valiant, and *inoffensive*, *vertuous* and *communicable*,
than by any fond ostentation of riches, or wanting
those vertues my self, boast that these were in my
Ancestors (and yet I grant that where a noble and
ancient descent and such merits meet in any man,
it is a double dignification of that person:) So if this
Antiquity of *Angling*, (which for my part I have not
forced,) shall, like an ancient family, be either an
honour or an ornament to this vertuous Art which I
profess to love and practice, I shall be the gladder
that I made an accidental mention of the antiquity of
it; of which I shall say no more but proceed to that
just commendation which I think it deserves.

And for that I shall tell you, that in ancient times
a debate hath risen, (and it remains yet unresolved)
Whether the happiness of man in this world doth
consist more in *Contemplation* or *action?*

Concerning which some have endeavoured to
maintain their opinion of the first, by saying, *That
the nearer we Mortals come to God by way of imitation,
the more happy we are.* And they say, *That God enjoys
himself only by a contemplation of his own infinitenesse,
Eternity, Power, and Goodness,* and the like. And
upon this ground many Cloysteral men of great
learning and devotion prefer *Contemplation* before
Action. And many of the fathers seem to approve
this opinion, as may appear in the Commentaries
upon the words of our Saviour to *Martha, Luke* 10.
41, 42.

And on the contrary, there want not men of equal
authority and credit, that prefer *action* to be the more
excellent, as namely *experiments in Physick, and the
application of it, both for the ease and prolongation of
mans life*; by which each man is enabled to act and

do good to others; either to serve his Countrey, or do good to particular persons; and they say also, *That action is Doctrinal, and teaches both art and vertue, and is a maintainer of humane society*; and for these, and other like reasons to be preferred before *contemplation*.

Concerning which two opinions I shall forbear to add a third by declaring my own, and rest my self contented in telling you (my very worthy friend) that both these meet together, and do most properly belong to the most *honest*, *ingenuous*, *quiet*, and *harmless* art of *Angling*.

And first, I shall tell you what some have observed, (and I have found it to be a real truth) that the very sitting by the Rivers side is not only the quietest and fittest place for *contemplation*, but will invite an Angler to it: and this seems to be maintained by the learned *Pet. du Moulin*, who (in his discourse of the fulfilling of Prophesies) observes, that when God intended to reveal any future events or high notions to his Prophets, he then carried them either to the *Desarts*, or the *Sea-shore*, that having so separated them from amidst the press of *people* and *business*, and the cares of the world, he might settle their mind in a quiet repose, and there make them fit for Revelation.

And this seems also to be intimated by the Children of *Israel*, (*Psal.* 137), who having in a sad condition banished all mirth and musick from their pensive hearts, and having hung up their then mute Harps upon the Willow-trees growing by the Rivers of *Babylon*, sat down upon those banks bemoaning the ruines of *Sion*, and contemplating their own sad condition.

And an ingenuous *Spaniard* says, *That Rivers and*

*the Inhabitants of the watry Element were made for
wise men to contemplate, and fools to pass by without
consideration.* And though I will not rank my self in
the number of the first, yet give me leave to free my
self from the last, by offering to you a short contemplation, first of *Rivers*, and then of *Fish*; concerning
which I doubt not but to give you many observations
that will appear very considerable: I am sure they
have appeared so to me, and made many an hour pass
away more pleasantly, as I have sate quietly on a
flowry Bank by a calm River, and contemplated what
I shall now relate to you.

And first concerning Rivers; there be so many
wonders reported and written of them, and of the
several Creatures that be bred and live in them; and,
those by Authors of so good credit, that we need not
to deny them an historical Faith.

As namely of a River in *Epirus*, that puts out any
lighted Torch, and kindles any Torch that was not
lighted. Some Waters being drank cause madness,
some drunkenness, and some laughter to death. The
River *Selarus* in a few hours turns a rod or wand to
stone: and our *Cambden* mentions the like in *England*,
and the like in *Lochmere* in *Ireland*. There is also a
river in *Arabia*, of which all the sheep that drink
thereof have their wool turned into a Vermilion
colour. And one of no less credit than *Aristotle*, tells
us of a merry River, (the River *Elusina*) that dances
at the noise of musick, for with musick it bubbles,
dances and grows sandy, and so continues till the
music ceases, but then it presently returns to its
wonted calmness and clearness. And *Cambden* tells
us of a Well near to *Kerby* in *Westmoreland*, that ebbs
and flows several times every day: and he tells us

of a River in Surry (it is called *Mole*) that after it has run several miles, being opposed by hills, finds or makes it self a way under ground, and breaks out again so far off, that the Inhabitants thereabout boast (as the *Spaniards* do of their river *Anus*) that they feed divers flocks of sheep upon a Bridge. And lastly, for I would not tire your patience, one of no less authority than *Josephus*, that learned Jew, tells us of a River in *Judea*, that runs swiftly all the six days of the week, and stands still and rests all their *Sabbath*.

But I will lay aside my Discourse of Rivers, and tell you some things of the Monsters, or Fish, call them what you will, that they breed and feed in them. *Pliny* the philosopher says, (in the third Chapter of his ninth Book) that in the *Indian Sea*, the fish call'd the *Balaena* or *Whirle-pool*, is so long and broad, as to take up more in length and bredth than two Acres of ground, and of other fish of two hundred cubits long; and that in the river *Ganges*, there be Eeles of thirty foot long. He says there, that these Monsters appear in that Sea only, when the tempestuous winds oppose the Torrents of Waters falling from the rocks into it, and so turning what lay at the bottom to be seen on the waters top. And he says, that the people of *Cadara* (an island near this place) make the Timber for their houses of those fish-bones. He there tells us, that there are sometimes a thousand of these great Eeles found wrapt, or interwoven together. He tells us there, that it appears that Dolphins love musick, and will come, when call'd for, by some men or boys, that know and use to feed them, and that they can swim as swift as an Arrow can be shot out of a Bow; and much of this is spoken concerning the

Dolphin, and other Fish, as may be *found also in learned Dr. Casaubons* Discourse of Credulity and Incredulity, printed by him about the year 1670.

I know, we Islanders are averse to the belief of these wonders: but there be so many strange Creatures to be now seen (many collected by *John Tredescant*, and others added by my friend *Elias Ashmole*, Esq.; who now keeps them carefully and methodically at his house near to *Lambeth* near *London*) as may get some belief of some of the other wonders I mentioned. I will tell you some of the wonders that you may now see, and not till then believe, unless you think fit.

You may there see the *Hog-fish*, the *Dog-fish*, the *Dolphin*, the *Cony-fish*, the *Parrot-fish*, the *Shark*, the *Poyson-fish*, *sword-fish*, and not only other incredible fish! but you may there see the *Salamander*, several sorts of *Barnacles*, of *Solan Geese*, the *bird* of *Paradise*, such sorts of Snakes, and such *birds-nests*, and of so various forms, and so wonderfully made, as may beget wonder and amusement in any beholder: and so many hundred of other rarities in that collection, as will make the other wonders I spake of, the less incredible; for, you may note, that the waters are natures store-house, in which she locks up her wonders.

But, Sir, lest this Discourse may seem tedious, I shall give it a sweet conclusion out of that holy Poet Mr. *George Herbert* his Divine Contemplation on Gods Providence.

> *Lord, who hath praise enough, nay, who hath any?*
> *None can express thy works, but he that knows them;*
> *And none can know thy works, they are so many,*
> *And so compleat, but only he that ows them.*

We all acknowledg both thy power and love
To be exact, transcendent and divine;
Who dost so strangely and so sweetly move,
Whilst all things have their end, yet none but thine.

Wherefore, most sacred Spirit, I here present,
For me, and all my fellows, praise to thee;
And just it is that I should pay the rent,
Because the benefit accrues to me.

And as concerning Fish, in that Psalm, (*Psal.* 104),
wherein for height of Poetry and Wonders, the prophet *David* seems even to exceed himself, how doth
he there express himself in choice Metaphors, even
to the amazement of a contemplative Reader, concerning the *Sea*, the *Rivers*, and the *Fish* therein contained? And the great Naturalist *Pliny* says, *That
Nature's great and wonderful power is more demonstrated in the Sea than on the Land.* And this may
appear by the numerous and various Creatures in-
habiting both in and about that Element; as to the
Readers of *Gesner, Rondeletius, Pliny, Ausonius, Aris-*
Dubartas in   *totle*, and others, may be demonstrated.
the fifth day.   But I will sweeten this discourse also out
of a Contemplation in Divine *Dubartas*, who says,

God quickned in the sea and in the rivers,
So many Fishes of so many features,
That in the waters we may see all creatures,
Even all that on the earth are to be found,
As if the world were in deep waters drown'd.
For seas (as well as skies) have Sun, Moon, Stars;
(As well as air) Swallows, Rooks, and Stares;
(As well as earth) Vines, Roses, Nettles, Melons,
Mushroms, Pinks, Gilliflowers, and many millions
Of other plants, more rare, more strange than these,
As very fishes, living in the seas;

As also Rams, Calves, Horses, Hares, and Hogs,
Wolves, Urchins, Lions, Elephants, and Dogs;
Yea Men and Maids, and, which I most admire,
The mitred Bishop, and the cowled Fryer:
Of which, Examples, but a few years since,
Were shewn the Norway *and* Polonian *Prince.*

These seem to be wonders, but have had so many confirmations from men of learning and credit, that you need not doubt them; nor are the number, nor the various shapes of fishes, more strange or more fit for *contemplation*, than their different natures, inclinations and actions; concerning which, I shall beg your patient ear a little longer.

The *Cuttle-fish* will cast a long gut out of her throat, which (like as an Angler doth his line) she sendeth forth and pulleth in again at her pleasure, according as she sees some little fish come near to her; and the *Cuttle-fish* (being then hid in the gravel) lets the smaller fish nibble and bite the end of it, at which time she *Mount. Essays, and others affirm this.* by little and little draws the smaller fish so near to her, that she may leap upon her, and then catches and devours her: and for this reason some have called this fish the *Sea-Angler*.

And there is a fish called a *Hermit*, that at a certain age gets into a dead fishes shell, and like a Hermite dwells there alone, studying the wind and weather, and so turns her shell, that she makes it defend her from the injuries that they would bring upon her.

There is also a fish called by *Ælian* (in his 9. book of Living Creatures, Chap. 16) the *Adonis*, or Darling of the Sea; so called, because it is a loving and innocent fish, a fish that hurts nothing that hath life,

and is at peace with all the numerous Inhabitants
of that vast watry Element; and truly, I think most
Anglers are so disposed to most of mankind.

And there are also lustful and chast fishes; of
which I shall give you examples.

And first, what *Dubartas* sayes of a fish called the
Sargus; which (because none can expresse it better
than he does) I shall give you in his own words,
supposing it shall not have the less credit for being
Verse, for he hath gathered this, and other observations out of Authors that have been great and industrious searchers into the secrets of Nature.

> *The Adult'rous* Sargus *doth not only change*
> *Wives every day in the deep streams, but (strange)*
> *As if the bony of Sea-love delight*
> *Could not suffice his ranging appetite,*
> *Goes courting she-Goats on the grassie shore,*
> *Horning their husbands that had horns before.*

And the same author writes concerning the *Cantharus*, that which you shall also hear in his own
words.

> *But, contrary, the constant* Cantharus
> *Is ever constant to his faithful Spouse,*
> *In nuptial duties spending his chaste life,*
> *Never loves any but his own dear Wife.*

Sir, but a little longer, and I have done.

Venat. Sir, take what liberty you think fit, for
your discourse seems to be Musick, and charms me to
an attention.

Pisc. Why then Sir, I will take a little liberty
to tell, or rather to remember you what is said of
Turtle-doves; First, that they silently plight their
troth and marry; and that then, the Survivor scorns

(as the *Thracian women* are said to do) to out-live his or her mate, and this is taken for a truth, and if the surviver shall ever couple with another, then not only the living, but the dead, (be it either the He or the she) is denyed the *name* and *honour* of a true *Turtle-dove*.

And to parallel this *Land-Rarity*, and teach man-kind moral faithfulness, and to condemn those that talk of Religion, and yet come short of the moral faith of fish and fowl; Men that violate the Law affirmed by St. *Paul* (*Rom*. 2. 14, 15) to be writ in their hearts, (and which, he says, shall at the last day condemn and leave them without excuse.) I pray hearken to what *Dubartas* sings, (for the hearing of such conjugal faithfulness, *Dubartas fifth day.* will be musick to all chast ears) and therefore I pray hearken to what *Dubartas* sings of the *Mullet*.

> *But for chast love the* Mullet *hath no peer;*
> *For, if the Fisher hath surpriz'd her pheer,*
> *As mad with wo, to shore she followeth,*
> *Prest to consort him, both in life and death.*

On the contrary, What shall I say of the *House-Cock*, which treads any Hen, and then (contrary to the *Swan*, the *Partridge*, and *Pigeon*) takes no care to hatch, to feed or to cherish his own brood, but is senseless though they perish.

And 'tis considerable, that the Hen (which be-cause she also takes any *Cock*, expects it not) who is sure the Chickens be her own, hath by a moral im-pression her care and affection to her own Brood more than doubled, even to such a height, that our Saviour in expressing his love to *Jerusalem* (*Mat*. 23. 37), quotes her for an example of tender affection; as his Father had done *Job* for a pattern of patience.

And to parallel this *Cock*, there be divers fishes that cast their Spawn on flags or stones, and then leave it uncovered, and exposed to become a prey, and be devoured by Vermine or other fishes: but other fishes (as namely the *Barbel*) take such care for the preservation of their seed, that (unlike to the *Cock*, or the *Cuckoe*) they mutually labour (both the Spawner and the Melter) to cover their spawn with sand, or watch it, or hide it in some secret place, unfrequented by Vermine or by any Fish but themselves.

Sir, these Examples may, to you and others, seem strange; but they are testified some by *Aristotle*, some by *Pliny*, some by *Gesner*, and by many others of credit, and are believed and known by divers, both of wisdom and experience, to be a Truth; and indeed are (as I said at the beginning) fit for the contemplation of a most serious and a most pious man. And doubtless this made the Prophet *David* say, *They that occupy themselves in deep waters see the wonderful works of God*: indeed such wonders and pleasures too as the land affords not.

And that they be fit for the contemplation of the most prudent, and pious, and peaceable men, seems to be testifyed by the practise of so many devout and contemplative men, as the *Patriarchs* and *Prophets* of old; and of the *Apostles* of our Saviour in our latter times; of which twelve, we are sure he chose four that were simple Fisher-men, whom he inspired and sent to publish his blessed Will to the *Gentiles, and inspir'd them also with a power to speak all languages, and by their powerful Eloquence to beget faith in the unbelieving Jews: and themselves to suffer for that Saviour whom their fore fathers and they had Crucified, and, in their sufferings, to preach freedom from the incumbrances of the Law, and a new way to everlasting life*: this was the imployment of these happy Fishermen. Concerning which choice, some have made these Observations.

First that he never reproved these for their Imployment or Calling, as he did the *Scribes* and the *Mony-changers*. And secondly, he found that the hearts of such men by nature were fitted for contemplation and quietnesse; men of mild, and sweet, and peaceable spirits, as indeed most Anglers are: these men our blessed Saviour, (who is observed to love to plant grace in good natures) though indeed nothing be too hard for him, yet these men he chose to call from their irreprovable imployment of Fishing, and gave them grace to be his Disciples, and to follow him and doe wonders, I say four of twelve.

And it is observable, that it was our Saviours will, that these our four Fishermen should have a priority of nomination in the Catalogue of his twelve Apostles, (*Mat.* 10.), as namely first St. *Peter*, St. *Andrew*, St. *James* and St. *John*, and then the rest in their order.

And it is yet more observable, that when our blessed Saviour went up into the Mount, when he left the rest of his Disciples, and chose only three to bear him company at his *Transfiguration*, that those three were all Fishermen. And it is to be believed, that all the other Apostles, after they betook themselves to follow Christ, betook themselves to be Fishermen too; for it is certain that the greater number of them were found together Fishing by Jesus after his Resurrection, as it is recorded in the 21. Chapter of St. *Johns* Gospel.

And since I have your promise to hear me with patience, I will take a liberty to look back upon an

observation that hath been made by an ingenuous
and learned man, who observes that God hath been
pleased to allow those, whom he himself hath appointed to write his holy Will in holy writ, yet to
express his Will in such metaphors as their former
affections or practice had inclined them to; and he
brings *Solomon* for an example, who before his conversion was remarkably carnally-amorous; and after
by Gods appointment wrote that spiritual Dialogue,
or holy amorous Love-song (the *Canticles*) betwixt
God and his Church; (in which he sayes, his beloved
had *Eyes like the fish-pools of Heshbon.*)

And if this hold in reason (as I see none to the
contrary,) then it may be probably concluded, that
Moses (who, I told you before, writ the Book of *Job*)
and the prophet *Amos*, who was a Shepherd, were
both Anglers; for you shall in all the Old Testament,
find Fish-hooks, I think but twice mentioned, namely,
by meek *Moses* the friend of God, and by the humble
prophet *Amos*.

Concerning which last, namely the Prophet *Amos*
I shall make but this Observation, That he that shall
read the *humble, lowly, plain style* of that *Prophet*, and
compare it with the *high, glorious, eloquent style* of the
prophet *Isaiah* (though they be both equally true)
may easily believe *Amos* to be, not only a shepherd,
but a good-natur'd, plain *Fisher-man*.

Which I do the rather believe by comparing the
affectionate, loving, lowly, humble Epistles of S.
Peter, S. *James* and S. *John*, whom we know were
all Fishers, with the glorious language and high
Metaphors of S. *Paul*, who we may believe was not.

And for the lawfulness of Fishing it may very well
be maintained by our Saviours bidding St. *Peter* cast

his hook into the water and catch a Fish, for mony to pay tribute to *Caesar*. And let me tell you, that Angling is of high esteem, and of much use in other Nations. He that reads the Voyages of *Ferdinand Mendez Pinto*, shall find, that there he declares to have found a King and several Priests a Fishing.

And he that reads *Plutarch*; shall find, that Angling was not contemptible in the days of *Mark Antony* and *Cleopatra*, and that they in the midst of their wonderful glory used Angling as a principal recreation. And let me tell you, that in the Scripture, Angling is always taken in the best sense, and that though hunting may be sometimes so taken, yet it is but seldom to be so understood. And let me add this more, he that views the ancient Ecclesiastical Canons, shall find *Hunting* to be forbidden to *Church-men*, as being a turbulent, toilsom, perplexing Recreation; and shall find *Angling* allowed to *Clergy-men*, as being a harmless Recreation, a recreation that invites them to *contemplation* and *quietness*.

I might here enlarge my self by telling you what commendations our learned *Perkins* bestows on Angling: and how dear a lover, and great a practiser of it, our learned Doctor *Whitaker* was, as indeed many others of great learning have been. But I will content my self with two memorable men, that lived near to our own time, whom I also take to have been ornaments to the Art of Angling.

The first is Doctor *Nowel*, sometimes *Dean of the Cathedral Church of St. *Pauls* in *London*, where his Monument stands yet undefaced, a man that   *1550. in the Reformation of Queen *Elizabeth* (not that of *Henry the VIII.*) was so noted for his meek spirit, deep learning, prudence and piety, that the then

Parliament and Convocation both, chose, enjoyned, and trusted him to be the man to make a Catechism for publick use, such a one as should stand as a rule for faith and manners to their posterity. And the good old man (though he was very learned, yet knowing that God leads us not to Heaven by many nor by hard questions) like an honest Angler, made that *good*, *plain*, *unperplext* Catechism which is printed with our good old Service Book. I say, this good man was a dear lover, and constant practicer of Angling, as any Age can produce; and his custom was to spend besides his fixed hours of prayer, (those hours which, by command of the Church were enjoyned the Clergy, and voluntarily dedicated to devotion by many Primitive Christians:) I say, besides those hours, this good man was observed to spend a tenth part of his time in Angling; and also (for I have conversed with those which have conversed with him) to bestow a tenth part of his Revenue, and usually all his fish, amongst the poor that inhabited near to those Rivers in which it was caught: saying often, *That charity gave life to Religion*: and at his return to his House would praise God he had spent that day free from worldly trouble; both harmlessly, and in a recreation that became a Church-man. And this good man was well content, if not desirous, that posterity should know he was an Angler, as may appear by his Picture, now to be seen, and carefully kept, in *Brasennose Colledge* (to which he was a liberal Benefactor) in which picture he is drawn leaning on a Desk, with his Bible before him; and on one hand of him his *lines*, *hooks*, and other *tackling*, lying in a round; and, on his other hand, are his Angle-rods of several sorts: and by them this is written, *That he died*.

13. *Feb.* 1601. *being aged 95 years, 44 of which he had been Dean of St.* Pauls *Church; and that his age had neither impair'd his hearing, nor dimm'd his eyes, nor weaken'd his memory, nor made any of the faculties of his mind weak, or useless.* 'Tis said that *angling* and *temperance* were great causes of these blessings, and I wish the like to all that imitate him, and love the memory of so good a man.

My next and last example shall be that under-valuer of mony, the late Provost of *Eton* Colledge, Sir *Henry Wotton*, (a man with whom I have often fish'd and convers'd) a man whose foreign Imployments in the service of this *Nation*, and whose *experience*, *learning*, *wit*, and *chearfulness*, made his company to be esteemed one of the delights of mankind; this man, whose very approbation of Angling were suffi-cient to convince any modest censurer of it, this man was also a most dear lover, and a frequent practiser of the art of Angling; of which he would say, '*Twas an imployment for his idle time, which was then not idly spent*: for Angling was after tedious Study, *a rest to his mind, a chearer of his spirits, a diverter of sadness, a calmer of unquiet thoughts, a moderator of passions, a procurer of contentedness*; and *that it begat habits of* peace *and* patience *in those that profess'd* and practis'd it. Indeed, my friend, you will find angling to be like the vertue of Humility, which has a calm-ness of spirit, and a world of other blessings attend-ing upon it.

Sir, this was the saying of that learned man, and I do easily believe that *peace*, and *patience*, and a calm *content*, did cohabit in the chearful heart of Sir *Henry Wotton*, because I know that when he was beyond seventy years of age, he made this description of a

part of the present pleasure that possess'd him, as he
sate quietly, in a Summers evening on a bank a Fishing; it is a description of the Spring, which, because
it glided as soft and sweetly from his pen, as that
river does at this time by which it was then made, I
shall repeat it unto you.

> *This day dame Nature seem'd in love:*
> *The lusty sap began to move;*
> *Fresh juice did stir th' embracing Vines;*
> *And birds had drawn their Valentines,*
> *The jealous* Trout, *that low did lye,*
> *Rose at a well-dissembled* flie;
> *There stood my friend with patient skill,*
> *Attending of his trembling quill.*
> *Already were the eaves possest*
> *With the swift* Pilgrims *dawbed nest;*
> *The Groves already did rejoyce,*
> *In* Philomels *triumphing voice:*
> *The showers were short, the weather mild,*
> *The morning fresh, the evening smil'd.*
>   Jone *takes her neatrub'd pail, and now,*
> *She trips to milk the sand-red* Cow;
> *Where, for some sturdy foot-ball* Swain,
> Jone *strokes a* sillibub *or twain,*
> *The fields and gardens were beset*
> *With* Tulips, Crocus, Violet,
> *And now, though late, the modest* Rose
> *Did more than half a blush disclose.*
> *Thus all looks gay, and full of chear,*
> *To welcome the new livery'd year.*

These were the thoughts that then possest the
undisturbed mind of Sir *Henry Wotton*. Will you
hear the wish of another Angler, and the commendation of his happy life which he also sings in Verse?
viz. Jo. Davors, Esq.

Let me live harmlessly, and near the brink
Of Trent *or* Avon *have a dwelling-place;*
Where I may see my quill *or* cork *down sink*
With eager bite of Perch, *or* Bleak, *or* Dace;
And on the world and my Creator think,
Whilst some men strive ill gotten goods t' embrace;
   And others spend their time in base excess
   Of wine, or worse, in war *and* wantonness.

Let them that list, these pastimes still pursue,
And on such pleasing fancies feed their fill,
So I the fields *and* Meadows *green may view,*
And daily by fresh Rivers *walk at will,*
Among the Daisies *and the* Violets *blew,*
Red Hiacynth, *and yellow* Daffadil,
   Purple Narcissus *like the morning rayes,*
   Pale Gandergrasse, *and azure* Culverkeyes.

I count it higher pleasure to behold
The stately compasse of the lofty skie;
And in the midst thereof (*like burning gold*)
The flaming Chariot of the Worlds great eye,
The watry clouds that in the air uprol'd
With sundry kinds of painted colours flie;
   And fair Aurora, *lifting up her head,*
   Still blushing, rise from old Tithonus *bed.*

The hills *and* mountains *raised from the* plains,
The plains *extended level with the* ground,
The grounds *divided into sundry veins,*
The veins *inclos'd with* rivers *running round;*
These rivers making way through natures chains
With headlong course into the sea profound;
   The raging sea, beneath the vallies low,
   Where lakes *and* rills *and* rivulets *do flow.*

The lofty woods the forrests wide and long,
Adorn'd with leaves and branches fresh and green,
In whose cool bowers the birds with many a song
Do welcome with their Quire *the* Summers Queen;

The Meadowes fair where Flora's *gifts among*
Are intermixt, with verdant grasse between;
    The silver-scaled fish that softly swim
    Within the sweet brooks chrystal, watry stream,
All these, and many more of his Creation
That made the Heavens, the Angler *oft doth see,*
Taking therein no little delectation,
To think how strange, how wonderful they be;
Framing thereof an inward contemplation,
To set his heart from other fancies free;
    And whilst he looks on these with joyful eye,
    His mind is rapt above the starry Skie.

Sir I am glad my memory has not lost these last Verses, because they are somewhat more pleasant and more sutable to *May-day* than my harsh Discourse, and I am glad your patience hath held out so long, as to hear them and me: for both together have brought us within the sight of the *Thatcht-house*: and I must be your Debtor (if you think it worth your attention) for the rest of my promised discourse, till some other opportunity, and a like time of leisure.

Venat. Sir, you have Angled me on with much pleasure to the *Thatcht-house*; and I now find your words true, *That good company makes the way seem short*, for trust me, Sir, I thought we had wanted three miles of this *House* till you shewed it to me: but now we are at it, we'l turn into it, and refresh our selves with a cup of drink, and a little rest.

Pisc. Most gladly (Sir) and we'l drink a civil cup to all the *Otter Hunters* that are to meet you to morrow.

Ven. That we will Sir, and to all the lovers of Angling too, of which number, I am now willing to be one my self, for, by the help of your good discourse and company, I have put on new thoughts both of the art of Angling, and of all that professe it: and if you will but meet me to morrow at the time and place appointed, and bestow one day with me and my friends in hunting the *Otter*, I will dedicate the next two dayes to wait upon you, and we two will for that time do nothing but angle, and talk of fish and fishing.

Pisc. 'Tis a match, Sir, I'l not fail you, God willing, to be at *Amwel-hill* to morrow morning before Sun-rising.

CHAP. II.

Observations of the Otter and Chub.

*V*Enat. My friend *Piscator*, you have kept time with my thoughts, for the Sun is just rising, and I my self just now come to this place, and the dogs have just now put down an *Otter*; look down at the bottom of the hill there in that Meadow, chequered with *water-Lillies* and *Lady-smocks*; there you may see what work they make; look! look! you may see all busie, men and dogs, dogs and men, all busie.

Pisc. Sir, I am right glad to meet you, and glad to have so fair an entrance into this dayes sport, and glad to see so many dogs, and more men all in pursuit of the *Otter*; lets complement no longer, but joyn unto them. Come, honest *Venator*, lets be gone, let us make hast; I long to be doing; no reasonable hedg or ditch shall hold me.

Ven. Gentleman Hunts-man, where found you this *Otter*.

Hunt. Marry (Sir) we found her a mile from this place a fishing; she has this morning eaten the greatest part of this *Trout*; she has only left thus much of it as you see, and was fishing for more; when we came we found her just at it: but we were here very early, we were here an hour before Sun-rise, and have given her no rest since we came; sure she will hardly escape all these dogs and men. I am to have the skin if we kill her.

Ven. Why, Sir, what's the skin worth?

Hunt. 'Tis worth ten shillings to make gloves; the gloves of an *Otter* are the best fortification for your hands that can be thought on against wet weather.

Pisc. I pray, honest Huntsman, let me ask you a pleasant question, do you hunt a beast or a fish?

Hunt. Sir, it is not in my power to resolve you, I leave it to be resolved by the Colledge of *Carthusians*, who have made vows never to eat flesh. But I have heard, the question hath been debated among many great Clerks, and they seem to differ about it; yet most agree that her tail is Fish: and if her body be fish too, then I may say, that a fish will walk upon land, (for an *Otter* does so) sometimes five or six, or ten miles in a night to catch for her young ones, or to glut herself with Fish, and I can tell you that *Pigeons* will fly forty miles for a breakfast, but, *Sir*, I am sure the *Otter* devours much Fish, and kills and spoils much more than he eats: And I can tell you, that this Dog-fisher (for so the Latins call him) can smell a Fish in the water an hundred yards from him (*Gesner* says much farther) and that his stones are good against the Falling-sickness: and that there is an herb *Benione*, which being hung in a linnen cloth near a Fish-pond, or any haunt that he uses, makes him to avoid the place; which proves he smells both by water and land; and I can tell you there is brave hunting this Water-dog in *Corn-wall*, where there have been so many, that our learned *Cambden* says, there is a River called *Ottersey*, which was so named by reason of the abundance of *Otters* that bred and fed in it.

And thus much for my knowledg of the *Otter*, which you may now see above water at vent, and the dogs close with him; I now see he will not last long, follow therefore my Masters, follow, for *Sweetlips* was like to have him at this last vent.

Ven. Oh me all the Horse are got over the River, what shall we do now? shall we follow them over the water?

Hunt. No, *Sir*, no, be not so eager, stay a little and follow me, for both they and the dogs will be suddenly on this side again, I warrant you: and the *Otter* too, it may be: now have at him with *Kilbuck*, for he vents again.

Ven. Marry so he do's, for look he vents in that corner. Now, now *Ringwood* has him: now he's gone again, and has bit the poor dog. Now *Sweetlips* has her; hold her, *Sweetlips*! now all the dogs have her, some above and some under water; but now, now she's tir'd, and past losing: come bring her to me, *Sweet-lips*. Look, 'tis a Bitch-*Otter*, and she has lately whelp'd, let's go to the place where she was *put down*, and not far from it you will find all her young ones, I dare warrant you, and kill them all too.

Hunt. Come, Gentlemen, come all! let's go to the place where we *put down* the *Otter*. Look you, hereabout it was that she kennell'd; look you, here it was indeed; for here's her young ones, no less than five; come, let's kill them all.

Pisc. No, I pray, Sir, save me one, and I'll try if I can make her tame, as I know an ingenuous Gentleman in *Leicester-shire* (Mr. *Nich. Seagrave*) has done; who hath not only made her tame, but to catch Fish, and do many other things of much pleasure.

Hunt. Take one with all my heart, but let us kill the rest. And now let's go to an honest Ale-house, where we may have a cup of good *Barley-wine*, and sing *Old Rose*, and all of us rejoyce together.

Venat. Come, my friend, *Piscator*, let me invite you along with us; I'll bear your charges this night, and you shall bear mine to morrow; for my intention is to accompany you a day or two in Fishing.

Pisc. Sir, your request is granted, and I shall be right glad, both to exchange such a courtesie, and also to enjoy your company.

Venat. Well, now let's go to your sport of Angling.

Pisc. Let's be going with all my heart. God keep you all, Gentlemen, and send you meet this day with another Bitch-Otter, and kill her merrily, and all her young ones too.

Ven. Now, *Piscator*, where will you begin to fish?

Pisc. We are not yet come to a likely place, I must walk a mile further yet, before I begin.

Venat. Well then, I pray, as we walk tell me freely, how do you like your lodging and mine Hoste and the company? is not mine Hoste a witty man?

Pisc. Sir, I will tell you presently what I think of your Hoste: but, first, I will tell you, I am glad these *Otters* were killed, and I am sorry there are no more *Otter-killers*, for I know that the want of *Otter-killers*, & the not keeping the *Fence months* for the preservation of *fish*, will in time prove the destruction of all *Rivers*; and those very few that are left, that make conscience of the Laws of the Nation, and of keeping days of abstinence, will be forced to eat flesh, or suffer more inconveniences than are yet foreseen.

Venat. Why, Sir, what be those that you call the Fence months?

Pisc. Sir, they be principally three, namely, *March*, *April*, and *May*, for these be the usual months that *Salmon* come out of the Sea to spawn in most fresh Rivers, and their Fry would about a certain time return back to the salt water, if they were not hindred by *wires* and *unlawful gins*, which the greedy Fisher-men set, and so destroy them by thousands; as they would (being so taught by nature) change the *fresh* for *salt water*. He that shall view the wise Statutes made in the 13 of *Edw. the I.* and the like in *Rich. the II.* may see several provisions made against the destruction of Fish: and though I profess no knowledg of the Law, yet I am sure the regulation of these defects might be easily mended. But I remember that a wise friend of mine did usually say, *That which is every bodies business, is no bodies business*. If it were otherwise, there could not be so many Nets and Fish that are under the Statute size, sold daily amongst us, and of which the *conservators* of the waters should be ashamed.

But above all, the taking Fish in Spawning time may be said to be against nature; it is like the taking the dam on the nest when she hatches her young: a sin so against nature, that Almighty God hath in the Levitical law made a law against it.

But the poor Fish have enemies enough beside such unnatural *Fisher-men*; as namely, the *Otters* that I spake of, the *Cormorant*, the *Bittern*, the *Osprey*, the *Sea-gull*, the *Hern*, the *Kingfisher*, the *Gorrara*, the *Puet*, the *Swan*, *Goose*, *Ducks*, and the *Craber*, which some call the Water-rat: against all which any honest man may make a just quarrel, but I will not, I will leave them to be quarrelled with, and killed by others; for I am not of a cruel nature, I love to kill nothing but Fish.

And now to your question concerning your Hoste, to speak truly, he is not to me a good companion: for most of his conceits were either Scripture jests, or lascivious jests; for which I count no man witty, for the Devil will help a man that way inclined, to the first; and his own corrupt nature (which he always carries with him) to the latter. But a companion that feasts the company with *wit* and *mirth*, and leaves out the sin (which is usually mixt with them) he is the man; and indeed such a companion should have his charges born; and to such company I hope to bring you this night; for at *Trout-hall*, not far from this place, where I purpose to lodge tonight, there is usually an Angler that proves good company: and let me tell you, good company and good discourse are the very sinews of vertue: but for such discourse as we heard last night, it infects others, the very boys will learn to talk and swear as they heard mine Host, and another of the company that shall be nameless; I am sorry the other is a Gentleman, for less Religion will not save their Souls than a beggars; I think more will be required at the last great day. Well, you know what Example is able to do, and I know what the Poet says in the like case, which is

worthy to be noted by all parents and people of
civility:

> ———*Many a one*
> *Owes to his Country his Religion:*
> *And in another would as strongly grow,*
> *Had but his nurse or mother taught him so.*

This is reason put into Verse, and worthy the
consideration of a wise man. But of this no more,
for though I love civility, yet I hate severe censures:
I'le to my own art, and I doubt not but at yonder tree
I shall catch a *Chub*: and then we'l turn to an honest
cleanly Hostess, that I know right well; rest our
selves there, and dress it for our dinner.

Venat. Oh Sir, a *Chub* is the worst Fish that swims,
I hoped for a *Trout* to my dinner.

Pisc. Trust me, *Sir*, there is not a likely place for
a *Trout*, hereabout, and we staid so long to take our
leave of your Huntsmen this morning, that the Sun
is got so high, and shines so clear, that I will not
undertake the catching of a *Trout* till evening; and
though a *Chub* be by you and many others, reckoned
the worst of *fish*, yet you shall see I'll make it a good
Fish by dressing it.

Ven. Why, how will you dress him?

Pisc. I'll tell you by and by, when I have caught
him. Look you here, Sir, do you see? (but you must
stand very close) there lye upon the top of the water
in this very hole twenty *Chubs*. I'll catch only one,
and that shall be the biggest of them all: and that I
will do so, I'll hold you twenty to one, and you shall
see it done.

Venat. Aye, marry Sir, now you talk like an
Artist, and I'll say you are one, when I shall see you
perform what you say you can do; but I yet doubt it.

Pisc. You shall not doubt it long, for you shall see me do it presently: look, the biggest of these *Chubs* has had some bruise upon his tail, by a Pike or some other accident, and that looks like a white spot; that very *Chub* I mean to put into your hands presently; sit you but down in the shade, and stay but a little while, and I'le warrant you I'le bring him to you.

Venat. I'le sit down and hope well, because you seem to be so confident.

Pisc. Look you Sir, there is a tryal of my skill, there he is, that very *Chub* that I shewed you with the white spot on his tail: and I'le be as certain to make him a good dish of meat, as I was to catch him: I'le now lead you to an honest Ale-house where we shall find a cleanly room, *Lavender* in the Windows, and twenty *Ballads* stuck about the wall; there my Hostess (which I may tell you, is both cleanly and handsome and civil) hath drest many a one for me, and shall now dress it after my fashion, and I warrant it good meat.

Ven. Come Sir, with all my heart, for I begin to be hungry, and long to be at it, and indeed to rest my self too; for though I have walk'd but four miles this morning, yet I begin to be weary; yesterdays hunting hangs still upon me.

Pisc. Well Sir, and you shall quickly be at rest, for yonder is the house I mean to bring you to.

Come Hostess, how do you? Will you first give us a cup of your best drink, and then dress this *Chub*, as you dressed my last, when I and my friend were here about eight or ten days ago? but you must do me one courtesie, it must be done instantly.

Host. I will do it, Mr. *Piscator*, and with all the speed I can.

Pisc. Now Sir, has not my Hostess made hast? and does not the fish look lovely?

Ven. Both, upon my word, Sir, and therefore let's say grace and fall to eating of it.

Pisc. Well, Sir, how do you like it?

Ven. Trust me, 'tis as good meat as I ever tasted: Now let me thank you for it, drink to you, and beg a courtesie of you; but it must not be deny'd me.

Pisc. What is it I pray Sir: you are so modest, that methinks I may promise to grant it before it is asked.

Ven. Why, Sir, it is, that from henceforth you would allow me to call you *Master*, and that really I may be your Scholar, for you are such a companion, and have so quickly caught, and so excellently cook'd this fish, as makes me ambitious to be your Scholar.

Pisc. Give me your hand; from this time forward I will be your Master, and teach you as much of this Art as I am able; and will, as you desire me, tell you somewhat of the nature of most of the Fish that we are to angle for, and I am sure I both can and will tell you more than any common *Angler* yet knows.

CHAP. III

How to fish for, and to dress the Chavender *or* Chub.

PIsc. The *Chub*, though he eat well thus drest, yet as he is usually drest, he does not: he is objected against, not only for being full of small forked bones, disperst through all his body, but that he eats watrish, and that the flesh of him is not firm, but short and tastless. The *French* esteem him so mean, as to call him *Un Villain*; nevertheless he may

be so drest as to make him very good meat; as
namely, if he be a large Chub, then dress him thus:

*First scale him, and then wash him clean, and then
take out his guts; and to that end make the hole as little
and near to his gills as you may conveniently, and
especially make clean his throat from the grass and weeds
that are usually in it (for if that be not very clean, it will
make him to taste very sour) having so done, put some
sweet herbs into his belly, and then tye him with two or
three splinters to a spit, and rost him, basted often with
Vinegar, or rather verjuice and butter, with good store
of salt mixt with it.*

Being thus drest, you will find him a much better
dish of meat than you, or most folk, even than
Anglers themselves do imagine; for this dries up
the fluid watry humor with which all *Chubs* do
abound.

But take this rule with you, That a *Chub* newly
taken and newly drest, is so much better than a *Chub*
of a days keeping after he is dead, that I can compare
him to nothing so fitly as to Cherries newly gathered
from a tree, and others that have been bruised and
lain a day or two in water. But the *Chub* being thus
used and drest presently, and not washed after he is
gutted (for note that lying long in water, and washing the blood out of any fish after they be gutted,
abates much of their sweetness) you will find the
Chub being drest in the blood and quickly, to be
such meat as will recompence your labour, and disabuse your opinion.

Or you may dress the *Chavender* or *Chub* thus:

*When you have scaled him, and cut off his tail and
fins, and washed him very clean, then chine or slit him
through the middle, as a salt fish is usually cut, then*

give him three or four cuts or scotches on the back with
your knife, and broil him on Char-coal, or Wood-coal
that are free from smoke, and all the time he is a broyling
baste him with the best sweet Butter, and good store of
salt mixt with it; and to this add a little Time cut ex-
ceeding small, or bruised into the butter. The Cheven
thus drest hath the watry tast taken away, for
which so many except against him. Thus was the
Cheven drest that you now liked so well, and commended so much. But note again, that if this Chub that
you eat of, had been kept till to morrow, he had not
been worth a rush. And remember that his throat be
washt very clean, I say very clean, and his body not
washt after he is gutted, as indeed no fish should be.

Well, Scholar, you see what pains I have taken to
recover the lost credit of the poor despised *Chub*.
And now I will give you some rules how to catch
him; and I am glad to enter you into the Art of fishing by catching a *Chub*, for there is no fish better to
enter a young Angler, he is so easily caught, but then
it must be this particular way:

Go to the same hole in which I caught my *Chub*,
where in most hot daies you will find a dozen or
twenty *Chevens* floating near the top of the water,
get two or three grasshoppers as you go over the
meadow, and get secretly behind the tree, and stand
as free from motion as is possible, then put a Grasshopper on your hook, and let your hook hang a
quarter of a yard short of the water, to which end
you must rest your rod on some bough of the tree,
but it is likely the Chubs will sink down towards the
bottom of the water at the first shadow of your Rod
(for a Chub is the fearfullest of fishes,) and will do
so if but a bird flies over him, and makes the least

shadow on the water: but they will presently rise up
to the top again, and there lie soaring till some
shadow affrights them again: I say when they lie
upon the top of the water, look out the best Chub,
(which you setting your self in a fit place, may very
easily see) and move your Rod, as softly as a Snail
moves, to that Chub you intend to catch; let your
bait fall gently upon the water three or four inches
before him, and he will infallibly take the bait, and
you will be as sure to catch him; for he is one of the
leather-mouth'd fishes, of which a hook does scarce
ever lose its hold; and therefore give him play
enough before you offer to take him out of the water.
Go your way presently, take my Rod, and do as I bid
you, and I will sit down and mend my tackling till
you return back.

Ven. Truly, my loving Master, you have offered
me as fair as I could wish. I'll go and observe your
directions.

Look you, Master, what I have done, that which
joys my heart, caught just such another *Chub* as
yours was.

Pisc. Marry, and I am glad of it: I am like to have
a towardly Scholar of you. I now see, that with advice and practice you will make an Angler in a short
time. Have but a love to it and I'le warrant you.

Venat. But Master, what if I could not have found
a *Grasshopper*?

Pisc. Then I may tell you, that a *black Snail*, with
his belly slit, to show his white: or a piece of soft
cheese, will usually do as well: nay, sometimes a *worm*
or any kind of *Flie*, as the *Ant-flie*, the *Flesh-flie*, or
Wall-flie, or the *Dor* or *Beetle*, (which you may find
under a Cow-tird) or a *Bob*, which you will find in

the same place, and in time will be a Beetle; it is a short white worm, like to and bigger than a Gentle, or a *Cod-worm*, or a *Case-worm*, any of these will do very well to fish in such a manner. And after this manner you may catch a *Trout* in a hot evening: when as you walk by a Brook, and shall see or hear him leap at flies, then if you get a *Grasshopper*, put it on your hook, with your line about two yards long, standing behind a bush or tree where his hole is, and make your bait stir up and down on the top of the water: you may, if you stand close, be sure of a bite, but not sure to catch him, for he is not a leather mouthed Fish: and after this manner you may fish for him with almost any kind of live flie, but especially with a *Grasshopper*.

Venat. But before you go further, I pray good Master, what mean you by a leather-mouthed Fish?

Pisc. By a leather-mouthed Fish, I mean such as have their teeth in their throat, as the *Chub* or *Cheven*, and so the *Barbel*, the *Gudgeon*, and *Carp*, and divers others have; and the hook, being stuck into the leather or skin of the mouth of such fish does very seldom or never lose its hold: But on the contrary, a *Pike*, a *Pearch*, or *Trout*, and so some other Fish, which have not their teeth in their throats, but in their mouths, (which you shall observe to be very full of bones, and the skin very thin, and little of it:) I say, of these fish the hook never takes so sure hold, but you often lose your fish, unless he have gorg'd it.

Ven. I thank you, good Master, for this observation; but now what shall be done with my *Chub* or *Cheven*, that I have caught?

Pisc. Marry, Sir, it shall be given away to some

poor body, for I'le warrant you I'le give you a *Trout*
for your supper: and it is a good beginning of your
Art to offer your first fruits to the poor, who will
both thank God and you for it, which I see by your
silence you seem to consent to. And for your willingness to part with it so charitably, I will also teach
more concerning Chub-fishing: you are to note that
in *March* and *April* he is usually taken with wormes;
in *May*, *June*, and *July* he will bite at any *fly*, or at
Cherries, or at *Beetles* with their legs and wings cut
off, or at any kind of *Snail*, or at the black *Bee* that
breeds in clay walls; and he never refuses a Grasshopper on the top of a swift stream, nor at the bottom the young *humble-bee* that breeds in long grasse,
and is ordinarily found by the Mower of it. In
August, and in the cooler months, a yellow *paste*,
made of the strongest cheese, and pounded in a
Mortar, with a little butter and saffron, (so much
of it as being beaten small will turn it to a lemon
colour.) And some make a paste for the Winter
months, at which time the Chub is accounted best,
(for then it is observed, that the forked bones are
lost, or turned into a kind of gristle, (especially if he
be baked) of Cheese and Turpentine; he will bite
also at a Minnow or Penk, as a Trout will: of which
I shall tell you more hereafter, and of divers other
baits. But take this for a rule, that in hot weather he
is to be fisht for towards the mid-water, or near the
top; and in colder weather nearer the bottom. And if
you fish for him on the top, with a Beetle or any *fly*,
then be sure to let your line be very long, and to keep
out of sight. And having told you that his spawn is
excellent meat, and that the head of a large Cheven,
the Throat being well washt, is the best part of him,

I will say no more of this Fish at the present, but wish you may catch the next you fish for.

But lest you may judg me too nice in urging to have the Chub drest so presently after he is taken, I will commend to your consideration how curious former times have been in the like kind.

You shall read in *Seneca* his natural Questions (*Lib.* 3, *cap.* 17.) that the Ancients were so curious in the newnesse of their Fish, that that seemed not new enough that was not put alive into the guests hand; and he says, that to that end they did usually keep them living in glass-bottles in their dining-rooms; and they did glory much in their entertaining of friends to have that Fish taken from under their table alive, that was instantly to be fed upon. And he says, they took great pleasure to see their Mullets change to several colours, when they were dying. But enough of this; for I doubt I have stayed too long from giving you some observations of the *Trout*, and how to fish for him, which shall take up the next of my spare time.

CHAP. IV

Observations of the nature and breeding of the Trout; and how to fish for him. And the Milk maids Song.

PIsc. The *Trout* is a fish highly valued both in this and forraign *Nations*: he may be justly said, (as the old Poet said of wine, and we English say of Venison) to be a generous Fish: a Fish that is so like the *Buck* that he also has his seasons, for it is observed, that he comes in and goes out of season with the *Stag* and *Buck*, *Gesner* says, his name is of a

Germane off-spring, and says he is a fish that feeds clean and purely, in the swiftest streams, and on the hardest gravel! and that he may justly contend with all fresh-water-Fish, as the Mullet may with all Sea-Fish for precedency and daintiness of taste, and that being in right season, the most dainty palats have allowed precedency to him.

And before I go farther in my Discourse, let me tell you, that you are to observe, that as there be some *barren Does*, that are good in Summer, so there be some *barren Trouts* that are good in Winter, but there are not many that are so, for usually they be in their perfection in the month of *May*, and decline with the *Buck*. Now you are to take notice, that in several Countries, as in *Germany* and in other parts, compar'd to ours, Fish do differ much in their bigness, and shape, and other ways, and so do *Trouts*; it is well known that in the Lake *Leman* (the Lake of *Geneva*) there are *Trouts* taken of three Cubits long, as is affirmed by *Gesner*, a Writer of good credit; and *Mercator* says, the *Trouts* that are taken in the Lake of *Geneva*, are a great part of the Merchandize of that famous City. And you are further to know, that there be certain waters that breed *Trouts* remarkable, both for their number and smallness. I know a little Brook in *Kent*, that breeds them to a number incredible, and you may take them twenty or forty in an hour, but none greater than about the size of a *Gudgion*. There are also in divers Rivers, especially that relate to, or be near to the Sea (as *Winchester*, or the *Thames* about *Windsor*) a little *Trout* called a *Samlet* or *Skegger Trout* (in both which places I have caught twenty or forty at a standing) that will bite as fast and as freely as *Minnows*; these be by some taken to be young *Salmons*, but in those waters they never grow to be bigger than a *Herring*.

There is also in *Kent* near to *Canterbury*, a *Trout* (call'd there a *Fordidge Trout*) a *Trout* (that bears the name of the Town where it is usually caught) that is accounted the rarest of Fish; many of them near the bigness of a *Salmon*, but known by their different colour, and in their best season they cut very white; and none of these have been known to be caught with an Angle, unless it were one that was caught by Sir *George Hastings* (an excellent Angler, and now with God) and he hath told me, he thought that *Trout* bit not for hunger but wantonness; and it is the rather to be believed, because both he then, and many others before him, have been curious to search into their bellies, what the food was by which they lived; and have found out nothing by which they might satisfie their curiosity.

Concerning which you are to take notice, that it is reported by good Authors, that *grasshoppers* and some Fish have no mouths, but are nourisht and take breath by the porousness of their Guills, Man knows not how; And this may be believed, if we consider that when the *Raven* hath hatcht her eggs, she takes no further care, but, leaves her young ones to the care of the God of Nature, who is said in the *Psalms*, *To feed the young Ravens that call upon him*. And they be kept alive, and fed by a *dew*, or *worms* that breed in their nests, or some other ways that we Mortals know not; and this may be believed of the *Fordidge Trout*, which (as it is said of the *Stork*, that he knows his season, so he) knows his times (I think almost his day) of coming into that River out of the Sea, where he lives (and it is like, feeds) nine months of the Year, and fasts three in the River of *Fordidge*. And you are to note, that those Townsmen are very punctual in observing the time of beginning to fish for them; and boast much that their River affords a Trout, that exceeds all others. And just so does *Sussex* boast of several Fish; as namely, a *Shelsey Cockle*, a *Chichester Lobster*, an *Arundel Mullet*, and an *Amerly Trout*.

And now for some confirmation of the *Fordidge* Trout, you are to know that this Trout is thought to eat nothing in the fresh water; and it may be the better believed, because it is well known, that *Swallows* and *Bats* and *Wagtails*, which are call'd half year birds, and not seen to flie in *England* for six months in the Year, but about *Michaelmas* leave us for a hotter Climate; yet some of them that have been left behind their fellows, have been found (many thousands at a time) in hollow trees, or clay-Caves, where they have been observed, to live and sleep *View Sir Fra.* out the whole Winter without meat; *Bacon, exper.* and so *Albertus* observes, that there is 899. one kind of *Frog* that hath her mouth naturally shut up about the end of *August*, and that *See Topsel,* she lives so all the Winter: and though *Of Frogs.* it be strange to some, yet it is known to too many among us to be doubted.

And so much for these *Fordidge trouts*, which never afford an *Angler* sport, but either live their time of being in the fresh water, by their meat formerly gotten in the Sea (not unlike the *Swallow* or *Frog*) or by the vertue of the fresh water only; or as the birds of *Paradise*, and the *Camelion* are said to live by the *Sun* and the *Air*.

There is also in *Northumberland* a *Trout* called a

Bull-trout, of a much greater length and bigness, than any in these Southern parts: and there are in many Rivers that relate to the Sea, *Salmon-trouts*, as much different from others, both in shape and in their spots, as we see sheep in some Countries differ one from another in their shape and bigness, and in the fineness of their wool: and certainly, as some pastures breed larger sheep, so do some Rivers, by reason of the ground over which they run, breed larger *Trouts*.

Now the next thing that I will commend to your consideration is, that the *Trout* is of a more sudden growth than other Fish: concerning which you are also to take notice, that he lives not so long as the *Pearch* and divers other Fishes do, as Sir *Francis Bacon* hath observed in his History of Life and Death.

And next you are to take notice, that he is not like the *Crocodile*, which if he lives never so long, yet always thrives till his death: but 'tis not so with the Trout; for after he is come to his full growth, he declines in his body, and keeps his bigness or thrives only in his head till his death. And you are to know, that he will about (especially before) the time of his Spawning, get almost miraculously through *Weires* and *Floud-gates* against the stream; even through such high and swift places as is almost incredible. Next, that the *Trout* usually Spawns about *October* or *November*, but in some Rivers a little sooner or later: which is the more observable, because most other fish Spawn in the Spring or Summer, when the Sun hath warmed both the earth and water, and made it fit for generation. And you are to note, that he continues many months out of season: for it may be observed of the Trout, that he is like the Buck or the Ox, that will not be fat in many months, though he go in the very same pastures that horses do, which will be fat in one month; and so you may observe, that most other Fishes recover strength, and grow sooner fat, and in season than the Trout doth.

And next, you are to note, that till the Sun gets to such a height as to warm the earth and the water, the Trout is sick and lean, and lowsie, and unwholesom: for you shall in winter find him to have a big head, and then to be lank, and thin, and lean; at which time many of them have sticking on them Sugs, or *Trout lice*, which is a kind of a worm, in shape like a clove or pin with a big head, and sticks close to him and sucks his moisture; those, I think, the *Trout* breeds himself, and never thrives till he free himself from them, which is when warm weather comes; and then, as he grows stronger, he gets from the dead, still water, into the sharp streams, and the gravel, and there rubs off these worms or lice; and then, as he grows stronger, so he gets him into swifter and swifter streams, and there lies at the watch for any flie or Minnow, that comes near to him; and he especially loves the *May-flie*, which is bred of the *Cod-worm*, or *Caddis*; and these make the Trout bold and lusty, and he is usually fatter and better meat at the end of that month, than at any time of the year.

Now you are to know, that it is observed, that usually the best *trouts* are either red or yellow, though some (as the *Fordidge Trout*) be white and yet good; but that is not usual: and it is a note observable, that the female *Trout* hath usually a less head, and a deeper body than the male *Trout*; and is usually the better meat: and note that a hogback, and a little head to either *Trout*, *Salmon*, or any other fish, is a sign that that fish is in season.

But yet you are to note, that as you see some Willows or palm-trees bud and blossom sooner than others do, so some Trouts be in Rivers sooner in season; and as some Hollies or Oaks are longer before they cast their leaves, so are some Trouts, in Rivers, longer before they go out of season.

And you are to note, that there are several kinds of *Trouts*, but these several kinds are not considered but by very few men, for they go under the general name of *Trouts*: just as Pigeons do in most places; though it is certain, there are tame, and wild Pigeons: and of the tame, there be *Helmits* and *Runts* and *Carriers* and *Cropers*, and indeed too many to name. Nay, the *Royal Society* have found and publisht lately, that there be thirty and three kinds of Spiders: and yet all, (for ought I know) go under that one general name of *Spider*. And 'tis so with many kinds of Fish, and of *Trouts* especially, which differ in their bigness and shape, and spots, and colour. The great *Kentish Hens* may be an instance, compared to other Hens; And doubtless there is a kind of small Trout, which will never thrive to be big, that breeds very many more than others do, that be of a larger size; which you may rather believe, if you consider, that the little *Wren* and *Titmouse* will have twenty young ones at a time, when usually the noble *Hawk*, or the Musical *Thrassal* or *Black-bird* exceed not four or five.

And now you shall see me try my skill to catch a Trout, and at my next walking either this evening, or to morrow morning, I will give you direction, how you your self shall fish for him.

Venat. Trust me, Master, I see now it is a harder matter to catch a *Trout* than a *Chub*: for I have put

on patience, and followed you these two hours, and
not seen a Fish stir, neither at your Minnow nor
your Worm.

Pisc. Well Scholar, you must endure worse luck
sometime, or you will never make a good Angler.
But what say you now? there is a *Trout* now, and
a good one too, if I can but hold him, and two or
three turns more will tire him: Now you see he lies
still, and the sleight is to land him: Reach me that
Landing Net. So (Sir) now he is mine own, what
say you now? is not this worth all my labour and your
patience?

Venat. On my word Master, this is a gallant
Trout, what shall we do with him?

Pisc. Marry e'en eat him to supper: we'l go to
my Hostess from whence we came; she told me, as
I was going out of door, that my brother *Peter*, a
good Angler and a chearful companion, had sent
word he would lodge there to night, and bring a
friend with him. My Hostess has two beds, and I
know, you and I may have the best: we'l rejoice
with my brother *Peter* and his friend, tell tales, or
sing Ballads, or make a Catch, or find some harmless
sport to content us, and pass away a little time without offence to God or man.

Venat. A match, good Master, lets go to that
house for the linnen looks white, and smells of
Lavender, and I long to lie in a pair of sheets that
smell so: lets be going, good Master, for I am
hungry again with fishing.

Pisc. Nay, stay a little good Scholar, I caught my
last *Trout* with a Worm, now I will put on a Minnow,
and try a quarter of an hour about yonder trees for
another, and so walk towards our Lodging. Look

you Scholar, thereabout we shall have a bite presently, or not at all: have with you (Sir!) o' my word
I have hold of him. Oh it is a great loggerheaded
Chub; Come, hang him upon that Willow twig, and
lets be going, But turn out of the way a little, good
Scholar, towards yonder high *honysuckle hedg*; there
we'll sit and sing whilst this showr falls so gently
upon the teeming earth, and gives yet a sweeter
smell to the lovely flowers that adorn these verdant
Meadows.

Look! under that broad *Beech-tree*, I sate down,
when I was last this way a fishing, and the birds
in the adjoyning Grove seemed to have a friendly
contention with an Eccho, whose dead voice seemed
to live in a hollow tree, near to the brow of that
Primrose-hill; there I sate viewing the silver streams
glide silently towards their center, the tempestuous
Sea; yet, sometimes opposed by rugged roots, and
pebble-stones, which broke their waves, and turned
them into foam: and sometimes I beguil'd time by
viewing the harmless Lambs, some leaping securely
in the cool shade, whilst others sported themselves
in the chearful Sun; and saw others craving comfort
from the swoln Udders of their bleating Dams. As
I thus sate, these and other sights had so fully
possesst my soul with content, that I thought as the
Poet has happily exprest it:

> *I was for that time lifted above earth;*
> *And possest joys not promis'd in my birth,*

As I left this place, and entered into the next
field, a second pleasure entertained me, 'twas a handsom milk-maid that had not yet attain'd so much age
and wisdom as to load her mind with any fears of

many things that will never be (as too many men too often do) but she cast away all care, and sung like a *Nightingale*: her voice was good, and the Ditty fitted for it; 'twas that smooth song, which was made by *Kit. Marlow*, now at least fifty years ago: and the *Milk-maids* Mother sung an answer to it, which was made by Sir *Walter Rawleigh* in his younger days.

They were old-fashioned Poetry, but choicely good, I think much better than the strong lines that are now in fashion in this critical age. Look yonder! on my word, yonder they both be a milking again, I will give her the *Chub*, and perswade them to sing those two songs to us.

God speed you good woman, I have been a-Fishing, and am going to *Bleak-Hall*, to my bed, and having caught more Fish than will sup my self and my friend, I will bestow this upon you and your Daughter, for I use to sell none.

Milk. Marry God requite you Sir, and we'll eat it chearfully: and if you come this way a Fishing two months hence, a grace of God I'le give you a Sillybub of new Verjuice in a new made Hay-cock, for it, And my *Maudlin* shall sing you one of her best *Ballads*, for she and I both love all *Anglers*, they be such honest, civil, quiet men; in the mean time will you drink a draught of *Red-Cows milk*, you shall have if freely.

Pisc. No, I thank you, but I pray do us a courtesie that shall stand you and your daughter in nothing, and yet we will think our selves still something in your debt: it is but to sing us a Song, that was sung by your daughter, when I last past over this Meadow, about eight or nine days since.

Milk. What Song was it, I pray? was it *Come*

Shepherds deck your herds, or *As at noon* Dulcina
rested, or Phillida *flouts me,* or *Chevy Chase,* or *Jonny
Armstrong* or *Troy Town?*

Pisc. No, it is none of those: it is a Song that your
daughter sung the first part, and you sung the answer
to it.

Milk. O, I know it now, I learn'd the first part in
my golden age, when I was about the age of my poor
daughter; and the latter part, which indeed fits me
best now, but two or three years ago, when the cares
of the World began to take hold of me: but you shall,
God willing, hear them both, and sung as well as
we can, for we both love Anglers. Come, *Maudlin,*
sing the first part to the Gentlemen, with a merry
heart, and I'le sing the second, when you have done.

The Milk-maids Song

> *Come live with me, and be my Love,*
> *And we will all the pleasures prove*
> *That valleys, groves, or hills, or fields,*
> *Or woods, and steepy mountains yeilds.*
>
> *Where we will sit upon the Rocks,*
> *And see the Shepherds feed our flocks,*
> *By shallow* Rivers, *to whose falls,*
> *Melodious birds sing* Madrigals.
>
> *And I will make thee beds of* Roses,
> *And then a thousand fragrant Posies,*
> *A Cap of flowers, and a Kirtle,*
> *Embroidered all with leaves of mirtle.*
>
> *A Gown made of the finest Wool*
> *Which from our pretty Lambs we pull;*
> *Slippers lin'd choicely for the cold,*
> *With buckles of the purest gold.*

A Belt of Straw, and Ivy-buds,
With Coral Clasps and Amber studs:
And if these pleasures may thee move,
Come live with me and be my Love.

Thy silver dishes for thy meat,
As precious as the Gods do eat,
Shall on an Ivory Table be
Prepar'd each day for thee and me.

The Shepherds Swains shall dance and sing
For thy delight each May-morning:
If these delights thy mind may move,
Then live with me, and be my Love.

Venat. Trust me, Master, it is a choice Song, and
sweetly sung by honest *Maudlin.* I now see it was
not without cause, that our good Queen *Elizabeth*
did so often wish her self a Milkmaid all the month
of *May*, because they are not troubled with fears and
cares, but sing sweetly all the day, and sleep securely
all the night: and without doubt, honest, innocent,
pretty *Maudlin* does so. I'le bestow Sir *Thomas
Overbury's* Milk-maid's wish upon her, *That she may
dye in the Spring, and being dead may have good store
of flowers stuck round about her winding sheet.*

The Milk-maids Mothers Answer

If all the world and Love were young,
And truth in every Shepherds tongue,
These pretty pleasures might me move
To live with thee, and be thy Love.

But Time drives flocks from field to fold,
When Rivers rage, and rocks grow cold,
Then Philomel *becometh dumb,*
And age complains of care to come.

The flowers do fade, and wanton fields
To wayward Winter reckoning yields,
A hony tongue, a heart of gall,
Is fancies spring, but sorrows fall;

Thy gowns, thy shoes, thy beds of roses,
Thy cap, thy kirtle, and thy posies,
Soon break, soon wither, soon forgotten,
In folly ripe, in reason rotten.

Thy Belt of Straw, and Ivy-buds,
Thy Coral clasps, and Amber-studs,
All these in me no means can move
To come to thee, and be thy Love.

What should we talk of dainties then,
Of better meat than's fit for men?
These are but vain: that's only good
Which God hath blest, and sent for food.

But could Youth last, and love still breed,
Had joys no date, nor age no need;
Then those delights my mind might move,
To live with thee, and be thy Love.

Mother. Well I have done my Song; but stay, honest *Anglers*, for I will make *Maudlin* to sing you one short Song more. *Maudlin*; sing that Song that you sung last night, when young *Corydon* the Shepherd plaid so purely on his *oaten pipe* to you and your cozen Betty.

Maud. I will Mother.

I married a Wife of late,
The more's my unhappy fate:
I married her for love,
As my fancy did me move,
And not for a worldly estate:

But Oh! the green-sickness
Soon changed her likeness;
   And all her beauty did fail.
     But 'tis not so
     With those that go
     Thro' frost and snow,
     As all men know,
   And, carry the Milking-pail.

Pisc. Well sung good Woman I thank you, I'le give you another dish of fish one of these days; and then beg another song of you. Come Scholar, let *Maudlin* alone: do not you offer to spoil her voice. Look, yonder comes mine *Hostess,* to call us to supper. How now? is my brother *Peter* come?

Hostess: Yes, and a friend with him, they are both glad to hear that you are in these parts, and long to see you, and long to be at supper, for they be very hungry.

CHAP. V

More Directions how to Fish for, and how to make for the Trout *an* Artificial Minnow, *and* Flies, *with some* Merriment.

PIsc. Well met Brother *Peter,* I heard you and a friend would lodge here to night, and that hath made me to bring my Friend to lodge here too. My Friend is one that would fain be *a Brother of the Angle,* he hath been an *Angler* but this day, and I have taught him how to catch a *Chub* by daping with a *Grass-hopper,* and the *Chub* he caught was a lusty one of nineteen inches long. But pray Brother *Peter* who is your companion?

Peter. Brother *Piscator*, my friend is an honest *Country-man*, and his name is *Coridon*, and he is a downright witty companion that met me here purposely to be pleasant and eat a *Trout*, And I have not yet wetted my Line since we met together? but I hope to fit him with a *Trout* for his breakfast, for I'le be early up.

Pisc. Nay Brother, you shall not stay so long: for look you here is a Trout

will fill six reasonable bellies. Come Hostess, dress it presently, and get us what other meat the house will afford, and give us some of your best *Barly-wine*, the good liquor that our honest Fore-fathers did use to drink of; the drink which preserved their health, and made them live so long, and to do so many good deeds.

Peter. O' my word this *Trout* is perfect in season. Come, I thank you, and here is a hearty draught to you, and to all the brothers of the Angle wheresoever they be, and to my young brothers good fortune to morrow: I will furnish him with a Rod, if you will furnish him with the rest of the Tackling: we will set him up and make him a Fisher.

And I will tell him one thing for his encouragement, that his fortune hath made him happy to be

Scholar to such a Master; a Master that knows as much both of the nature and breeding of fish as any man: and can also tell him as well how to catch and cook them, from the *Minnow* to the *Salmon*, as any that I ever met withall.

Pisc. Trust me, brother *Peter*, I find my Scholar to be so sutable to my own humour, which is to be free and pleasant, and civilly merry, that my resolution is to hide nothing that I know from him. Believe me, Scholar, this is my resolution; and so here's to you a hearty draught, and to all that love us, and the honest art of Angling.

Ven. Trust me, good Master, you shall not sow your seed in barren ground, for I hope to return you an increase answerable to your hopes; but however you shall find me obedient, and thankful, and serviceable to my best abilitie.

Pisc. 'Tis enough, honest Scholar, come, lets to supper. Come my friend *Coridon* this *Trout* looks lovely, it was twentie two inches when it was taken, and the belly of it looked some part of it as yellow as a Marigold, and part of it as white as a lilly, and yet methinks it looks better in this good sawce.

Cor. Indeed honest friend, it looks well, and tastes well, I thank you for it, and so doth my friend *Peter*, or else he is to blame.

Pet. Yes, and so I do, we all thank you, and when we have supt, I will get my friend *Coridon* to sing you a Song for requital.

Cor. I will sing a song, if any body will sing another; else, to be plain with you, *I will sing none*: I am none of those that sing for meat, but for company: I say, *'Tis merry in Hall, when men sing all*.

Pisc. I'le promise you I'l sing a song that was

lately made at my request, by Mr. *William Basse*, one that hath made the choice songs of the *Hunter in his cariere*, and of *Tom of Bedlam*, and many others of note; and this that I will sing is in praise of Angling.

Cor. And then mine shall be the praise of a Country mans life. What will the rest sing of?

Pet. I will promise you, I will sing another song in praise of Angling to morrow night; for we will not part till then, but Fish to morrow, and sup together, and the next day every man leave Fishing, and fall to his businesse.

Venat. 'Tis a match, and I will provide you a Song or a Catch against then too, which shall give some addition of mirth to the company; for we will be civil and as merry as beggers.

Pisc. 'Tis a match my Masters, let's ev'n say Grace, and turn to the fire, drink the other cup to wet our whistles, and so sing away all sad thoughts.

Come on my Masters, who begins? I think it is best to draw cuts, and avoid contention.

Pet. It is a match. Look, the shortest cut falls to *Coridon*.

Cor. Well then, I will begin, for I hate contention.

CORIDONS Song

Oh the sweet contentment
The country-man doth find
  high trolollie loe
  high trolollie lee,
That quiet contemplation
Possesseth all my mind:
  Then care away,
  And wend along with me.

For Courts are full of flattery,
As hath too oft been tri'd;
   high trolollie lollie lee, &c.
The City full of wantonness,
And both are full of pride:
   Then care away, &c.

But oh, the honest Country-man
Speaks truely from his heart,
   high trolollie lollie lee, &c.
His pride is in his tillage,
His horses and his cart:
   Then care away, &c.

Our cloathing is good sheep skins,
Gray russet for our wives,
   high trolollie lollie lee, &c.
'Tis warmth and not gay cloathing
That doth prolong our lives:
   Then care away, &c.

The ploughman, though he labour hard,
Yet on the Holy-Day,
   High trolollie lollie lee, &c.
No Emperour so merrily
Does passe his time away:
   Then care away, &c.

To recompence our tillage,
The Heavens afford us showers;
   High trolollie lollie lee, &c.
And for our sweet refreshments
The earth affords us bowers:
   Then care away, &c.

The Cuckow and the Nightingale
Full merrily do sing,
   High trolollie lollie lee, &c.
And with their pleasant roundelaies
Bid welcome to the Spring:
   Then care away, &c.

> *This is not half the happiness*
> *The country-man enjoyes;*
>   *high trolollie lollie lee, &c.*
> *Though others think they have as much,*
> *Yet he that says so lies:*
>   Then come away, turn
>   Country man with me.
>   *Jo. Chalkhill.*

Pisc. Well sung *Coridon*, this song was sung with mettle; and it was choicely fitted to the occasion; I shall love you for it as long as I know you; I would you were a brother of the Angle, for a companion that is chearful, and free from swearing and scurrilous discourse, is worth gold. I love such mirth as does not make friends ashamed to look upon one another next morning; nor men (that cannot well bear it) to repent the money they spend when they be warmed with drink: and take this for a rule, You may pick out such times and such companies, that you make your selves merrier for a little than a great deal of money; for, *'Tis the company and not the charge that makes the feast*; and such a companion you prove, I thank you for it.

But I will not complement you out of the debt that I owe you, and therefore I will begin my Song and wish it may be so well liked.

The Anglers Song

> *As inward love breeds outward talk,*
> *The* Hound *some praise, and some the* Hawk:
> *Some better pleas'd with private sport,*
> *Use* Tennis, *some a* Mistress *court:*
>   *But these delights I neither wish,*
>   *Nor envy, while I freely fish.*

Who Hunts, *doth oft in danger ride;*
Who Hawks, *lures oft both far and wide;*
Who uses Games *shall often prove*
A loser, but who falls in love,
    Is fettered in fond Cupids *snare:*
    My Angle breeds me no such care.

Of Recreation there is none
So free as Fishing is alone;
All other pastimes do no lesse
Than mind and body both possesse:
    My hand alone my work can doe,
    So I can fish and study too.

I care not, I, to fish in seas
Fresh rivers best my mind do please,
Whose sweet calm course I contemplate,
And seek in life to imitate:
    In civil bounds I fain would keep,
    And for my past offences weep.

And when the timorous Trout *I wait*
To take, and he devours my bait,
How poor a thing sometimes I find
Will captivate a greedy mind:
    And when none bite, I praise the wise,
    Whom vain allurements ne're surprise.

But yet though while I fish I fast;
I make good fortune my repast,
And thereunto my friend invite,
In whom I more than that delight:
    Who is more welcom to my dish,
    Than to my angle was my fish,

As well content no prize to take,
As use of taken prize to make:
For so our Lord was pleased when
He fishers made fishers of men:
    Where (which is in no other game)
    A man may fish and praise his name.

> *The first men that our Saviour dear*
> *Did chuse to wait upon him here,*
> *Blest Fishers were, and fish the last*
> *Food was, that he on earth did taste.*
>   *I therefore strive to follow those,*
>   *Whom he to follow him hath chose,*

Cor. Well sung, brother, you have paid your debt in good coin, we Anglers are all beholden to the good man that made this Song. Come Hostess, give us more Ale, and lets drink to him.

And now lets every one go to bed that we may rise early; but first lets pay our reckoning, for I will have nothing to hinder me in the morning for my purpose is to prevent the Sun-rising.

Pet. A match; Come *Coridon*, you are to be my Bed-fellow. I know, brother, you and your Scholar will lie together; but where shall we meet to morrow night? for my friend *Coridon* and I will go up the water towards *Ware*.

Pisc. And my Scholar and I will go down towards *Waltham*.

Cor. Then lets meet here, for here are fresh sheets that smell of *Lavender*, and I am sure we cannot expect better meat, or better usage in any place.

Pet. 'Tis a match. Good night to every body.

Pisc. And so say I.

Venat. And so say I.

Pisc. Good morrow good Hostess, I see my brother *Peter* is still in bed: Come give my Scholar and me a Morning-drink, and a bit of meat to breakfast, and be sure to get a good dish of meat or two against supper, for we shall come home as hungry as Hawks. Come Scholar, lets be going.

Venat. Well now, good Master, as we walk towards the River give me direction, according to your promise, how I shall fish for a *Trout*.

Pisc. My honest Scholar, I will take this very convenient opportunity to do it.

The Trout is usually caught with a worm or a *Minnow*, (which some call a *Penk*) or with a *flie*, *viz*. either a *natural* or an *artificial flie*: concerning which three I will give you some observations and directions.

And first for Worms: Of these there be very many sorts, some breed only in the earth, as the *Earth-worm*; others of or amongst Plants, as the *Dug-worm*; and others breed either out of Excrements, or in the bodies of living creatures, as in the horns of Sheep or Deer; or some of dead flesh, as the *Mag-got* or *gentle*, and others.

Now these be most of them particularly good for particular Fishes: but for the *Trout*, the *dew-worm* (which some also call the *Lob-worm*) and the *Brandling* are the chief; and especially the first for a great Trout, and the latter for a less. There be also of *Lob-worms* some called *squirrel-tailes*, (a worm that has a red head, a streak down the back and a broad tail) which are noted to be the best, because they are the toughest and most lively, and live longest in the water; for you are to know, that a dead worm is but a dead bait and like to catch nothing, compared to a lively, quick, stirring worm: And for a *Brandling*, he is usually found in an old dunghil, or some very rotten place near to it: but most usually in Cow-dung, or hogs-dung, rather than horse-dung, which is somewhat too hot and dry for that worm. But the best of them are to be found in the bark of the Tanners which they cast up in heaps after they have used it about their leather.

There are also divers other kinds of worms which for colour and shape alter even as the ground out of which they are got, as the *marsh-worm*, the *tag-tail*, the *stag-worm*, the *dock-worm*, the *oak-worm*, the *gilt-tayle*, the *twachel* or *lob-worm* (which of all others is the most excellent bait for a *Salmon*) and too many to name, even as many sorts as some think there be of several hearbs or shrubs, or of several kinds of birds in the air; of which I shall say no more, but tell you, that what worms soever you fish with, are the better for being well scowred, that is long kept, before they be used; and in case you have not been so provident, then the way to cleanse and scowr them quickly, is to put them all night in water, if they be *Lob-worms*, and then put them into your bag with fennel: but you must not put your Brandlings above an hour in water, and then put them into fennel for suddain use: but if you have time and purpose to keep them long, then they be best preserved in an earthen pot with good store of *Mosse*, which is to be fresh every three or four dayes in Summer, and every week or eight dayes in Winter: or at least the mosse taken from them, and clean washed, and wrung betwixt your hands till it be dry, and then put it to them again. And when your worms, especially the Brandling, begins to be sick, and lose of his bigness, then you may recover him, by putting a little milk or cream (about a spoonful in a day) into them by drops on the mosse; and if there be added to the cream an egg beaten and boiled in it, then it will both fatten and preserve them long. And note, that when the *knot*, which is near to the middle of the *brandling*, begins to swell, then he is sick, and, if he be not well look'd to, is near dying. And for mosse, you are to note, that there be divers kinds of it, which I could name to you, but will onely tell you, that that which is likest a *Bucks-Horn* is the best, except it be soft white moss, which grows on some heaths, and is hard to be found. And note, that in a very dry time, when you are put to an extremity for worms, Walnut-tree leaves squeez'd into water, or salt in water, to make it bitter or salt, and then that water poured on the ground, where you shall see worms are used to rise in the night, will make them to appear above ground presently. And you may take notice, some say that *Camphire* put into your bag with your mosse and worms, gives them a strong and so tempting a smell, that the fish fare the worse and you the better for it.

And now I shall show you how to bait your hook with a worm, so as shall prevent you from much trouble, and the loss of many a hook too; when you fish for a *Trout* with a running line: that is to say, when you fish for him by hand at the ground, I will direct you in this as plainly as I can, that you may not mistake.

Suppose it be a big Lob-worm, put your hook into him somewhat above the middle, and out again a little below the middle: having so done, draw your worm above the arming of your hook; but note that at the entring of your hook it must not be at the head-end of the worm, but at the tail-end of him, (that the point of your hook may come out toward the head-end) and having drawn him above the arming of your hook, then put the point of your hook again into the very head of the worm, till it come near to the place where the point of the hook first came out: and then draw back that part of the worm that was above the shank or arming of your hook, and so fish with it. And if you mean to fish with two worms, then put the second on before you turn back the hooks-head of the first worm; you cannot lose above two or three worms before you attain to what I direct you; and having attain'd it, you will find it very useful, and thank me for it: For you will run on the ground without tangling.

Now for the *Minnow* or *Penk*, he is not easily found and caught till *March*, or in *April*, for then he appears first in the River, Nature having taught him to shelter and hide himself in the Winter in ditches that be near to the River, and there both to hide and keep himself warm in the mud or in the weeds, which rot not so soon as in a running River, in which place if he were in Winter, the distempered Floods that are usually in that season, would suffer him to take no rest, but carry him head-long to Mills and Weires to his confusion. And of these *Minnows*, first you are to know, that the biggest size is not the best; and next, that the middle size and the whitest are the best: and then you are to know, that your *Minnow* must be so put on your hook that it must turn round when 'tis drawn against the stream, and that it may turn nimbly, you must put it on a big-sized hook as I shall now direct you, which is thus. Put your hook in at his mouth and out at his gill, then having drawn your hook 2 or 3 inches beyond or through his gill, put it again into his mouth, and the point and beard out at his taile, and then tie the hook and his taile about very neatly with a white thred, which will make it the apter to turn quick in the water: that done, pull back that part of your line which was slack when you did put your hook into the *Minnow* the second time: I say pull that part of your line back so that it shall fasten the head, so that the body of the *Minnow* shall be almost streight on your hook; this

done, try how it will turn by drawing it cross the
water or against a stream, and if it do not turn
nimbly, then turn the tail a little to the right or left
hand, and try again, till it turn quick; for if not? you
are in danger to catch nothing; for know, that it is
impossible that it should turn too quick: And you are
yet to know, that in case you want a *Minnow*, then a
small *Loch*, or a *Sticklebag*, or any other small fish
that will turn quick will serve as well: And you are
yet to know, that you may salt them, and by that
means keep them ready and fit for use three or four
days, or longer, and that of salt, bay-salt is the best.

And here let me tell you, what many old Anglers
know right well, that at some times, and in some
waters, a *Minnow* is not to be got, and therefore let
me tell you, I have (which I will shew to you) an
artificial Minnow, that will catch a Trout as well as
an *artificial Flie*, and it was made by a handsom
Woman that had a fine hand, and a live *Minnow* lying
by her: *the mould or body of the Minnow was cloth,
and wrought upon or over it thus with a needle: the back
of it with very sad French green silk, and paler green
silk towards the belly, shadowed as perfectly as you can
imagine, just as you see a Minnow; the belly was wrought
also with a needle, and it was a part of it white silk, and
another part of it with silver thred; the tail and fins were
of a quill, which was shaven thin, the eyes were of two
little black beads, and the head was so shadowed, and all
of it so curiously wrought, and so exactly dissembled,
that it would beguile any sharpe sighted Trout in a
swift stream. And this Minnow I will now shew you,
(look here it is) and if you like it, lend it you, to have two
or three made by it, for they be easily carryed about an
Angler, and be of excellent use; for note, that a large*

*Trout will come as fiercely at a Minnow, as the highest-
mettled Hawk doth seize on a Partridge, or a Greyhound
on a Hare.* I have been told, that 160 *Minnows* have
been found in a *Trouts* belly: either the *Trout* had
devoured so many; or the Miller that gave it a friend
of mine had forced them down his throat after he had
taken him.

Now for *Flies*, which is the third bait wherewith
Trouts are usually taken. You are to know, that
there are so many sorts of Flies as there be of Fruits:
I will name you but some of them, as the *dun-flie*, the
stone-flie, the *red-flie*, the *moor-flie*, the *tawnie-flie*, the
shell-flie, the *cloudy*, or *blackish-flie*, the *flag-flie*, the
vine-flie; there be of *flies*, *Caterpillars*, and *Canker-
flies*, and *Bear-flies*, and indeed too many either for
me to name or for you to remember: and their breeding is so various and wonderful, that I might easily
amaze my self, and tire you in a relation of them.

And yet I will exercise your promised patience by
saying a little of the *Caterpillar*, or the *Palmer-flie* or
worm, that by them you may guess what a work it
were in a Discourse but to run over those very many
flies, worms, and little living creatures with which the
Sun and Summer adorn and beautifie the River banks
and Meadows; both for the recreation and contemplation of us Anglers, pleasures which (I think) my self
enjoy more than any other man that is not of my
profession.

Pliny holds an opinion, that many have their birth
or being from a dew that in the Spring falls upon the
leaves of trees; and that some kinds of them are from
a dew left upon herbs or flowers; and others from
a dew left upon Coleworts or Cabbages: All which
kinds of dews being thickned and condensed, are by

the Suns generative heat most of them hatch'd, and
in three days made living creatures; and these of
several shapes and colours; some being hard and
tough, some smooth and soft; some are horned in
their head, some in their tail, some have none; some
have hair, some none: some have sixteen feet, some
less, and some have none, but (as our *Topsel* hath
In his history with great diligence observed) those
of Serpents. which have none, move upon the earth
or upon broad leaves, their motion being not unlike
to the waves of the Sea. Some of them he also
observes to be bred of the Eggs of other Caterpillars,
and that those in their time turn to be *Butter-flies*:
and again, that their Eggs turn the following year
to be *Caterpillars*. And some affirm, that every plant
has his particular flie or Caterpillar, which it breeds
and feeds. I have seen, and may therefore affirm it,
a green Caterpillar, or worm, as big as a small Peascod, which had fourteen legs; eight on the belly,
four under the neck, and two near the tail. It was
found on a hedge of Privet, and was taken thence,
and put into a large Box, and a little branch or two
of Privet put to it, on which I saw it feed as sharply
as a dog gnaws a bone: it lived thus five or six daies,
and thrived, and changed the colour two or three
times, but by some neglect in the keeper of it, it then
dyed, and did not turn to a flie: but if it had lived,
it had doubtless turned to one of those flies that
some call flies of prey, which those that walk by the
Rivers may, in Summer, see fasten on smaller flies,
and I think, make them their food. And 'tis observable, that as there be these *flies of prey* which be very
large, so there be others very little, created, I think,
only to feed them, and breed out of I know not what;

whose life, they say, Nature intended not to exceed an hour, and yet that life is thus made shorter by other flies, or accident.

'Tis endless to tell you what the curious searchers into Natures productions have observed of these Worms and Flies: But yet I shall tell you what *Aldrovandus*, our *Topsel*, and others say of the *Palmerworm*, or *Caterpillar*, That whereas others content themselves to feed on particular herbs or leaves, (for most think those very leaves that gave them life and shape, give them a particular feeding and nourishment, and that upon them they usually abide) yet he observes, that this is called a *pilgrim* or *palmer-worm*, for his very wandring life and various food; not contenting himself (as others do) with any one certain place for his abode, nor any certain kind of herb or flower for his feeding; but will boldly and disorderly wander up and down, and not endure to be kept to a diet, or fixed to a particular place.

Nay, the very colours of *Caterpillars* are, as one has observed, very elegant and beautiful: I shall (for a taste of the rest) describe one of them, which I will sometime the next month shew you feeding on a Willow-tree, and you shall find him punctually to answer this very description; *His lips and mouth somewhat yellow, his eyes black as Jet, his forehead purple, his feet and hinder parts green, his tail twoforked and black, the whole body stained with a kind of red spots which run along the neck and shoulderblade, not unlike the form of St.* Andrew's *Cross, or the letter* X, *made thus cross-wise, and a white line drawn down his back to his tail; all which add much beauty to his whole body.* And it is to me observable, that at a fixed age this *Caterpillar* gives over to eat, and towards

Winter comes to be covered over with a strange
shell or crust called an *Aurelia,* and so lives a kind of
View Sir Fra.
Bacon exper.
728 & 90, in
his Natural
History. dead life, without eating all the Winter;
and (as others of several kinds turn to
be several kinds of flies and vermin the
Spring following) so this *Caterpillar*
then turns to be a *painted Butter-fly.*

Come, come, my Scholar, you see the River stops
our morning walk, and I will also here stop my discourse, only as we sit down under this *Honeysuckle*
hedg, whilst I look a Line to fit the Rod that our
brother *Peter* hath lent you, I shall, for a little confirmation of what I have said, repeat the observation
of *Du Bartas:*

6th Day of   *God not contented to each kind to give,*
Du Bartas.   *And to infuse the vertue generative,*
     By his wise power made many creatures breed
     Of liveless bodies, without Venus *deed.*

     So the cold humor breeds the Salamander,
     who (in effect) like to her births commander,
     With child with hundred winters, with her touch
     Quencheth the fire though glowing ne'r so much.

     So in the fire in burning furnace springs
     The Fly Perausta *with the flaming wings;*
     Without the fire it dyes, in it it joyes,
     Living in that which all things else destroyes.

View Gerh.   *So slow* Boôtes *underneath him sees*
Herbal and   *In th' Icy Islands goslings hatcht of trees,*
Cambden.   *Whose fruitful leaves falling into the water,*
     Are turn'd, ('tis known) to living fowls soon after.

     So rotten planks of broken ships do change
     To Barnacles. *O transformation strange!*
     'Twas first a green tree, then a broken hull,
     Lately a mushrome, now a flying Gull.

Venat. O my good Master, this morning-walk has been spent to my great pleasure and wonder: but I pray, when shall I have your direction how to make artificial flies, like to those that the *Trout* loves best? and also how to use them?

Pisc. My honest Scholar, it is now past five of the Clock, we will fish till nine, and then go to breakfast: Go you to yonder *Sycamore-tree*, and hide your Bottle of drink under the hollow root of it; for about that time, and in that place, we will make a brave breakfast with a piece of powder'd Beef, and a Radish or two, that I have in my Fish-bag: we shall, I warrant you, make a good, honest, wholsome, hungry breakfast. And I will then give you direction for the making and using of your flies: and in the mean time, there is your Rod and Line, and my advice is, that you fish as you see me do, And let's try which can catch the first Fish.

Venat. I thank you Master. I will observe and practise your direction as far as I am able.

Pisc. Look you Scholar, you see I have hold of a good Fish: I now see it is a Trout, I pray, put that Net under him, and touch not my line for if you do, then we break all. Well done Scholar; I thank you.

Now for another. Trust me, I have another bite: come Scholar, come lay down your Rod, and help me to land this as you did the other. So, now we shall be sure to have a good dish of Fish for supper.

Venat. I am glad of that; but I have no fortune: sure, Master, yours is a better Rod, and better tackling.

Pisc. Nay, then take mine, and I will fish with yours. Look you, Scholar, I have another; come, do as you did before. And now I have a bite at another:

Oh me! he has broke all; there's half a line and a good hook lost.

Venat. I and a good *Trout* too.

Pisc. Nay, the *Trout* is not lost, for pray take notice no man can lose what he never had.

Venat. Master, I can neither catch with the first nor second Angle: I have no fortune.

Pisc. Look you, Scholar, I have yet another: and now, having caught three brace of Trouts, I will tell you a short Tale as we walk towards our breakfast: *A Scholar (a preacher I should say) that was to preach to procure the approbation of a Parish that he might be their Lecturer, had got from his Fellow-pupil the copy of a Sermon that was first preached with great commendation by him that composed it; and though the borrower of it preach'd it word for word, as it was at first, yet it was utterly disliked as it was preached by the second to his Congregation: which the sermon-borrower complained of to the lender of it, and was thus answered; I lent you indeed my* Fiddle, *but not my* Fiddlestick; *for you are to know, that every one cannot make musick with my words, which are fitted for my own mouth.* And so, my Scholar, you are to know, that as the ill pronunciation or ill accenting of words in a Sermon spoils it, so the ill carriage of your line, or not fishing even to a foot in a right place, makes you lose your labour: and you are to know, that though you have my *Fiddle*, that is, my very Rod and Tacklings with which you see I catch Fish; yet you have not my *Fiddlestick*, that is, you yet have not skill to know how to carry your hand and line, nor how to guide it to a right place: and this must be taught you (for you are to remember I told you, Angling is an Art) either by practice, or a long observation or both. But take this for a rule, when you fish for a Trout with a Worm, let your line have so much, and not more Lead than will fit the stream in which you fish; that is to say; more in a great troublesom stream than in a smaller that is quieter; as near as may be, so much as will sink the bait to the bottom, and keep it still in motion, and not more.

But now lets say Grace and fall to breakfast: what say you, Scholar, to the providence of an old Angler? does not this meat taste well? and was not this place well chosen to eat it? for this Sycamore-tree will shade us from the Suns heat.

Venat. All excellent good, and my stomach excellent good too. And I now remember and find that true which devout *Lessius* says, *That poor men, and those that fast often, have much more pleasure in eating than rich men and gluttons, that always feed before their stomachs are empty of their last meat, and call for more: for by that means they rob themselves of that pleasure that hunger brings to poor men.* And I do seriously approve of that saying of yours, *That you had rather be a civil, well govern'd, well grounded, temperate, poor Angler, than a drunken Lord.* But I hope there is none such; however I am certain of this, that I have been at many very costly dinners that have not afforded me half the content that this has done, for which I thank God and you.

And now good Master, proceed to your promised direction for making and ordering my Artificial flie.

Pisc. My honest Scholar, I will do it, for it is a debt due unto you by my promise: and because you shall not think your self more engaged to me than indeed you really are, I will freely give you such directions as were lately given to me by an ingenuous brother of the Angle, an honest man, and a most excellent *Flie-fisher*.

You are to note, that there are twelve kinds of Artificial made Flies to Angle with upon the top of the water. Note by the way, that the fittest season of using these is in a blustering windy day, when the waters are so troubled that the natural fly cannot be seen, or rest upon them. The first is the *dun-flie*, in *March*, the body is made of *dun wool*, the wings of the Partridges feathers. The second is another *dun-flie*, the body of *Black wool*, and the wings made of the black Drakes feathers, and of the feathers under his tail. The third is the *stone-flie*, in *April*, the body is made of *black wool* made yellow under the wings and under the tail, and so made with wings of the Drake. The fourth is the *ruddy Flie*, in the beginning of *May*, the body made of *red wool* wrapt about with black silk, and the feathers are the wings of the Drake, with the feathers of a red Capon also, which hang dangling on his sides next to the tail. The fifth is the *yellow* or *greenish-flie* (in *May* likewise) the body made of *yellow wool*, and the wings made of the red cocks hackle or tail. The sixth is, the *black flie*, in *May* also, the body made of *black wool* and lapt about with the herl of a Peacocks tail: the wings are made of the wings of a brown Capon with his blew feathers in his head. The seventh is the sad *yellow-flie* in *June*, the body is made of *black wool*, with a yellow list on either side, and the wings taken off the wings of a *Buzzard*, bound with black braked hemp. The eighth is the *moorish flie*; made with the body of dusk-ish Wool, and the wings made of the blackish mail of the Drake. The ninth is the *tawny-flie*, good until the middle of *June*; the body made of *tawny-wool*, the wings made contrary one against the other, made of the whitish mail of the wild Drake. The tenth is the *Wasp-flie* in *July*, the body made of *black wool*, lapt about with yellow silk, the wings made of the feathers of the Drake, or of the Buzzard. The Eleventh is the *shell-flie*, good in mid *July*: the body made of greenish wool, lapt about with the herle of a Peacocks tail: and the wings made of the wings of the Buzzard. The twelfth is the dark *Drake-flie*, good in *August*, the body made with *black Wool*, lapt about with black silk; his wings are made with the mail of the black Drake, with a black head. Thus have you a Jury of flies likely to betray and condemn all the Trouts in the River.

I shall next give you some other Directions for Flie-fishing, such as are given by Mr. *Thomas Barker*, a Gentleman that hath spent much time in Fishing: but I shall do it with a little variation.

First, let your Rod be light, and very gentle, I take the best to be of two pieces, and let not your Line exceed (especially for three or four links next to the hook) I say, not exceed three or four hairs at the most, though you may fish a little stronger above in the upper part of your line: but if you can attain to angle with one hair, you shall have more rises, and catch more Fish. Now you must be sure not to cumber your self with too long a Line, as most do: and before you begin to Angle, cast to have the wind on your back, and the Sun (if it shines) to be before you, and to fish down the stream; and carry the point or top of your Rod downward, by which means the shadow of your self, and Rod too will be the least offensive to the Fish, for the sight of any shade amazes the fish, and spoils your sport, of which you must take a great care.

In the middle of *March* (till which time a man should not in honesty catch a Trout) or in *April*, if the weather be dark, or a little windy or cloudy, the best fishing is with the *Palmer-worm*, of which I last spoke to you, but of these there be divers kinds, or at least of divers colours; these and the *May-flie* are the ground of all Flie-angling, which are to be thus made.

First, you must arm your hook with the line in the inside of it, then take your Scissars, and cut so much of a brown Mallards feather as in your own reason, will make the wings of it, you having withal regard to the bigness or littleness of your hook, then lay the outmost part of your feather next to your hook, then the point of your feather next the shank of your hook; and having so done, whip it three or four times about the hook with the same Silk, with which your hook was armed; and having made the Silk fast, take the hackle of a *Cock* or *Capons* neck, or a *Plovers* top, which is usually better: take off the one side of the feather, and then take the hackle, Silk, or Crewel, Gold or Silver thred, make these fast at the bent of the hook, that is to say, below your arming; then you must take the hackle, the Silver or Gold thred, and work it up to the wings, shifting or still removing your finger, as you turn the Silk about the hook: and still looking, at every stop or turn, that your Gold, or what materials soever you make your *Flie* of, do lie right and neatly; and if you find they do so, then when you have made the head, make all fast, and then work your hackle up to the head, and make that fast: and then with a needle or pin divide the wing into two, and then with the arming Silk whip it about cross-waies betwixt the wings; and then with your thumb you must turn the point of the feather towards the bent of the hook, and then work three or four times about the shank of the hook, and then view the proportion, and if all be neat and to your liking, fasten.

I confess, no direction can be given to make a man of a dull capacity able to make a flie well: and yet I know, this with a little practice will help an ingenuous Angler in a good degree: but to see a Flie made by an Artist in that kind, is the best teaching to make it, and then an ingenuous Angler may walk by the River, and mark what flies fall on the water that day, and catch one of them, if he see the *Trouts* leap at a fly of that kind: and then having alwaies hooks ready hung with him, and having a bag also always with him, with Bears hair, or the hair of a brown or sad-coloured Heifer, hackles of a Cock or Capon, several coloured Silk and Crewel to make the body of the flie, the feathers of a Drakes head, black or brown Sheeps wool, or Hogs wool, or hair, thred of Gold and of Silver: Silk of several colours (especially sad coloured to make the flies head:) and there be also other coloured feathers both of little birds and of speckled fowl. I say, having those with him in a bag, and trying to make a flie, though he miss at first, yet shall he at last hit it better, even to such a perfection, as none can well teach him, and if he hit to make his flie right, and have the luck to hit also where there is store of *Trouts*, a dark day, and a right wind, he will catch such store of them, as will encourage him to grow more and more in love with the art of *Fly-making*.

Venat. But my loving master, if any wind will not serve, then I wish I were in *Lapland*, to buy a good wind of one of the honest Witches, that sell so many winds there, and so cheap.

Pisc. Marry Scholar, but I would not be there, nor indeed from under this tree: for look how it begins to rain, and by the clouds, if I mistake not we shall presently have a smoaking showre, and therefore sit close, this *Sycamore-tree* will shelter us: and I will tell you, as they shall come into my mind, more observations of flie-fishing for a Trout.

But first for the wind, you are to take notice, that of the winds the *Southwind* is said to be best. One observes, That

——————*When the wind is South,*
· *It blows your bait into a fishes mouth.*

Next to that, the *West* wind is believed to be the best: and having told you that the *East* wind is the worst, I need not tell you which wind is the best in the third degree: And yet (as *Solomon* observes) that *He that considers the wind shall never sow:* so he that busies his head too much about them, (if the weather be not made extream cold by an East wind) shall be a little superstitious: For as it is observed by some, That there is no good horse of a bad colour; so I have observed that if it be a cloudy day, and not extream cold, let the Wind sit in what corner it will and do its worst I heed it not. And yet take this for a rule, that I would willingly fish standing on the Lee-shore: and you are to take notice, that the Fish lies or swims nearer the bottom, and in deeper water, in Winter than in Summer; and also nearer the bottom in any cold day, and then gets nearest the Lee-side of the water.

But I promised to tell you more of the Flie-fishing for a *Trout*; which I may have time enough to do, for you see it rains *May-butter*: First for a *May-flie*: you may make his body with greenish coloured Crewel, or Willowish colour; darkning it in most places with waxed Silk, or rib'd with black hair, or some of them rib'd with silver thred; and such Wings for the colour as you see the flie to have at that season; nay, at that very day on the water. Or you may make the Oak-flie with an Orange-tawny and black ground, and the brown of a Mallards feather for the Wings; and you are to know, that these two are most excellent flies, that is, the *May-flie* and the *Oak-flie*. And let me again tell you, that you keep as far from the water as you can possibly, whether you fish with a flie or worm, and fish down the stream; and when you fish with a flie, if it be possible, let no part of your line touch the water, but your flie only; and be still moving your fly upon the water, or casting it into the water, you your self being also always moving down the stream. Mr. *Barker* commends several sorts of the *Palmer* flies, not only those rib'd with silver and gold, but others that have their bodies all made of black, or some with red, and a red hackle; you may also make the *Hawthorn-flie*: which is all black, and not big, but very small, the smaller the better; or the *Oak-flie*, the body of which is Orange-colour and black Crewel, with a brown Wing; or a flie made with a *Peacocks* feather, is excellent in a bright day: You must be sure you want not in your *Magazine-bag* the *Peacocks* feather, and grounds of such wool and Crewel as will make the Grasshopper; and note that usually the smallest flies are the best; and note also, that the light flie does usually make most sport in a dark day, and the darkest and least fly in a bright or clear day; and lastly note, that you are to repair upon any occasion to your *Magazine-bag*, and upon any occasion vary and make them lighter or sadder according to your fancy or the day.

And now I shall tell you, that the fishing with a natural flie is excellent, and affords much pleasure; they may be found thus, the *May-flie* usually in and about that month near to the River side, especially against rain; the *Oak-Flie*, on the butt or body of an *Oak* or *Ash*, from the beginning of *May* to the end of *August*; it is a brownish flie, and easie to be so found, and stands usually with his head downward, that is to say, towards the root of the tree; the small black flie, or Hawthorn flie, is to be had on any Hawthorn bush after the leaves be come forth: with these and a short Line (as I shewed to Angle for a *Chub*) you may dape or dop, and also with a *Grasshopper* behind a tree, or in any deep hole, still making it to move on the top of the water, as if it were alive, and still keeping your self out of sight, you shall certainly have sport if there be *Trouts*; yea, in a hot day, but especially in the evening of a hot day, you will have sport.

And now, Scholar, my direction for flie-fishing is ended with this showre, for it has done raining; and now look about you, and see how pleasantly that Meadow looks; nay, and the Earth smells as sweetly too. Come, let me tell you what holy Mr. *Herbert* says of such days and flowers as these, and then we will thank God that we enjoy them, and walk to the River and sit down quietly, and try to catch the other brace of *Trouts*.

Sweet day, so cool, so calm, so bright,
The bridal of the earth and skie,
Sweet dews shall weep thy fall to night,
        for thou must die.

Sweet Rose, whose hew, angry and brave
Bids the rash gazer wipe his eye,
Thy root is ever in its grave,
        and thou must die.

Sweet Spring, full of sweet days and roses,
A box where sweets compacted lye;
My Musick shews you have your closes,
        and all must dye.

Only a sweet and vertuous soul,
Like seasoned Timber never gives,
But when the whole world turns to coal,
        then chiefly lives.

Venat. I thank you, good Master, for your good direction for Flie-fishing, and for the sweet enjoyment of the pleasant day, which is so far spent without offence to God or man: and I thank you for the sweet close of your discourse with Mr. *Herberts* Verses, who I have heard loved Angling; and I do the rather believe it, because he had a spirit suitable to Anglers, and to those primitive Christians, that you love, and have so much commended.

Pisc. Well my loving Scholar, and I am pleased, to know that you are so well pleased with my direction and discourse.

And since you like these Verses of Mr. *Herberts* so well, let me tell you what a reverend and learned Divine that professes to imitate him (and has indeed done so most excellently) hath writ of our *Book* of

Common Prayer, which I know you will like the
better, because he is a friend of mine, and I am sure
no enemy to Angling.

> *What? pray'r by th' book? and common? Yes, why not?*
> *The Spirit of grace*
> *And supplication*
> *Is not left free alone*
> *For time and place,*
> *But manner too: to read or speak by rote,*
> *Is all alike to him, that prayes*
> *In's heart, what with his mouth he says.*
>
> *They that in private, by themselves alone*
> *Do pray, may take*
> *What liberty they please,*
> *In chusing of the ways*
> *Wherein to make*
> *Their souls most intimate affections known*
> *To him that sees in secret, when*
> *Th' are most conceal'd from other men.*
>
> *But he, that unto others leads the way*
> *In publick prayer,*
> *Should do it so*
> *As all that hear may know*
> *They need not fear*
> *To tune their hearts unto his tongue, and say,*
> *Amen: not doubt they were betray'd*
> *To blaspheme, when they meant to have pray'd.*
>
> *Devotion will add Life unto the Letter,*
> *And why should not*
> *That which Authority*
> *Prescribes, esteemed be*
> *Advantage got?*

If th' prayer be good, the commoner the better,
Prayer in the Churches words, as well
As sense, of all prayers bears the bell.

CH. HARVIE.

And now, Scholar, I think it will be time to repair to our Angle-rods, which we left in the water, to fish for themselves, and you shall chuse which shall be yours; and it is an even lay, one of them catches.

And let me tell you, this kind of fishing with a dead rod, and laying night-hooks, are like putting money to Use, for they both work for the Owners, when they do nothing but sleep, or eat, or rejoyce; as you know we have done this last hour, and sate as quietly and as free from cares under this *Sycamore*, as *Virgils Tityrus* and his *Melibœus* did under their broad *Beech-tree*: No life, my honest Scholar, no life so happy and so pleasant, as the life of a well governed *Angler*; for when the *Lawyer* is swallowed up with business, and the *Statesman* is preventing or contriving plots, then we sit on *Cowslip-banks*, hear the birds sing, and possess our selves in as much quietness as these silent silver streams, which we now see glide so quietly by us. Indeed my good Scholar, we may say of *Angling*, as Dr. *Boteler* said of *Strawberries*, *Doubtless God could have made a better berry, but doubtless God never did*: And so (if I might be Judge) *God never did make a more calm, quiet, innocent recreation than Angling*.

I'll tell you, Scholar, when I sate last on this *Primrose-bank*, and looked down these Meadows, I thought of them as *Charles* the Emperor did of the City of *Florence*: *That they were too pleasant to be looked on, but only on Holy-days*. As I then sate on this very

grass, I turned my present thoughts into verse:
'twas a Wish, which I'll repeat to you:

The Anglers wish

I in these flowry meads wou'd be:
These chrystal streams should solace me;
To whose harmonious bubbling noise,
I with my Angle wo'd rejoice:
Sit here and see the Turtle-dove,
Court his chast Mate to acts of love,
Or, on that bank, feel the west wind
Breath health and plenty, please my mind
To see sweet dew-drops kiss these flowers,
And then, washt off by April-showers:
Like Hermit   Here bear my Kenna sing a song;
poor.   *There see a* Black-bird *feed her young,*
Or a Leverock *build her nest:*
Here give my weary spirits rest,
And raise my low pitcht thoughts above
Earth, or what poor mortals love:
     Thus, free from Law-suits, *and the noise*
     Of Princes Courts, *I would rejoyce.*

Or, with my Bryan, *and a book,*
Loyter long days near Shawford-brook;
There sit by him, and eat my meat,
There see the Sun both rise and set:
There bid good morning to next day,
There meditate my time away:
     And angle on, and beg to have
     A quiet passage to a welcome grave.

When I had ended this composure, I left this
place, and saw a Brother of the Angle sit under that
bony-suckle-hedg (one that will prove worth your acquaintance) I sate down by him, and presently we

met with an accidental piece of merriment, which I
will relate to you; for it rains still.

On the other side of this very hedge sate a gang
of *Gypsies*, and near to them sate a gang of *Beggars*:
the *Gypsies* were then to divide all the money that
had been got that week, either by stealing linnen or
poultrie, or by Fortune-telling or Legerdemain, or
indeed, by any other sleights and secrets belonging
to their mysterious Government. And the sum that
was got that week proved to be but twenty and
some odd shillings. The odd money was agreed to
be distributed amongst the poor of their own Corporation; and for the remaining twenty shillings,
that was to be divided unto four Gentlemen *Gypsies*,
according to their several degrees in their Commonwealth.

And the first or chiefest *Gypsie* was, by consent,
to have a third part of the twenty shillings; which
all men know is 6*s*. 8*d*.

The second was to have a fourth part of the 20*s*.
which all men know to be 5*s*.

The third was to have a fifth part of the 20*s*. which
all men know to be 4*s*.

The fourth and last *Gypsie* was to have a sixth part
of the 20*s*., which all men know to be 3*s*. 4*d*.

> As for example,
> 　　3 times 6*s*. 8*d*. is　　.　　.　　20*s*.
> And so is 4 times 5*s*. .　　.　　20*s*.
> And so is 5 times 4*s*. .　　.　　20*s*.
> And so is 6 times 3*s*. 4*d*.　　.　　20*s*.

And yet he that divided the money was so very
a *Gypsie*, that though he gave to every one these said
sums, yet he kept one shilling of it for himself.

As for Example,	s.	d.
	6	8
	5	0
	4	0
	3	4
make but	19	0

But now you shall know, that when the four *Gyp-sies* saw that he had got one shilling by dividing the money, though not one of them knew any reason to demand more, yet like Lords and Courtiers every *Gypsie* envied him that was the gainer, and wrangled with him, and every one said the *remaining shilling belonged to him*: and so they fell to so high a contest about it, as none that knows the faithfulness of one *Gypsie* to another, will easily believe; only we that have lived these last twenty years, are certain that money has been able to do much mischief. However the *Gypsies* were too wise to go to Law, and did therefore chuse their choice friends *Rook* and *Shark*, and our late English *Gusman*, to be their Arbitrators and Umpires; and so they left this *Hony-suckle-hedg*, and went to *tell fortunes*, and *cheat*, and get more money and lodging in the next Village.

When these were gone we heard as high a contention among the *beggars*, *Whether it was easiest to rip a Cloak, or to unrip a Cloak?* One *beggar* affirmed it was all one. But that was denied by asking her, *If doing and undoing were all one?* then another said, *'Twas easiest to unrip a Cloak*, for that was to let it alone. But she was answered, by asking her, how she unript it, if she let it alone? and she confest her self mistaken. These and twenty such like questions

were proposed and answered with as much beggarly
Logick and earnestness, as was ever heard to proceed
from the mouth of the most pertinacious Schismatick;
and sometimes all the Beggars (whose number was
neither more nor less than the Poets nine Muses)
talk'd all together about this ripping and unripping,
and so loud that not one heard what the other said;
but at last one beggar crav'd audience, and told them
that old Father *Clause*, whom *Ben Johnson*, in his
Beggars-Bush created King of their Corporation, was
that night to lodg at an Ale-house (called *Catch-her-
by-the-way*) not far from *Waltham-Cross*, and in the
high-road towards *London*; and he therefore desired
them to spend no more time about that and such like
questions, but refer all to Father *Clause* at night, for
he was an upright *Judge*, and in the mean time draw
cuts what Song should be next sung, and who should
sing it; They all agreed to the motion, and the lot
fell to her that was the youngest, and veriest Virgin
of the Company, and she sung *Frank Davisons* Song,
which he made forty years ago, and all the others of
the company joyned to sing the burthen with her:
the Ditty was this, but first the burthen.

> *Bright shines the Sun, play beggars, play,*
> *Here's scraps enough to serve to day.*

> *What noise of viols is so sweet,*
> *As when our merry clappers ring?*
> *What mirth doth want when beggars meet?*
> *A beggar's life is for a King:*
>   *Eat, drink and play, sleep when we list,*
>   *Go where we will, so stocks be mist.*
>   *Bright shines the Sun, play beggars play,*
>   *Here's scraps enough to serve to day.*

The world is ours, and ours alone,
For we alone have world at will;
We purchase not, all is our own,
Both fields and streets we beggars fill:
    Play beggars play, play beggers play;
    Here's scraps enough to serve to day.

A hundred herds of black and white
Upon our Gowns securely feed
And yet if any dare us bite,
He dies therefore as sure as Creed.
Thus beggars Lord it as they please,
And only beggars live at ease:
    Bright shines the sun, play beggars play,
    Here's scraps enough to serve to day.

Venat. I thank you good Master, for this piece of merriment, and this Song, which was well humoured by the Maker, and well remembered by you.

Pisc. But I pray forget not the Catch which you promised to make against night, for our Countryman, honest *Coridon*, will expect your Catch and my Song, which I must be forced to patch up, for it is so long since I learnt it, that I have forgot a part of it. But come, now it hath done raining, let's stretch our legs a little in a gentle walk to the River, and try what interest our Angles will pay us for lending them so long to be used by the *Trouts*, lent them indeed, like Usurers, for our profit and their destruction.

Venat. Oh me, look you Master, a fish, a fish, oh las Master, I have lost her!

Pisc. I marry Sir, that was a good fish indeed: if I had had the luck to have taken up that Rod, then 'tis twenty to one, he should not have broke my line by running to the rods end as you suffered him: I would have held him within the bent of my Rod (unless he had been fellow to the great *Trout* that is near an ell long, which was of such a length and depth, that he had his picture drawn, and now is to be seen at mine Host *Rickabies*, at the *George* in *Ware*,) and it may be, by giving that very great *Trout* the Rod, that is, by casting it to him into the water, I might have caught him at the long run, for so I use alwayes to do when I meet with an overgrown fish, and you will learn to do so too hereafter: for I tell you, Scholar, fishing is an Art, or, at least, it is an Art to catch fish.

Venat. But Master, I have heard that the great *Trout* you speak of is a *Salmon*.

Pisc. Trust me Scholar, I know not what to say to it. There are many Country people that believe *Hares* change Sexes every year: And there be very many learned men think so too, for in their dissecting them they find many reasons to incline them to that belief. And to make the wonder seem yet less that Hares change Sexes, note that Dr. *Mer. Casaubon* affirms in his book of credible and incredible things, that *Gasper Peuseus*, a learned Physician, tells us of a people that once a year turn wolves, partly in shape, and partly in conditions. And so whether this were a *Salmon* when he came into the fresh water, and his not returning into the Sea hath altered him to another colour or kind, I am not able to say; but I am certain he hath all the signs of being a *Trout* both for his *shape*, *colour*, and *spots*, and yet many think he is not.

Venat. But Master, will this *Trout* which I had hold of die? for it is like he hath the hook in his belly.

Pisc. I will tell you, Scholar, that unless the hook

be fast in his very Gorge, 'tis more than probable
he will live, and a little time with the help of the
water, will rust the hook, and it will in time wear
away: as the gravel doth in the horse hoof, which
only leaves a false quarter.

And now Scholar, lets go to my rod. Look you,
Scholar, I have a fish too, but it proves a loggerheaded *Chub*, and this is not much amiss, for this will
pleasure some poor body, as we go to our lodging to
meet our brother *Peter* and honest *Coridon*. Come,
now bait your hook again, and lay it into the water,
for it rains again; and we will ev'n retire to the
Sycamore tree, and there I will give you more directions concerning Fishing: for I would fain make you
an Artist.

Venat. Yes, good Master, I pray let it be so.

Pisc. Well Scholar, now we are sate down and
are at ease, I shall tell you a little more of *Trout*
fishing, before I speak of the *Salmon* (which I purpose shall be next,) and then of the *Pike* or *Luce*.
You are to know, there is night as well as day-fishing
for a *Trout*, and that, in the night, the best *Trouts*
come out of their holes: And the manner of taking
them, is on the top of the water with a great *Lob* or
Garden-worm, or rather two, which you are to fish
with in a place where the waters run somewhat
quietly (for in a stream the bait will not be so well
discerned.) I say in a *quiet* or dead place near to
some swift, there draw your bait over the top of the
water to and fro, and if there be a good *Trout* in the
hole, he will take it, especially if the night be dark:
for then he is bold and lies near the top of the water,
watching the motion of any *Frog* or *Water-rat* or
Mouse that swims betwixt him and the skie; these he

hunts after, if he sees the water but wrinkle, or move in one of these dead holes, where these great old *Trouts* usually lie near to their holds: for you are to note, that the great old *Trout* is both subtil and fearful, and lies close all day, and does not usually stir out of his hold, but lies in it as close in the day, as the *timorous Hare* does in her form: for the chief feeding of either is seldom in the day, but usually in the night, and then the great *Trout* feeds very boldly.

And you must fish for him with a strong Line, and not a little hook; and let him have time to gorge your hook, for he does not usually forsake it, as he oft will in the day-fishing: and if the night be not dark, then Fish so with an *Artificial flie* of a light-colour, and at the snap: nay, he will sometimes rise at a dead Mouse, or a piece of cloth, or any thing, that seems to swim cross the water, or to be in motion: this is a choice way, but I have not oft used it, because it is void of the pleasures, that such dayes as these, that we two now enjoy, afford an Angler.

And you are to know, that in *Hampshire*, which I think exceeds all *England* for swift shallow, clear, pleasant Brooks, and store of *Trouts*, they use to catch *Trouts* in the night, by the light of a torch or straw, which when they have discovered, they strike with a *Trout-spear*, or other wayes. This kind of way they catch very many, but I would not believe it till I was an eye-witness of it, nor do I like it now I have seen it.

Venat. But Master, do not *Trouts* see us in the night?

Pisc. Yes, and hear, and smell too, both then and in the day time: for *Gesner* observes, the *Otter* smells a Fish forty furlongs off him in the water: and that it may be true, seems to be affirmed by Sir *Francis Bacon* (in the eighth Century of his Natural History) who there proves, that waters may be the *Medium* of sounds, by demonstrating it thus, *That if you knock two stones together very deep under the water, those that stand on a bank near to that place may hear the noise without any diminution of it by the water.* He also offers the like experiment concerning the letting an *Anchor* fall by a very long cable or rope on a rock, or the sand within the Sea: And this being so well observed, and demonstrated, as it is by that learned man, has made me to believe that *Eeles* unbed themselves, and stir at the noise of Thunder, and not only, as some think, by the motion or stirring of the earth which is occasioned by that Thunder.

And this reason of Sir *Francis Bacon* (*Exper.* 792) has made me crave pardon of one that I laught at for affirming that he knew *Carps* come to a certain place in a Pond, to be fed at the ringing of a Bell or the beating of a Drum: And however, it shall be a rule for me to make as little noise as I can when I am fishing, untill Sir *Francis Bacon* be confuted, which I shall give any man leave to do.

And, lest you may think him singular in this opinion, I will tell you, this seems to be believed by our learned Doctor *Hackwell*, who (in his *Apology of Gods Power and Providence*, f. 360) quotes *Pliny* to report, that one of the Emperors had particular Fishponds, and in them several Fish, that appeared and came when they were called by their particular names: and St. *James* tells us (chap. 1 and 7) that all things in the Sea have been tamed by Mankind. And *Pliny* tells us (*lib.* 9. 35) that *Antonia* the Wife of *Drusus*, had a *Lamprey*, at whose gills she hung Jewels or

Ear-rings; and that others have been so tender-hearted as to shed tears at the death of Fishes, which they have kept and loved. And these Observations, which will to most hearers seem wonderful, seem to have a further confirmation from *Martial* (*lib*. 4. *epigr*. 30), who writes thus:

Piscator fuge ne nocens, &c.

Angler! *would'st thou be guiltless? then forbear,*
For these are sacred fishes *that swim here;*
Who know their Sovereign, and will lick his hand;
Than which none's greater in the world's command:
Nay more, th' have names, & when they called are,
Do to their several Owners Call repair.

All the further use that I shall make of this, shall be, to advise Anglers to be patient, and *forbear swearing, lest they be heard and catch no Fish.*

And so I shall proceed next to tell you, it is certain, that certain fields near *Lemster*, a Town in *Herefordshire*, are observed to make the sheep that graze upon them more fat than the next, and also to bear finer wool; that is to say, that, that year in which they feed in such a particular pasture, they shall yield finer wool than they did that year before they came to feed in it and coarser again if they shall return to their former pasture; and again return to a finer wool being fed in the fine-wool-ground. Which I tell you, that you may the better believe that I am certain, if I catch a *Trout* in one Meadow, he shall be *white* and *faint*, and very like to be *lowsie*; and, as certainly, if I catch a *Trout* in the next Meadow, he shall be *strong*, and *red*, and *lusty*, and much better meat: Trust me, Scholar, I have caught many a *Trout* in a particular Meadow, that the very shape and the enamell'd colour of him hath been such, as hath joyed me to look on him: and I have then with much pleasure concluded with *Solomon, Every thing is beautiful in his season.*

I should by promise speak next of the *Salmon,* but I will, by your favour say a little of the *Umber* or *Grayling*; which is so like a *Trout* for his shape and feeding, that I desire I may exercise your patience with a short discourse of him, and then the next shall be of the *Salmon.*

CHAP. VI

Observations of the Umber *or* Grayling, *and directions how to fish for them.*

P*isc.* The *Umber* and *Grayling* are thought by some to differ as the *Herring* and *Pilcher* do. But though they may do so in other Nations, I think those in *England* differ nothing but in their names. *Aldrovandus* says, they be of a Trout kind: and *Gesner* says, that in his Country (which is *Swisserland*) he is accounted the choicest of all Fish. And in *Italy,* he is in the month of *May* so highly valued, that he is sold then at a much higher rate than any other Fish. The *French* (which call the *Chub Un Villain*) call the *Umber* of the Lake *Leman, Un Umble Chevalier*; and they value the *Umber* or Grayling so highly, that they say he feeds on Gold, and say that many have been caught out of their famous River of *Loyre,* out of whose bellies grains of Gold have been often taken. And some think that he feeds on *Water-time,* and smells of it at his first taking out of the water; and they may think so with as good reason as we do, that our Smelts smell like Violets at their being first caught; which I think is a truth. *Aldrovandus* says, the *Salmon*, the *Grayling*, and *Trout*, and all fish that live in clear and sharp streams, are made by their mother *Nature* of such exact shape and pleasant colours, purposely to invite us to a joy and contentedness in feasting with her. Whether this is a truth or not, is not my purpose to dispute: but 'tis certain, all that write of the *Umber* declare him to be very medicinable. And *Gesner* says, that the fat of an *Umber* or *Grayling* being set with a little Hony a day or two in the Sun in a little glass, is very excellent against redness, or swarthiness, or any thing that breeds in the eyes. *Salvian* takes him to be called *Umber* from his swift swimming or gliding out of sight, more like a shadow or a Ghost than a fish. Much more might be said both of his smell and tast, but I shall only tell you that St. *Ambrose* the glorious bishop of *Millan* (who liv'd when the Church kept Fasting-days), calls him the *flower-fish*, or flower of Fishes, and that he was so far in love with him, that he would not let him pass without the honour of a long Discourse; but I must; and pass on to tell you how to take this dainty fish.

First, Note, that he grows not to the bigness of a Trout; for the biggest of them do not usually exceed eighteen inches. He lives in such Rivers as the Trout does, and is usually taken with the same baits as the Trout is, and after the same manner, for he will bite both at the *Minnow*, or *Worm*, or *Fly*, (though he bites not often at the Minnow) and is very gamesom at the *Fly*, and much simpler, and therefore bolder than a *Trout*, for he will rise twenty times at a fly, if you miss him, and yet rise again. He has

been taken with a fly made of the red feathers of a
Parakita, a strange outlandish bird, and he will rise
at a fly not unlike a gnat or a small moth, or indeed,
at most flies that are not too big. He is a Fish that
lurks close all winter, but is very pleasant and jolly
after mid-*April*, and in *May*, and in the hot months:
he is of a very fine shape, his flesh is white, his teeth,
those little ones that he has, are in his throat, yet he
has so tender a mouth, that he is oftner lost after an
Angler has hooked him, than any other Fish. Though
there be many of these Fishes in the delicate River
Dove, and in *Trent*, and some other smaller Rivers,
as that which runs by *Salisbury*, yet he is not so general
a Fish as the *Trout*, nor to me so good to eat or to
angle for. And so I shall take my leave of him, and
now come to some Observations of the *Salmon*, and
how to catch him.

CHAP. VII.

Observations of the Salmon, *with directions how to
fish for him*.

Pisc. The *Salmon* is accounted the King of fresh-
water fish, and is ever bred in Rivers relating to
the Sea, yet so high or far from it as admits of no
tincture of salt, or brackishness; He is said to breed
or cast his spawn in most Rivers in the month of
August: some say, that then they dig a hole or grave
in a safe place in the gravel, and there place their
eggs or spawn (after the Melter has done his natural
Office) and then hide it most cunningly, and cover it
over with gravel and stones; and then leave it to
their Creators protection, who, by a gentle heat

which he infuses into that cold element makes it
brood and beget life in the spawn, and to become
Samlets early in the spring next following.

The *Salmons* having spent their appointed time,
and done this Natural Duty in the fresh waters; they
then haste to the Sea before Winter; both the Melter
and Spawner: but, if they be stopped by *Flood-gates*
or *Weires*, or lost in the fresh waters, then those so
left behind, by degrees grow *sick*, and *lean*, and *un-
seasonable*, and *kipper*; that is to say, have bony gristles
grow out of their lower chaps (not unlike a Hawks
beak) which hinders their feeding, and in time such
Fish so left behind, pine away and dye. 'Tis observed,
that he may live thus one year from the Sea; but he
then grows insipid, and tasteless, and loses both his
blood and strength, and pines and dies the second
year. And 'tis noted, that those little *Salmons* called
Skeggers, which abound in many Rivers relating to
the *Sea*, are bred by such sick *Salmons*, that might
not go to the *Sea*, and that though they abound, yet
they never thrive to any considerable bigness.

But if the old *Salmon* gets to the Sea, then that
gristle which shews him to be *kipper*, wears away, or
is cast off (as the *Eagle* is said to cast his bill) and
he recovers his strength, and comes next Summer to
the same River (if it be possible) to enjoy the former
pleasures that there possest him; for (as one has
wittily observed) he has (like some persons of
Honour and Riches, which have both their Winter
and Summer houses) the fresh Rivers for Summer,
and the salt water for Winter, to spend his life in;
which is not (as Sir *Francis Bacon* hath observed in
his *History of Life and Death*) above ten years: And
it is to be observed, that though the *Salmon* does

grow big in the Sea, yet he grows not fat but in fresh Rivers; and it is observed, that the farther they get from the Sea, they be both the fatter and better.

Next, I shall tell you, that though they make very hard shift to get out of the fresh Rivers into the Sea: yet they will make harder shift to get out of the salt into the fresh Rivers, to spawn, or possess the pleasures that they have formerly found in them: to which end, they will force themselves through *Floodgates*, or over *Weires*, or *hedges*, or *stops* in the water, even to a height beyond common belief. *Gesner* speaks of such places as are known to be above eight foot high above water. And our *Cambden* mentions (in his *Britannia*) the like wonder to be in *Pembrokeshire*, where the river *Tivy* falls into the Sea, and that the fall is so down-right, and so high, that the people stand and wonder at the strength and slight by which they see the *Salmon* use to get out of the Sea into the said River; and the manner and height of the place is so notable, that it is known far by the name of the *Salmon-leap*; concerning which, take this also out of *Michael Draiton*, my honest old friend. As he tells it you in his *Polyalbion*.

> *And when the* Salmon *seeks a fresher stream to find,*
> *(Which hither from the Sea comes yearly by his kind)*
> *As he towards season grows, & stems the watry tract*
> *Where* Tivy *falling down, makes an high cataract,*
> *Forc'd by the rising rocks that there her course oppose*
> *As tho within her bounds they meant her to inclose;*
> *Here, when the labouring fish does at the foot arrive,*
> *And finds that by his strength he does but vainly strive,*
> *His tail takes in his mouth, & bending like a bow*
> *That's to full compass drawn, aloft himself doth throw,*
> *Then springing at his height, as doth a little wand,*
> *That bended end to end, and started from mans hand,*

Far off it self doth cast; so does the Salmon *vault:*
And if at first he fail, his second Summer-salt,
He instantly essaies, and, from his nimble ring,
Still yerking, never leaves untill himself he fling
Above the opposing stream.——

This *Michael Drayton* tells you of this leap or *Summer-salt* of the *Salmon*.

And next I shall tell you, that it is observed by *Gesner* and others, that there is no better *Salmon* than in *England*: and that though some of our Northern Countries have as fat and as large as the River *Thames*, yet none are of so excellent a tast.

And as I have told you that Sir *Francis Bacon* observes, the age of a *Salmon* exceeds not ten years, so let me next tell you, that his growth is very sudden: it is said, that after he is got into the Sea, he becomes from a *Samlet*, not so big as a Gudgion, to be a *Salmon*, in as short a time as a Gosling becomes to be a Goose. Much of this has been observed by tying a *Ribband* or some known *tape* or *thred*, in the tail of some young *Salmons* which have been taken in Weirs as they have swimm'd toward the salt water, and then by taking a part of them again with the known mark at the same place at their return from the Sea, which is usually about six months after; and the like experiment hath been tryed upon young *Swallows*, who have after six months absence, been observed to return to the same chimney, there to make their nests and habitations for the Summer following: which has inclined many to think, that every *Salmon* usually returns to the same River in which it was bred, as young *Pigeons* taken out of the same *Dove-cote*, have also been observed to do.

And you are yet to observe further, that the Hee

Salmon is usually bigger than the Spawner, and that he is more kipper, and less able to endure a winter in the fresh water, than the She is, yet she is at that time of looking less kipper and better, as watry, and as bad meat.

And yet you are to observe, that as there is no general rule without an exception, so there are some few Rivers in this Nation, that have *Trouts* and *Salmons* in season in winter, as 'tis certain there be in the River *Wy* in *Monmouth-shire*, where they be in season (as *Cambden* observes) from *September* till *April*. But, my Scholar, the observation of this and many other things, I must in manners omit, because they will prove too large for our narrow compass of time, and therefore I shall next fall upon my direction *how to fish for this Salmon*.

And for that first, you shall observe, that usually he staies not long in a place (as *Trouts* will) but (as I said) covets still to go nearer the Spring head; and that he does not (as the *Trout* and many other fish) lie near the water side or bank or roots of trees, but swims in the deep and broad parts of the water, and usually in the middle, and near the ground; and that there you are to fish for him, and that it is to be caught as the *Trout* is, with a *Worm*, a *Minnow*, (which some call a *Penk*) or with a *Flie*.

And you are to observe, that he is very seldom observed to bite at a *Minnow*, (yet sometimes he will) and not usually at a *Flie*, but more usually at a *Worm*, and then most usually at a *Lob* or *Garden-worm*, which should be well scoured that is to say, kept seven or eight daies in Moss before you fish with them: and if you double your time of eight into sixteen twenty or more daies, it is still the better,

for the worms will still be clearer, tougher, and more
lively, and continue so longer upon your hook, and
they may be kept longer by keeping them cool, and
in fresh Moss, and some advise to put Camphire
into it.

Note also, that many use to fish for a *Salmon* with
a ring of wire on the top of their Rod, through which
the Line may run to as great a length as is needful
when he is hook'd. And to that end, some use a
wheel about the middle of their Rod, or near their
hand, which is to be observed better by seeing one
of them, than by a large demonstration of words.

And now I shall tell you, that which may be called
a secret: I have been a-fishing with old *Oliver Henly*,
(now with God) a noted fisher both for *Trout* and
Salmon, and have observed, that he would usually
take three or four worms out of his bag, and put
them into a little box in his pocket, where he would
usually let them continue half an hour or more, before
he would bait his hook with them; I have asked him
his reason, and he has replyed, *He did but pick the best
out to be in readiness against he baited his hook the next
time*: But he has been observed both by others, and
my self, to catch more fish than I, or any other body,
that has ever gone a fishing with him, could do; and
especially *Salmons*; And I have been told lately by
one of his most intimate and secret friends, that the
box in which he put those worms, was anointed with
a drop, or two or three, of the Oyl of *Ivy-berries*,
made by expression or infusion; and told that by the
worms remaining in that box an hour, or a like time,
they had incorporated a kind of smell that was irresis-
tibly attractive, enough to force any Fish within the
smell of them, to bite. This I heard not long since

from a friend, but have not tryed it; yet I grant it probable, and refer my Reader to Sir *Francis Bacons* Natural History, where he proves fishes may hear and doubtless can more probably smell: and I am certain *Gesner* says, the *Otter* can smell in the water, and I know not but that Fish may do so too: 'tis left for a lover of Angling, or any that desires to improve that Art, to try this conclusion.

I shall also impart two other Experiments (but not tryed by myself) which I will deliver in the same words that they were given me by an excellent Angler and a very friend, in writing; he told me the latter was too good to be told, but in a learned language, lest it should be made common.

'*Take the stinking oil drawn out of* Polypody *of the Oak by a retort, mixt with* Turpentine, *and* Hive-honey, *and anoint your bait therewith, and it will doubtless draw the fish to it.*'

The other is this: *Vulnera hederæ grandissimæ inflicta sudant Balsamum oleo gelato, albicantique persimile, odoris vero longe suavissimi.*

'Tis supremely sweet to any fish, and yet *Asafœtida* may do the like.

But in these things I have no great faith, yet grant it probable, and have had from some chymical men (namely, from Sir *George Hastings* and others) an affirmation of them to be very advantageous: but no more of these, especially not in this place.

I might here, before I take my leave of the *Salmon*, tell you, that there is more than one sort of them, as namely, a *Tecon*, and another called in some places a *Samlet*, or by some, a *Skegger*: but these (and others which I forbear to name) may be Fish of another kind, (and differ, as we know a *Herring* and a *Pilcher* do,) which I think are as different, as the Rivers in which they breed, and must by me be left to the disquisitions of men of more leisure, and of greater abilities, than I profess my self to have.

And lastly, I am to borrow so much of your promised patience, as to tell you that the *Trout* or *Salmon* being in season, have, at their first taking out of the water (which continues during life) their bodies adorned, the one with such red spots, and the other with such black or blackish spots, as give them such an addition of natural beauty as, I think, was never given to any woman by the Artificial Paint or Patches in which they so much pride themselves in this Age. And so I shall leave them both and proceed to some Observations of the *Pike*.

CHAP. VIII.

Observations of the Luce *or* Pike, *with directions how to fish for him.*

PIsc. The mighty *Luce* or *Pike* is taken to be the Tyrant (as the *Salmon* is the King) of the fresh waters. 'Tis not to be doubted, but that they are bred, some by generation, and some not: as namely, of a Weed called *Pickerel-weed*, unless learned *Gesner* be much mistaken, for he says, this weed and other glutinous matter, with the help of the Suns heat in some particular Months, and some Ponds apted for it by nature, do become *Pikes*. But doubtless divers *Pikes* are bred after this manner, or are brought into some Ponds some such other wayes as is past mans finding out, of which we have daily testimonies.

Sir *Francis Bacon*, in his History of Life and Death,

observes the *Pike* to be the longest lived of any fresh-
water-fish, and yet he computes it to be not usually
above forty years; and others think it to be not above
ten years: and yet *Gesner* mentions a *Pike* taken in
Swedeland in the Year 1449. with a Ring about his
neck, declaring he was put into that pond by *Frederick*
the second, more than two hundred years before he
was last taken, as by the Inscription in that Ring
(being Greek) was interpreted by the then Bishop
of *Worms*. But of this no more, but that it is observed,
that the old or very great Pikes have in them more
of state than goodness; the smaller or middle sized
Pikes being by the most and choicest Palates observed to be the best meat; and contrary, the Eel is
observed to be the better for age and bigness.

All Pikes that live long prove chargeable to their
Keepers, because their life is maintained by the death
of so many other Fish, even those of their own kind,
which has made him by some Writers to be called
the *Tyrant* of the Rivers, or the *Fresh-water-wolf*, by
reason of his bold, greedy, devouring disposition,
which is so keen, as *Gesner* relates, a man going to a
Pond (where it seems a *Pike* had devoured all the
fish) to water his Mule, had a *Pike* bit his Mule by
the lips; to which the *Pike* hung so fast, that the
Mule drew him out of the water; and by that accident
the owner of the Mule angled out the *Pike*. And the
same *Gesner* observes, that a maid in *Poland* had a
Pike bit her by the foot, as she was washing clothes
in a Pond. And I have heard the like of a woman in
Killingworth Pond not far from *Coventry*. But I have
been assured by my friend Mr. *Seagrave*, (of whome
I spake to you formerly,) that keeps tame *Otters*,
that he hath known a *Pike* in extream hunger fight

with one of his Otters for a Carp that the Otter had caught and was then bringing out of the water. I have told you who relates these things, and tell you they are persons of credit; and shall conclude this observation, by telling you what a wise man has observed, *It is a hard thing to persuade the belly, because it has no ears.*

But if these relations be disbelieved, it is too evident to be doubted, that a *Pike* will devour a Fish of his own kind, that shall be bigger than his belly or throat will receive, and swallow a part of him, and let the other part remain in his mouth till the swallowed part be digested, and then swallow that other part that was in his mouth, and so put it over by degrees; which is not unlike the Ox and some other beasts, taking their meat not out of their mouth immediately into their belly, but first into some place betwixt, and then chaw it, or digest it by degrees after, which is called *Chewing the Cud.* And doubtless *Pikes* will bite when they are not hungry, but as some think even for very anger, when a tempting bait comes near to them.

And it is observed, that the *Pike* will eat venemous things (as some kind of *Frogs* are) and yet live without being harmed by them: for, as some say, he has in him a natural Balsom or Antidote against all poison: and he has a strange heat, that though it appear to us to be cold, can yet digest or put over, any Fish-flesh by degrees without being sick. And others observe, that he never eats the venemous *Frog* till he have first killed her, and then (as *Ducks* are observed to do to *Frogs* in spawning time at which time some *Frogs* are observed to be *venemous*) so throughly washt her, by tumbling her up and down in the water, that he may devour her without danger. And *Gesner* affirms, that a *Polonian* Gentleman, did faithfully assure him, he had seen two young Geese at one time in the belly of a *Pike*. And doubtless a *Pike* in his height of hunger will bite at and devour a dog that swims in a Pond, and there have been examples of it, or the like; for as I told you, *The belly has no ears when hunger comes upon it*.

The *Pike* is also observed to be a solitary, melancholy and a bold Fish: Melancholy, because he always swims or rests himself alone, and never swims in sholes or with company, as *Roach* and *Dace*, and most other Fish do: And bold, because he fears not a shadow, or to see or be seen of anybody, as the *Trout* and *Chub*, and all other Fish do.

And it is observed by *Gesner*, that the Jaw-bones, and Hearts, and Galls of *Pikes*, are very medicinable for several diseases, or to stop blood, to abate Fevers, to cure Agues, to oppose or expel the infection of the Plague, and to be many ways medicinable and useful for the good of Mankind; but he observes, that the biting of a *Pike* is venemous and hard to be cured.

And it is observed, that the *Pike* is a fish that breeds but once a year, and that other fish (as namely *Loaches*) do breed oftner: as we are certain tame Pigeons do almost every month, and yet the *Hawk* (a Bird of Prey, as the *Pike* is of Fish) breeds but once in twelve months: and you are to note, that his time of breeding or spawning is usually about the end of *February*, or somewhat later, in *March*, as the weather proves colder or warmer; and to note, that his manner of breeding is thus, a He and a She *Pike* will usually go together out of a River into some ditch or creek, and that there the Spawner casts her eggs, and the Melter hovers over her all that time that she is casting her spawn, but touches her not.

I might say more of this, but it might be thought curiosity or worse, and shall therefore forbear it, and take up so much of your attention, as to tell you, that the best of *Pikes* are noted to be in *Rivers*, next those in great *Ponds* or *Meres*, and the worst in small Ponds.

But before I proceed further, I am to tell you that there is a great antipathy betwixt the *Pike* and some *Frogs*; and this may appear to the Reader of *Dubravius* (a Bishop in *Bohemia*) who in his Book of Fish and Fish-ponds, relates what, he says, he saw with his own eyes, and could not forbear to tell the Reader. Which was:

As he and the Bishop Thurzo *were walking by a large Pond in* Bohemia, *they saw a Frog, when the Pike lay very sleepily and quiet by the shore side, leap upon his head, and the Frog having exprest malice or anger by his swoln cheeks and staring eyes, did stretch out his legs and embraced the* Pikes *head, and presently reached them to his eyes, tearing with them and his teeth those tender parts; the* Pike *moved with anguish, moves up and down the water, and rubs himself against weeds, and whatever he thought might quit him of his enemy; but all in vain, for the frog did continue to ride triumphantly, and to bite and torment the* Pike, *till his strength failed, and then the frog sunk with the Pike to the bottom of the water; then presently the frog appeared again at the top, and croaked, and seemed to rejoice like a Conqueror, after which he presently retired to his secret hole. The Bishop, that had beheld the battel, called his fisherman to fetch his nets, and by all means to get the* Pike *that they might declare what had hapned: and the Pike was drawn forth, and both his eyes eaten out, at which when they began to wonder, the Fisherman wished them to forbear, and assured them he was certain that* Pikes *were often so served.*

I told this, (which is to be read in the sixth chapter of the book of *Dubravius*) unto a friend, who replied, *It was as improbable as to have the mouse scratch out the cats eyes.* But he did not consider, that there be fishing Frogs (which the *Dalmatians* call the Water-Devil) of which I might tell you as wonderful a story, but I shall tell you, that 'tis not to be doubted, but that there be some Frogs so fearful of the Water-snake, that, when they swim in a place in which they fear to meet with him, they then get a reed across into their mouths, which if they two meet by accident, secures the frog from the strength and malice of the *Snake*, and note, that the frog usually swims the fastest of the two.

And let me tell you, that as there be *Water* and *Land-frogs*, so there be *Land* and *Water-Snakes*. Concerning which take this observation, that the Land-snake breeds, and hatches her eggs, which become young Snakes, in some old dunghill, or a like hot place; but the Water-snake, which is not venemous (and as I have been assured by a great observer of such secrets) does not hatch but breed her young alive, which she does not then forsake, but bides with them, and in case of danger will take them all into her mouth and swim away from any apprehended danger, and then let them out again when she thinks all danger to be past; These be accidents that we Anglers sometimes see and often talk of.

But whither am I going? I had almost lost my self by remembering the Discourse of *Dubravius*. I will therefore stop here, and tell you according to my promise how to catch this *Pike*.

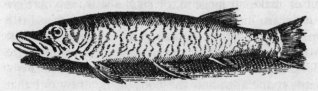

His feeding is usually of *fish* or *frogs*, and sometimes a weed of his own called Pickrell-weed. Of which I told you some think some *Pikes* are bred; for they have observed, that where none have been put into Ponds, yet they have there found many: and that there has been plenty of that weed in those Ponds, and that that weed both breeds and feeds them; but whether those *Pikes* so bred will ever breed by generation as the others do, I shall leave to the disquisitions of men of more curiosity and leasure than I profess my self to have; and shall proceed to tell you that you may fish for a *Pike*, either with a *ledger* or a *walking-bait*; and you are to note, that I call that a Ledger bait, which is fixed, or made to rest in one certain place when you shall be absent from it: and I call that a walking bait, which you take with you, and have ever in motion. Concerning which two, I shall give you this direction; that your ledger-bait is best to be a living bait, though a dead one may catch, whether it be a fish or a frog; and that you may make them live the longer, you may, or indeed you must, take this course.

First, for your live bait of fish, a *Roach* or *Dace* is (I think) best and most tempting, and a *Pearch* is the longest-lived on a hook, and having cut off his fin on his back, which may be done without hurting him, you must take your knife (which cannot be too sharp) and betwixt the head and the fin on the back, cut or make an incision, or such a scar, as you may put the arming wire of your hook into it, with as little bruising or hurting the fish as art and diligence will enable you to do; and so carrying your arming wire along his back, unto, or near the tail of your Fish, betwixt the skin and the body of it, draw out that wire or arming of your hook at another scar near to his tail: then ty him about it with thred, but no harder than of necessity, to prevent hurting the fish; and the better to avoid hurting the fish, some have a kind of probe to open the way, for the more easy entrance and passage of your wire or arming: but as for these, time, and a little experience will teach you better than I can by words; therefore I will for the present say no more of this, but come next to give you some directions, how to bait your hook with a frog.

Ven. But, good Master, did you not say even now, that some *Frogs* were venemous, and is it not dangerous to touch them?

Pisc. Yes, but I will give you some Rules or Cautions concerning them: And first, you are to note, that there are two kinds of *Frogs*; that is to say (if I may so express my self) a *flesh*, and a *fish-frog*. By *flesh-frogs*, I mean *frogs* that breed and live on the land; and of these there be several sorts also and of several colours, some being peckled, some greenish, some blackish, or brown: the green *Frog*, which is a small one, is, by *Topsel* taken to be venemous; and so is the *padock*, or *Frog-padock*, which usually keeps or breeds on the land, and is very large and bony, and big, especially the She frog of that kind; yet these will sometimes come into the water, but it is not often: and the land frogs are some of them observed by him, to breed by laying eggs: and others to breed of the slime and dust of the earth, and that in winter they turn to slime again, and that the next summer that very Slime returns to be a living creature; this is the opinion of *Pliny*: And *Cardanus* In his 19 Book, undertakes to give a reason for the *De subtil. ex.* raining of Frogs: but if it were in my power, it should rain none but water-Frogs, for those I think are not venemous, especially the right water-Frog, which about *February* or *March* breeds in ditches by slime, and blackish eggs in that slime: about which time of breeding the He and She frogs are observed to use divers *Simber-salts*, and to croak and make a noise, which the land-frog, or Padock-frog, never does. Now of these water-frogs, if you intend to fish with a frog for a Pike, you are to chuse the yellowest that you can get, for that the Pike ever likes best. And thus use your frog, that he may continue long alive:

Put your hook into his mouth, which you may easily do from the middle of *April* till *August*, and then the frogs mouth grows up, and he continues so for at least six moneths without eating, but is sustained, none but he whose name is Wonderful, knows how: I say, put your hook, I mean the arming wire, through his mouth, and out at his gills, and then with a fine needle and silk sew the upper part of his leg with only one stitch to the arming wire of your hook, or tie the frogs leg above the upper joynt, to the armed wire; and in so doing, use him as though you loved him, that is, harm him as little as you may possibly, that he may live the longer.

And now, having given you this direction for the baiting your ledger hook with a live Fish or frog, my next must be to tell you, how your hook thus baited must or may be used: and it is thus. Having fastened your hook to a line, which if it be not fourteen yards long, should not be less than twelve; you are to fasten that line to any bough near to a hole where a Pike is, or is likely to lie, or to have a haunt, and then wind your line on any forked stick, all your line, except half a yard of it or rather more, and split that forked stick with such a nick or notch at one end of it, as may keep the line from any more of it ravelling from about the stick, than so much of it as you intend; and choose your forked stick to be of that bigness as may keep the Fish or frog from pulling the forked stick under the water till the Pike bites, and then the Pike having pulled the line forth of the clift or nick of that stick in which it was gently fastened, he will have line enough to go to his hold and pouch the bait: and if you would have this ledger bait to keep at a fixt place, undisturbed by wind or other accidents which may drive it to the shore side, (for you are to note, that it is likeliest to catch a Pike in the midst of the water) then hang a small Plummet of lead, a stone, or piece of tile, or a turf in a string, and cast it into the water, with the forked stick, to hang upon the ground, to be a kind of Anchor to keep the forked stick from moving out of your intended place till the Pike come. This I take to be a very good way, to use so many ledger-baits as you intend to make trial of.

Or if you bait your hooks thus with live Fish or Frogs, and in a windy day, fasten them thus to a bough or bundle of straw, and by the help of that

wind can get them to move cross a *Pond* or *mere*, you
are like to stand still on the shore and see sport presently if there be any store of *Pikes*; or these live
baits may make sport, being tied about the body or
wings of a *Goose* or *Duck*, and she chased over a *Pond*:
and the like may be done with turning three or four
live baits thus fastened to bladders, or boughs, or
bottles of hay or flags, to swim down a River, whilst
you walk quietly alone on the shore, and are still in
expectation of sport. The rest must be taught you
by practice, for time will not allow me to say more
of this kind of fishing with live baits.

And for your dead bait for a *Pike*, for that you may
be taught by one daies going a fishing with me, or any
other body that fishes for him, for the baiting your
hook with a dead *Gudgeon* or a *Roach*, and moving it
up and down the water, is too easie a thing to take up
any time to direct you to do it; and yet, because I cut
you short in that, I will commute for it, by telling
you that that was told me for a secret: it is this.

Dissolve Gum *of* Ivy *in Oyl of* Spike, *and therewith
anoynt your dead bait for a* Pike, *and then cast it into
a likely place, and when it has lain a short time at the
bottom, draw it towards the top of the water and so up
the stream, and it is more than likely that you have a*
Pike *follow with more than common eagerness*.

And some affirm, that any bait anointed with the
marrow of the Thigh-bone of an *Hern* is a great
temptation to any Fish.

These have not been tryed by me, but told me by a
friend of note, that pretended to do me a courtesie, but
if this direction to catch a *Pike* thus, do you no good,
yet I am certain this direction how to roast him when
he is caught, is choicely good, for I have tryed it, and

it is somewhat the better for not being common, but with my direction you must take this Caution, that your *Pike* must not be a small one, that is, it must be more than half a Yard, and should be bigger.

First open your Pike *at the gills, and if need be, cut also a little slit towards the belly; out of these, take his guts, and keep his liver, which you are to shred very small with* Time, Sweet-Marjoram, *and a little* Winter-savoury; *to these put some pickled* Oysters, *and some* Anchovies, *two or three, both these last whole* (*for the Anchovies will melt, and the Oysters should not*) *to these you must adde also a pound of sweet butter, which you are to mix with the herbs that are shred, and let them all be well salted* (*if the* Pike *be more than a yard long, then you may put into these herbs more than a pound, or if he be less, then less Butter will suffice:*) *these being thus mixt with a blade or two of* Mace, *must be put into the* Pikes *belly, and then his belly so sowed up, as to keep all the Butter in his belly if it be possible, if not, then as much of it as you possibly can, but take not off the scales; then you are to thrust the spit through his mouth, out at his tail. And then take four or five or six split sticks, or very thin lathes, and a convenient quantity of Tape or Filleting, these lathes are to be tyed round about the* Pikes *body from his head to his tail, and the Tape tyed somewhat thick to prevent his breaking or falling off from the spit; let him be roasted very leasurely, and often basted with Claret wine, and Anchovyes, and butter mixt together, and also with what moisture falls from him into the pan: when you have rosted him sufficiently you are to hold under him,* (*when you unwind or cut the Tape that ties him*) *such a dish as you purpose to eat him out of; and let him fall into it with the sawce that is roasted in his belly, and by this means the* Pike *will be kept unbroken and compleat: then, to the sawce which was within, and also that sawce in the pan, you are to add a fit quantity of the best Butter, and to squeeze the juyce of three or four Oranges: Lastly, you may either put into the* Pike, *with the* Oysters, *two cloves of* Garlick, *and take it whole out, when the* Pike *is cut off the spit, or, to give the sawce a* hogo, *let the dish (into which you let the* Pike *fall) be rubbed with it: the using or not using of this Garlick is left to your discretion.*

M. B.

This dish of meat is too good for any but Anglers or very honest men; and I trust, you will prove both, and therefore I have trusted you with this secret.

Let me next tell you, that *Gesner* tells us there are no Pikes in *Spain*, and that the largest are in the Lake *Thrasimene* in *Italy*; and the next, if not equall to them, are the Pikes of *England*, and that in *England*, *Lincolnshire* boasteth to have the biggest. Just so doth *Sussex* boast of four sorts of fish; namely, an *Arundel Mullet*, a *Chichester Lobster*, a *Shelsey Cockle*, and an *Amerly Trout*.

But I will take up no more of your time with this relation, but proceed to give you some observations of the *Carp*, and how to angle for him, and to dress him, but not till he is caught.

CHAP. IX.

Observations of the Carp, *with Directions how to fish for him.*

P*Isc.* The *Carp* is the Queen of Rivers: a stately, a good, and a very subtil fish, that was not at first bred, nor hath been long in *England*, but is now naturalized. It is said, they were brought hither by one Mr. *Mascal* a Gentleman, that then lived at *Plumsted* in *Sussex*, a County that abounds more with this fish than any in this Nation.

You may remember that I told you, *Gesner* says, there are no *Pikes* in *Spain*; and doubtless, there was a time, about a hundred or a few more years ago, when there were no *Carps* in *England*, as may seem to be affirmed by *S. Richard Baker*, in whose Chronicle you may find these Verses.

> *Hops and Turkies, Carps and Beer*
> *Came into* England *all in a year*.

And doubtless as of Sea-fish the *Herring* dies soonest out of the water, and of fresh-water fish the *Trout*, so (except the Eel) the *Carp* endures most hardness, and lives longest out of his own proper Element. And therefore the report of the Carps being brought out of a forraigne Country into this Nation is the more probable.

Carps and Loaches are observed to Breed several months in one year, which Pikes and most other fish do not. And this is partly proved by tame and wild *Rabbets*, as also by some *Ducks*, which will lay eggs nine of the twelve months, and yet there be other *Ducks* that lay not longer than about one month. And it is the rather to be believed, because you shall scarce or never take a *Male-Carp* without a *Melt*, or a *Female* without a *Roe* or *spawn*, and for the most part very much; and especially all the Summer season; and it is observed, that they breed more naturally in ponds than in running waters, (if they breed there at all;) and that those that live in Rivers are taken by men of the best palats to be much the better meat.

And it is observed, that in some ponds *Carps* will not breed, especially in cold ponds; but where they will breed, they breed innumerably; *Aristotle* and *Pliny* say, six times in a year, if there be no *Pikes* nor *Pearch* to devour their spawn, when it is cast upon grass, or flags or weeds, where it lies ten or twelve dayes before it be enlivened.

The *Carp*, if he have water-room and good feed, will grow to a very great bigness and length: I have heard, to be much above a yard long. 'Tis said, (by *Jovius*, who hath writ of Fishes) that in the Lake *Lurian* in *Italy*, *Carps* have thriven to be more than fifty pound weight, which is the more probable, for as the *Bear* is conceiv'd and born suddenly; and being born is but short-liv'd: So, on the contrary, the *Elephant* is said to be two years in his dams belly (some think he is ten years in it) and being born grows in bigness twenty years; and 'tis observ'd too that he lives to the Age of a hundred years. And 'tis also observ'd that the *Crocodile* is very long-liv'd, and more than that, that all that long life he thrives in bigness, and so I think some *Carps* do, especially in some places; though I never saw one above 23. inches, which was a great and a goodly Fish; But have been assured there are of a far greater size, and in *England* too.

Now, as the increase of *Carps* is wonderful for their number; so there is not a reason found out, I think by any, why they should breed in some ponds, and not in others of the same nature, for soil and all other circumstances: and as their breeding, so are their decays also very mysterious: I have both read it, and been told by a Gentleman of tryed honesty, that he has known sixty or more large *Carps* put into several ponds near to a house; where by reason of the stakes in the ponds, and the Owners constant being near to them, it was impossible they should be stole away from him: and that when he has after three or four years emptyed the pond, and expected an increase from them by breeding young ones (for that they might do so, he had, as the rule is, put in three Melters for one Spawner) he has, I say, after three or four years, found neither a young nor old *Carp* remaining. And the like I have known of one that has almost watched the pond, and, at a like distance of time, at the fishing of a pond, found of seventy or eighty large *Carps* not above five or six: and that he had forborn longer to fish the said pond, but that he saw, in a hot day in summer, a large *Carp* swim near the top of the water with a Frog upon his head, and that he upon that occasion caused his pond to be let dry: and I say, of seventy or eighty *Carps*, only found five or six in the said pond, and those very sick and lean, and with every one a Frog sticking so fast on the head of the said *Carps*, that the frog would not be got off without extreme force or killing: and the Gentleman that did affirm this to me, told me he saw it, and did declare his belief to be, (and I also believe the same) that he thought the other *Carps* that were so strangely lost, were so killed by frogs, and then devoured.

And a person of honour, now living in *Worcester-* Mr. Fr. Ru. *shire*, assur'd me he had seen a necklace or collar of Tadpoles hang like a chaine or necklace of beads about a *Pikes* neck, and to kill him; whether it were for meat or malice, must be to me a question.

But I am faln into this Discourse by accident, of which I might say more, but it has proved longer than

I intended, and possibly may not to you be considerable; I shall therefore give you three or four more
short observations of the *Carp*, and then fall upon
some directions how you shall fish for him.

The age of *Carps* is by Sir *Francis Bacon* (in his
History of Life and Death) observed to be but ten
years; yet others think they live longer. *Gesner* saies
a *Carp* has been known to live in the *Palatinate* above
a hundred years: But most conclude, that (contrary
to the *Pike* or *Luce*) all *Carps* are the better for age
and bigness; the tongues of *Carps* are noted to be
choice and costly meat, especially to them that buy
them: but *Gesner* saies, *Carps* have no tongue like
other Fish, but a piece of flesh-like-Fish in their
mouth like to a tongue, and should be called a palate:
But it is certain it is choicely good, and that the *Carp*
is to be reckoned amongst those leather-mouthed
fish which I told you have their teeth in their throat,
and for that reason he is very seldom lost by breaking
his hold, if your hook be once stuck into his chaps.

I told you that Sir *Francis Bacon* thinks that the
Carp lives but ten years: but *Janus Dubravius* has
writ a Book of Fish and Fish-ponds, in which he saies,
That *Carps* begin to Spawn at the age of three years,
and continue to do so till thirty: he says also, that in
the time of their breeding, which is in Summer, when
the sun hath warmed both the earth and water, and
so apted them also for generation: that then three or
four Male-*Carps* will follow a Female, and that then
she putting on a seeming coyness, they force her
through weeds and flags, where she lets fall her
Eggs or Spawn, which sticks fast to the weeds, and
then they let fall their Melt upon it, and so it becomes in a short time to be a living Fish; and as I

told you, it is thought the *Carp* does this several months in the year, and most believe that most fish breed after this manner, except the Eel: and it has been observed, that when the Spawner has weakened her self by doing that natural office, that two or three Melters have helped her from off the weeds, by bearing her up on both sides, and guarding her into the deep. And you may note, that though this may seem a curiosity not worth observing, yet others have judged it worth their time and costs, to make *Glass-hives*, and order them in such a manner as to see how *Bees* have bred and made their *Honeycombs*, and how they have obeyed their King, and governed their Commonwealth. But it is thought that all *Carps* are not bred by generation, but that some breed other ways, as some *Pikes* do.

The physicians make the *galls* and *stones* in the heads of *Carps* to be very medicinable; but 'tis not to be doubted but that in *Italy* they make great profit of the Spawn of *Carps*, by selling it to the *Jews*, who make it into red *Caviare*, the *Jews* not being by their Law admitted to eat of *Caviare* made of the *Sturgeon*, that being a Fish that wants scales, and (as may appear in *Levit*. 11.) by them reputed to be unclean.

Much more might be said out of him, and out of *Aristotle*, which *Dubravius* often quotes in his Discourse of Fishes; but it might rather perplex than satisfie you, and therefore I shall rather chuse to direct you how to catch, than spend more time in discoursing either of the nature or the breeding of this CARP, or of any more circumstances concerning him; but yet I shall remember you of what I told you before, that he is a very subtil Fish, and hard to be caught.

And my first direction is, that if you will Fish for
a *Carp*, you must put on a very large measure of
patience; especially to fish for a *River Carp*: I have
known a very good Fisher angle diligently four or
six hours in a day, for three or four daies together
for a *River Carp*, and not have a bite: and you are to

note, that in some ponds it is as hard to catch a Carp
as in a River; that is to say, where they have store of
feed, and the water is of a clayish colour: But you
are to remember, that I have told you there is no
rule without an exception, and therefore being possest with that hope and patience which I wish to all
Fishers, especially to the *Carp-Angler*, I shall tell
you with what bait to fish for him. But first you are
to know, that it must be either early or late; and let
me tell you, that in hot weather (for he will seldom
bite in cold) you cannot be too early or too late at
it. And some have been so curious as to say, the
10. of *April* is a fatal day for Carps.

The Carp bites either at worms or at paste, and
of worms I think the blewish Marsh or Meadow
worm is best; but possibly another worm not too big
may do as well, and so may a green Gentle: And as

for pastes, there are almost as many sorts as there are Medicines for the Toothach; but doubtless sweet pastes are best; I mean, pastes made with honey or with sugar: which, that you may the better beguile this crafty Fish, should be thrown into the Pond or place in which you fish for him some hours or longer before you undertake your tryal of skill with the Angle-rod; and doubtless if it be thrown into the water a day or two before, at several times and in small pellets, you are the likelier when you fish for the Carp to obtain your desired sport; or in a large Pond to draw them to any certain place, that they may the better and with more hope be fished for, you are to throw into it in some certain place, either Grains or Blood mixt with Cow dung or with Bran; or any Garbage, as Chickens guts or the like, and then some of your small sweet pellets with which you purpose to angle: and these small pellets being a few of them also thrown in as you are Angling will be the better.

And your paste must be thus made: Take the flesh of a Rabbet or Cat cut small, and Bean-flowre; and if that may not be easily got, get other flowre, and then mix these together, and put to them either Sugar, or Honey, which I think better, and then beat these together in a Mortar, or sometimes work them in your hands, (your hands being very clean) and then make it into a Ball, or two, or three, as you like best for your use; but you must work or pound it so long in the Mortar; as to make it so tough as to hang upon your hook without washing from it, yet not too hard; or, that you may the better keep it on your hook, you may knead with your paste a little (and not much) white or yellowish wool.

And if you would have this paste keep all the year for any other Fish, then mix with it *Virgin wax* and *clarified honey*, and work them together with your hands, before the Fire, then make these into balls, and they will keep all the year.

And if you fish for a Carp with Gentles, then put upon your hook a small piece of Scarlet about this bigness ▇, it being soked in, or anointed with *Oyl of Peter*, called by some *Oyl of the Rock*, and if your Gentles be put two or three dayes before into a box or horn anointed with honey, and so put upon your hook as to preserve them to be living, you are as like to kill this crafty fish this way as any other. But still, as you are fishing chaw a little white or brown bread in your mouth, and cast it into the pond about the place where your Flote swims. Other baits there be, but these with diligence, and patient watchfulness, will do it better than any that I have ever practised, or heard of: And yet I shall tell you, that the crumbs of white bread and honey made into a paste is a good bait for a *Carp*, and you know it is more easily made. And having said thus much of the *Carp*, my next discourse shall be of the *Bream*, which shall not prove so tedious, and therefore I desire the continuance of your attention.

But first I will tell you how to make this *Carp* that is so curious to be caught, so curious a dish of meat, as shall make him worth all your labour and patience; and though it is not without some trouble and charges, yet it will recompence both.

Take a Carp (*alive if possible*) *scour him, and rub him clean with water and salt, but scale him not, then open him, and put him, with his bloud and his liver* (*which you must save when you open him*) *into a small pot or kettle; then take sweet Marjoram, Time and Parsley, of each half a handful, a sprig of Rosemary, and another of Savoury, bind them into two or three small bundles, and put them to your Carp, with four or five whole Onyons, twenty pickled Oysters, and three Anchovies. Then pour upon your Carp as much Claret wine as will only cover him; and season your Claret well with salt, Cloves, and Mace, and the rinds of Oranges and Lemons, that done, cover your pot and set it on a quick-fire, till it be sufficiently boiled; then take out the Carp and lay it with the broth into the dish, and pour upon it a quarter of a pound of the best fresh butter melted and beaten with half a dozen spoonfuls of the broth, the yolks of two or three eggs, and some of the herbs shred: garnish your dish with Lemons, and so serve it up, and much good do you.* Dr. *T.*

CHAP. X.

Observations of the Bream, *and directions to catch him.*

P*Isc.* The *Bream* being at a full growth is a large and stately Fish: he will breed both in Rivers and Ponds: but loves best to live in ponds, and where, if he likes the water and Air, he will grow not only to be very large, but as fat as a Hog: he is by *Gesner* taken to be more pleasant or sweet than wholesome; this Fish is long in growing, but breeds exceedingly in a water that pleases him; yea, in many Ponds so fast, as to over-store them, and starve the other Fish.

He is very broad with a forked tail, and his scales set in excellent order, he hath large eyes and a narrow sucking mouth; he hath two sets of teeth, and a lozenge like bone, a bone to help his grinding.

The Melter is observed to have two large Melts, and the Female two large bags of eggs or spawn.

Gesner reports, that in *Poland* a certain, and a great number of large Breams were put into a Pond, which in the next following winter were frozen up into one intire ice, and not one drop of water remaining, nor one of these fish to be found, though they were diligently searcht for; and yet the next Spring, when the ice was thawed, and the weather warm, and fresh water got into the pond, he affirms they all appeared again. This *Gesner* affirms, and I quote my Author, because it seems almost as incredible as the *Resurrection* to an *Atheist*. But it may win something in point of believing it, to him that considers the breeding or renovation of the Silk-worm and of many insects. And that is considerable which Sir *Francis Bacon* observes in his History of Life and Death (*fol.* 20), that there be some herbs that die and spring every year, and some endure longer.

But though some do not, yet the *French* esteem this Fish highly, and to that end have this Proverb, *He that hath Breams in his pond is able to bid his friend welcome*. And it is noted, that the best part of a Bream is his belly and head.

Some say, that *Breams* and *Roaches* will mix their eggs, and melt together, and so there is in many places a Bastard breed of *Breams*, that never come to be either large or good, but very numerous.

The Baits good to catch this BREAM are many. I. Paste made of brown bread and hony, gentles, or the brood of wasps that be young, (and then not unlike gentles) and should be hardned in an oven, or dried on a tile before the fire to make them tough; or there is, at the root of docks, or flags, or rushes, in watry places, a worm not unlike a Maggot, at which Tench will bite freely. Or he will bite at a Grass-hopper with his legs nipt off in *June* and *July*, or at several flies under water, which may be found on flags that grow near to the water side. I doubt not but that there be many other baits that are good, but

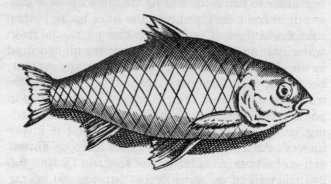

I will turn them all into this most excellent one, either for a *Carp* or *Bream*, in any River or Mere: it was given to me by a most honest and excellent Angler, and hoping you will prove both, I will impart it to you.

1. Let your bait be as big a *red worm* as you can find, without a knot, get a pint or quart of them in an evening in garden walks, or Chalky Commons after a showre of rain; and put them with clean Moss well washed and picked, and the water squeezed out of the Moss as dry as you can, into an earthen pot or pipkin set dry, and change the Moss fresh every three or four dayes for three weeks or a month together; then your bait will be at the best, for it will be clear and lively.

2. Having thus prepared your baits, get your

tackling ready and fitted for this sport. Take three long Angling Rods, and as many and more silk, or silk and hair, lines, and as many large Swan or Goose-quil floats. Then take a piece of Lead made after this manner, and fasten them to the low ends of your Lines. Then fasten your link-hook also to the lead; and let there be about a foot or ten inches between the lead and the hook; but be sure the lead be heavy enough to sink the float or quil a little under the water, and not the quil to bear up the Lead, for the lead must lie on the ground. Note, that your link next the hook may be smaller than the rest of your line, if you dare adventure for fear of taking the *Pike* or *Pearch*, who will assuredly visit your hooks, till they be taken out (as I will shew you afterwards) before either *Carp* or *Bream* will come near to bite. Note also, that when the worm is well baited, it will crawl up and down, as far as the Lead will give leave, which much enticeth the Fish to bite without suspicion.

3. Having thus prepared your baits, and fitted your tackling, repair to the River, where you have seen them to swim in skuls or shoals in the summer-time, in a hot afternoon, about three or four of the clock, and watch their going forth of their deep holes and returning (which you may well discern) for they return about four of the clock most of them seeking food at the bottom, yet one or two will lie on the top of the water, rolling and tumbling themselves whilst the rest are under him at the bottom, and so you shall perceive him to keep Sentinel; then mark where he plays most, and stays longest, (which commonly is in the broadest and deepest place of the River) and there, or, near thereabouts, at a clear bottom, and a

convenient landing place, take one of your Angles ready fitted as aforesaid, and sound the bottom, which should be about eight or ten foot deep (two yards from the bank is the best.) Then consider with your self, whether that water will rise or fall by the next morning, by reason of any Water-mills near, and, according to your discretion take the depth of the place, where you mean after to cast your ground-bait, and to fish, to half an inch; that the Lead lying on or near the ground-bait, the top of the float may only appear upright half an inch above the water.

Thus you having found and fitted for the place and depth thereof, then go home and prepare your ground-bait, which is next to the fruit of your labours, to be regarded.

The Ground-Bait.

You shall take a peck, or a peck and a half (according to the greatness of the stream, and deepness of the water, where you mean to Angle) of sweet grossground barly-malt, and boil it in a kettle (one or two warms is enough) then strain it through a Bag into a tub (the liquor whereof hath often done my Horse much good) and when the bag and malt is near cold, take it down to the water-side about eight or nine of the clock in the evening, and not before; cast in two parts of your ground-bait, squeezed hard between both your hands, it will sink presently to the bottom, and be sure it may rest in the very place where you mean to Angle; if the stream run hard or move a little, cast your malt in handfuls a little the higher, upwards the stream. You may between your hands close the Malt so fast in handfuls, that the water will hardly part it with the fall.

Your ground thus baited, and tackling fitted, leave your bag with the rest of your tackling and ground-bait near the sporting-place all night, and in the morning about three or four of the clock visit the water-side (but not too near) for they have a cunning Watch-man, and are watchful themselves too.

Then gently take one of your three rods, and bait your hook, casting it over your ground-bait, and gently and secretly draw it to you till the Lead rests about the middle of the ground-bait.

Then take a second Rod and cast in about a yard above, and your third a yard below the first Rod, and stay the Rods in the ground, but go your self so far from the water-side, that you perceive nothing but the top of the floats, which you must watch most diligently; then when you have a bite, you shall perceive the top of your float to sink suddenly into the water; yet nevertheless be not too hasty to run to your Rods, until you see that the Line goes clear away, then creep to the water-side, and give as much Line as possibly you can: if it be a good *Carp* or *Bream*, they will go to the farther side of the River, then strike gently, and hold your rod at a bent a little while; but if you both pull together, you are sure to lose your Game, for either your line, or hook, or hold will break; and after you have overcome them, they will make noble sport, and are very shie to be landed. The *Carp* is far stronger and more mettlesom than the *Bream*.

Much more is to be observed in this kind of Fish and Fishing, but it is far fitter for experience and discourse than paper. Only thus much is necessary for you to know, and, to be mindful and careful of; that if the *Pike* or *Pearch* do breed in that River, they will be sure to bite first, and must first be taken. And for the most part they are very large, and will repair to your ground-bait, not that they will eat of it, but will feed and sport themselves amongst the young Fry that gather about and hover over the Bait.

The way to discern the *Pike* and to take him, if you mistrust your *Bream*-hook (for I have taken a *Pike* a yard long several times at my *Bream*-hooks, and sometimes he hath had the luck to share my line) may be thus.

Take a small *Bleak*, or *Roach*, or *Gudgion*, and bait it, and set it alive among your Rods two foot deep from the Cork, with a little red worm on the point of the hook, then take a few crumbs of White-bread, or some of the ground-bait, and sprinkle it gently amongst your Rods. If Mr. *Pike* be there; then the little fish will skip out of the water at his appearance but the live-set Bait is sure to be taken.

Thus continue your sport from four in the morning till eight, and if it be a gloomy, windy day, they will bite all day long. But this is too long to stand to your rods at one place and it will spoil your evening sport that day, which is this.

About four of the clock in the Afternoon repair to your baited place, and as soon as you come to the water-side, cast in one half of the rest of your ground-bait, and stand off: then whilst the Fish are gathering together (for there they will most certainly come for their supper) you may take a pipe of Tobacco; and then in with your three rods as in the morning: You will find excellent sport that evening till eight of the clock; then cast in the residue of your ground-bait, and next morning, by four of the clock visit them again for four hours, which is the best sport of all;

and after that let them rest till you and your friends have a mind to more sport.

From St. *James* Tide until *Bartholomew* Tide is the best, when they have had all the Summers food, they are the fattest.

Observe lastly, that after three or four days fishing together, your Game will be very shie and wary, and you shall hardly get above a bite or two at a baiting; then your only way is to desist from your sport about two or three days; and in the mean time (on the place you late baited, and again intend to bait) you shall take a turf of green, but short grass, as big or bigger than a round Trencher; to the top of this turf, on the green side, you shall, with a Needle and green thred, fasten one by one as many little red worms as will near cover all the turf: Then take a round board or Trencher, make a hole in the middle thereof, and through the turf placed on the board or Trencher, with a string or cord as long as is fitting, tied to a pole, let it down to the bottom of the water for the Fish to feed upon without disturbance about two or three days; and after that you have drawn it away, you may fall to, and enjoy your former recreation.   **B. A.**

CHAP. XI.

Observations of the Tench, *and advice how to Angle for him.*

PIsc. The *Tench*, the Physician of Fishes, is observed to love Ponds better than Rivers, and to love pits better than either; yet *Cambden* observes there is a river in *Dorsetshire* that abounds with

Tenches, but doubtless they retire to the most deep and quiet places in it.

This fish hath very large Fins, very small and smooth Scales, a red circle about his Eyes, which are big and of a gold colour, and from either Angle of his mouth there hangs down a little Barb; in every *Tenches* head there are two little stones, which forraign Physicians make great use of, but he is not commended for wholesom meat, though there be very much use made of them, for outward applications. *Rondelitius* says. That at his being at *Rome, he saw a great cure done by applying a Tench to the feet of a very sick man*. This he says was done after an unusual manner by certain Jews. And it is observed that many of those people have many secrets, yet unknown to Christians; secrets that have never yet been written, but have been since the days of their *Solomon* (who knew the nature of all things, even from the Cedar to the Shrub) delivered by tradition from the Father to the Son, and so from generation to generation without writing, or (unless it were casually) without the least communicating them to any other Nation or Tribe : for to do that they account a prophanation. And yet it is thought that they, or some Spirit worse than they, first told us, that Lice swallowed alive were a certain cure for the Yellow-Jaundice. This, and many other medicines were discover'd by them or by revelation, for, doubtless we attain'd them not by study.

Well, this fish, besides his eating, is very useful, both dead and alive for the good of mankind. But, I will meddle no more with that, my honest humble Art teaches no such boldness; there are too many foolish medlers in Physick and Divinity, that think themselves fit to meddle with hidden secrets, and so bring destruction to their followers. But I'le not meddle with them any farther than to wish them wiser; and shall tell you next (for, I hope, I may be so bold) that the *Tench* is the Physician of fishes, for the *Pike* especially, and that the *Pike*, being either sick or hurt, is cured by the touch of the *Tench*. And

it is observed, that the Tyrant *Pike* will not be a Wolf to his Physician, but forbears to devour him though he be never so hungry.

This fish that carries a natural Balsome in him to cure both himself and others, loves yet to feed in very foul water, and amongst weeds. And yet I am sure he eats pleasantly, and, doubtless, you will think so too, if you tast him. And I shall therefore proceed to give you some few, and but a few directions how to catch this *Tench*, of which I have given you these observations.

He will bite at a Paste made of brown bread and honey, or at a marsh worm, or a Lob-worm; he inclines very much to any paste with which Tar is mixt, and he will bite also at a smaller worm, with his head nipp'd off, and a Cod-worm put on the hook before that worm; and I doubt not but that he will also, in the three hot months (for in the nine colder

he stirs not much) bite at a Flag-worm, or at a green
Gentle, but can positively say no more of the *Tench*,
he being a Fish that I have not often Angled for; but
I wish my honest Scholar may, and be ever fortunate
when he fishes.

CHAP. XII.

Observations of the Pearch, *and directions how to fish
for him.*

PIsc. The *Pearch* is a very good, and a very bold
biting fish; He is one of the Fishes of prey, that
like the *Pike* and *Trout*, carries his teeth in his mouth:
which is very large, and he dare venture to kill and
devour several other kinds of fish: he has a hook't
or hog back, which is armed with sharp and stiff
bristles, and all his skin armed or covered over with
thick, dry, hard scales, and hath (which few other
Fish have) two Fins on his back: He is so bold that
he will invade one of his own kind, which the *Pike*
will not do so willingly, and, you may therefore easily
believe him to be a bold biter.

The *Pearch* is of great esteem in *Italy* saith *Aldrovandus*, and especially the least are there esteemed a dainty
dish. And *Gesner* prefers the *Pearch* and *Pike* above the
Trout, or any fresh-water Fish: he says the *Germans*
have this Proverb, *More wholesom than a Pearch of
Rhine*: and he says the River-*Pearch* is so wholesom,
that Physicians allow him to be eaten by wounded men
or by men in Feavers, or by Women in Child-bed,

He spawns but once a year, and is, by Physicians,
held very nutritive: yet by many to be hard of digestion: They abound more in the river *Poe* and in

England (says *Rondelitius*) than other parts, and have in their brain a stone, which is, in forraign parts sold by Apothecaries, being there noted to be very medicinable against the stone in the reins: These be a part of the commendations which some Philosophical brains have bestowed upon the fresh-water *Pearch*: yet they commend the Sea-*Pearch*, which is known by having but one fin on his back (of which they say, we *English* see but a few) to be a much better fish.

The *Pearch* grows slowly, yet will grow, as I have been credibly informed, to be almost two foot long; for an honest informer told me, such a one was not long since taken by Sir *Abraham Williams*, a Gentleman of worth, and a Brother of the Angle (that yet lives, and I wish he may:) this was a deep bodied Fish: and doubtless durst have devoured a *Pike* of half his own length: for I have told you, he is a bold Fish, such a one as but for extreme hunger, the *Pike* will not devour: for to affright the *Pike* and save himself, the *Pearch* will set up his fins, much like as a *Turkie-Cock* will sometimes set up his tail.

But, my Scholar, the *Pearch* is not only valiant to defend himself, but he is (as I said) a bold biting fish, yet he will not bite at all seasons of the year; he is very abstemious in Winter, yet will bite then in the midst of the day, if it be warm: and note that all Fish bite best about the midst of a warm day in Winter, and he hath been observed by some, not usually to bite till the *Mulberry-tree* buds; that is to say, till extreme frosts be past the Spring; for when the *Mulberry-tree* blossoms, many Gardeners observe their forward fruit to be past the danger of Frosts, and some have made the like observation of the *Pearches* biting.

But bite the *Pearch* will, and that very boldly: and as one has wittily observed, if there be twenty or forty in a hole, they may be at one standing all catch'd one after another; they being, as he says, like the wicked of the world, not afraid though their fellows and companions perish in their sight. And you may observe,

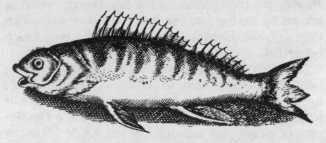

that they are not like the solitary *Pike*, but love to accompany one another, and march together in troops.

And the baits for this bold Fish are not many; I mean, he will bite as well at some, or at any of these three, as at any, or all others whatsoever: a *Worm*, a *Minnow*, or a little *Frog* (of which you may find many in hay-time) and of *worms*, the Dunghil-worm called a *Brandling* I take to be best, being well scowred in Moss or Fennel; or he will bite at a worm that lies under a cow-turd with a blewish head. And if you *rove* for a *Pearch* with a *Minnow*, then it is best to be alive, you sticking your hook through his back-fin; or a *Minnow* with the hook in his upper lip, and letting him swim up and down about mid-water, or a little lower, and you still keeping him to about that depth, by a Cork, which ought not to be a very little one: and the like way you are to Fish for the *Pearch*, with a small frog, your hook being fastned through the skin of his leg, towards the upper part of it: And lastly, I will give you but this advice, that you give the *Pearch* time enough when he bites, for there was scarce any Angler that has given him too much. And now I think best to rest my self, for I have almost spent my spirits with talking so long.

Venat. Nay, good Master, one fish more, for you see it rains still, and you know our Angles are like mony put to usury; they may thrive, though we sit still and do nothing but talk and enjoy one another. Come, come the other fish, good Master.

Pisc. But Scholar, have you nothing to mix with this discourse, which now grows both tedious and tiresom? shall I have nothing from you that seem to have both a good memory, and a chearful Spirit?

Ven. Yes, Master, I will speak you a Copy of Verses that were made by Doctor *Donne*, and made to shew the world that he could make soft and smooth Verses when he thought smoothness worth his labour; and I love them the better, because they allude to Rivers, and fish and fishing. They be these:

> *Come live with me, and be my Love,*
> *And we will some new pleasures prove,*
> *Of golden sands, and Chrystal brooks,*
> *With silken lines, and silver hooks.*
>
> *There will the River whispering run,*
> *Warm'd by thy eyes more than the Sun;*
> *And there the enamel'd fish will stay,*
> *Begging themselves they may betray.*
>
> *When thou wilt swim in that live bath,*
> *Each fish, which every channel hath,*
> *Most amorously to thee will swim,*
> *Gladder to catch thee, than thou him.*
>
> *If thou, to be so seen, beest loath*
> *By Sun or Moon, thou darknest both,*

And if mine eyes have leave to see,
I need not their light, having thee.

Let others freeze with Angling reeds,
And cut their legs with shells and weeds,
Or treacherously poor fish beset,
With strangling snares, or windowy net.

Let course bold hands, from slimy nest,
The bedded fish in banks outwrest,
Let curious Traytors sleave silk flies,
To 'witch poor wandring fishes eyes.

For thee, thou needst no such deceit,
For thou thy self art thine own bait:
That fish that is not catcht thereby,
Is wiser far, alas, than I.

Pisc. Well remembred, honest Scholar, I thank
you for these choice Verses, which I have heard
formerly, but had quite forgot, till they were recovered by your happy memory. Well, being I have
now rested my self a little, I will make you some
requital, by telling you some observations of the *Eel*,
for it rains still, and because (as you say) our *Angles*
are as mony put to Use that thrives when we play,
therefore we'l sit still and enjoy our selves a little
longer under this *honey-suckle-hedg*.

CHAP. XIII.

Observations of the Eel, *and other fish that want scales,*
and how to fish for them.

P*Isc.* It is agreed by most men, that the *Eel* is a
most daintie fish; the Romans have esteemed her
the *Helena* of their feasts, and some *The Queen of*
palat pleasure. But most men differ about their breeding: some say they breed by generation, as other fish

do, and others, that they breed (as some worms do) of mud, as Rats and Mice, and many other living creatures are bred in *Egypt*, by the Suns heat when it shines upon the overflowing of the river *Nilus*: or out of the putrefaction of the earth, and divers other wayes. Those that deny them to breed by generation as other fish do; ask: if any man ever saw an *Eel* to have a Spawn or Melt? and they are answered, that they may be as certain of their breeding as if they had seen Spawn: for they say, that they are certain that *Eels* have all parts fit for generation, like other fish, but so small as not to be easily discerned, by reason of their fatness, but that discerned they may be, and that the He and the She *Eel* may be distinguished by their fins. And *Rondelitius* says, he has seen *Eels* cling together like *Dew-worms*.

And others say, that *Eels* growing old breed other *Eels* out of the corruption of their own age, which Sir *Francis Bacon* sayes, exceeds not ten years. And others say, that as *Pearls* are made of glutinous dewdrops, which are condensed by the Suns heat in those Countries, so *Eels* are bred of a particular dew falling in the months of *May* or *June* on the banks of some particular Ponds or Rivers (apted by nature for that end), which in a few dayes are by the Suns heat, turned into *Eels*, and some of the Ancients have called the *Eels* that are thus bred, *The Off-spring of Jove*. I have seen in the beginning of *July*, in a River not far from *Canterbury*, some parts of it covered over with young *Eels*, about the thickness of a straw; and these *Eels* did lie on the top of that water, as thick as motes are said to be in the Sun: and I have heard the like of other Rivers, as namely in *Severn*, (where they are called *Yelvers*) and in a *pond* or *mere* near unto *Stafford-shire*, where, about a set time in Summer, such small *Eels* abound so much, that many of the poorer sort of people that inhabit near to it take such *Eels* out of this Mere with sieves or sheets, and make a kind of Eel-cake of them, and eat it like as Bread. And *Gesner* quotes Venerable *Bede* to say, that in *England* there is an island called *Ely*, by reason of the innumerable number of *Eels* that breed in it. But that *Eels* may be bred as some worms, and some kind of *Bees* and *Wasps* are, either of *dew*, or out of the corruption of the earth, seems to be made probable by the *Barnacles* and young *Goslings* bred by the Suns heat, and the rotten planks of an old Ship, and hatched of trees; both which are related for truths by *Dubartas* and *Lobel*, and also by our learned *Cambden*, and laborious *Gerard* in his *Herbal*.

It is said by *Rondelitius*, that those *Eels* that are bred in Rivers that relate to, or be nearer to the Sea, never return to the fresh waters (as the *Salmon* does always desire to do) when they have once tasted the salt water; and I do the more easily believe this, because I am certain that powdered Beef is a most excellent bait to catch an *Eel*: And though Sir *Francis Bacon* will allow the *Eels* life to be but ten years; yet he, in his History of Life and Death, mentions a *Lamprey* belonging to the *Roman* Emperour, to be made tame, and so kept for almost threescore years: and that such useful and pleasant observations were made of this *Lamprey*, that *Crassus* the Orator (who kept her) lamented her Death. And we read (in Doctor *Hackwel*) that *Hortensius* was seen to weep at the death of a *Lamprey* that he had kept long, and loved exceedingly.

It is granted by all, or most men, that *Eels*, for

about six months (that is to say, the six cold months of the year) stir not up and down, neither in the Rivers, nor in the Pools in which they usually are, but get into the soft earth or mud, and there many of them together bed themselves, and live without feeding upon any thing (as I have told you some *Swallows* have been observed to do in hollow trees for those six cold months:) and this the *Eel* and *Swallow* do, as not being able to endure winter weather: for *Gesner* quotes *Albertus*, to say, that in the year 1125, (that years winter being more cold than usually) *Eels* did, by natures instinct get out of the water into a stack of hay in a Meadow upon drie ground, and there bedded themselves, but yet at last a frost kill'd them. And our *Cambden* relates, that in *Lancashire* Fishes were dig'd out of the earth with Spades, where no water was near to the place. I shall say little more of the Eel, but that, as it is observed he is impatient of cold; so it hath been observed, that in warm weather an *Eel* has been known to live five days out of the water.

And lastly, let me tell you that some curious searchers into the natures of Fish, observe that there be several sorts or kinds of *Eels*, as the *silver Eel*, and green or *greenish Eel* (with which the River of *Thames* abounds, and those are called Grigs;) and a *blackish Eel*, whose head is more flat and bigger than ordinary *Eels*; and also an *Eel* whose Fins are reddish and but seldom taken in this Nation, (and yet taken sometimes:) These several kinds of *Eels* are (say some) diversely bred, as namely, out of the corruption of the earth, and some by dew, and other ways, (as I have said to you:) and yet it is affirmed by some for a certain, that the *silver Eel* is bred by generation, but not by Spawning as other Fish do, but that her brood come alive from her, being then little live Eels no bigger nor longer than a pin; and I have had too many testimonies of this to doubt the truth of it my self, and if I thought it needful I might prove it, but I think it is needless.

And this Eel, of which I have said so much to you, may be caught with divers kinds of Baits: as namely with powdered Beef, with a *Lob* or *Garden-worm*, with a *Minnow*, or gut of a *Hen*, *Chicken*, or the guts of any Fish, or with almost any thing, for he is a greedy Fish; but the Eel may be caught especially with a little, a very little *Lamprey* which some call a *Pride*, and may in the hot months be found many of them in the River *Thames*, and in many mud-heaps in other Rivers, yea, almost as usually as one finds worms in a dunghill.

Next note, that the Eel seldom stirs in the day, but then hides himself, and therefore he is usually caught by night with one of these baits of which I have spoken, and may be then caught by laying hooks, which you are to fasten to the bank or twigs of a tree; or by throwing a string cross the stream with many hooks at it, and those baited with the aforesaid Baits, and a clod, or plummet, or stone, thrown into the River with this line, that so you may in the morning find it near to some fixt place, and then take it up with a Drag-hook or otherwise: but these things are indeed too common to be spoken of, and an hours fishing with any Angler will teach you better, both for these and many other common things in the practical part of *Angling*, than a week's discourse. I shall therefore conclude this direction for taking the *Eel*, by telling you, that in a warm day in

Summer I have taken many a good Eel by *snigling* and have been much pleased with that sport.

And because you that are but a young Angler know not what snigling is, I will now teach it to you. You remember I told you that Eels do not usually stir in the day time, for then they hide themselves under some covert, or under boards or planks about Floodgates, or Weires, or Mills, or in holes in the River banks: so that you observing your time in a warm day, when the water is lowest, may take a strong small hook tied to a strong line, or to a string about a yard long; and then into one of these holes, or between any boards about a Mill, or under any great stone or plank, or any place where you think an Eel may hide or shelter her self, you may, with the help of a short stick put in your bait, but leasurely, and as far as you may conveniently: and it is scarce to be doubted, but that if there be an Eel within the sight of it, the Eel will bite instantly, and as certainly gorge it: and you need not doubt to have him if you pull him not out of the hole too quickly, but pull him out by degrees, for he lying folded double in his hole, will with the help of his tail break all, unless you give him time to be wearied with pulling, and so get him out by degrees, not pulling too hard.

And to commute for your patient hearing this long Direction I shall next tell you how to make this EEL a most excellent dish of meat:

First, wash him in water and salt, then pull off his skin below his vent or navel, and not much further: having done that, take out his guts as clean as you can, but wash him not: then give him three or four scotches with a knife, and then put into his belly and those scotches, sweet herbs, an Anchovy, and a little Nutmeg grated or cut very

*small, and your herbs and Anchovis must also be cut very
small, and mixt with good butter and salt; having done
this, then pull his skin over him all but his head, which
you are to cut off, to the end you may tie his skin about
that part where his head grew, and it must be so tyed as
to keep all his moisture within his skin: and having done*

*this, tie him with Tape or Packthred to a spit, and rost
him leasurely, and baste him with water and salt till
his skin breaks, and then with Butter: and having rosted
him enough, let what was put into his belly, and what he
drips be his sawce.*　　　　　　　　　　　　　　　S. F.

When I go to dress an Eel thus, I wish he were as
long and big, as that which was caught in *Peter-
borough* River in the year 1667. which was a yard
and three quarters long. If you will not believe me?
then go and see at one of the *Coffee-houses* in *King
street* in *Westminster*.

But now let me tell you, that though the Eel thus
drest be not only excellent good, but more harmless
than any other way, yet it is certain, that Physicians
account the Eel dangerous meat; I will advise you
therefore, as *Solomon* says of Honey, Prov. 25. *Hast
thou found it, eat no more than is sufficient, lest thou
surfeit, for it is not good to eat much honey.* And let me
add this that the uncharitable *Italian* bids us, *Give
Eels, and no wine to our enemies.*

And I will beg a little more of your attention to tell you that *Aldrovandus* and divers Physicians commend the Eel very much for medicine though not for meat. But let me tell you one observation; That the Eel is never out of season, as *Trouts* and most other fish are set time, at least most Eels are not.

I might here speak of many other Fish whose shape and nature are much like the Eel, and frequent both the *Sea* and fresh Rivers; as namely, the *Lamprel*, the *Lamprey* and the *Lamperne*: as also of the mighty *Conger*, taken often in *Severn*, about *Glocester*; and might also tell in what high esteem many of them are for the curiosity of their taste; But these are not so proper to be talk'd of by me, because they make us Anglers no sport, therefore I will let them alone as the Jews do, to whom they are forbidden by their Law.

And Scholar, there is also a Flounder, a Sea-fish, which will wander very far into fresh Rivers, and there lose himself, and dwell and thrive to a hands breadth, and almost twice so long, a fish without scales, and most excellent meat, and a fish that affords much sport to the Angler, with any small worm, but especially a little blewish worm, gotten out of Marsh-ground or Meadows, which should be well scowred, but this though it be most excellent meat, yet it wants scales, and is as I told you therefore an abomination to the Jews.

But Scholar, there is a fish that they in *Lancashire* boast very much of, called a *Char*; taken there, (and I think there only) in a Mere called *Winander Mere*; a Mere, says *Cambden*, that is the largest in this Nation, being ten miles in length, and some say as smooth in the bottom as if it were paved with polisht marble: this fish never exceeds fifteen or sixteen inches in length; and 'tis spotted like a *Trout*, and has scarce a bone but on the back: But this, though I do not know whether it make the Angler sport, yet I would have you take notice of it, because it is a rarity, and of so high esteem with persons of great note.

Nor would I have you ignorant of a rare fish called a *Guiniad*, of which I shall tell you what *Cambden* and others speak. The river *Dee* (which runs by *Chester*) springs in *Merionethshire*; and as it runs toward *Chester* it runs through *Pemble-Mere*, which is a large water: And it is observed, that though the river *Dee* abounds with *Salmon*, and *Pemble-Mere* with the *Guiniad*, yet there is never any *Salmon* caught in the *Mere*, nor a *Guiniad* in the River. And now my next observation shall be of the *Barbel*.

CHAP. XIV.

Observations of the Barbel, *and directions how to fish for him.*

P*isc.* The *Barbel* is so called (says *Gesner*) by reason of his Barb or Wattels at his mouth, which are under his nose or chaps. He is one of those leather-mouthed Fishes that I told you of, that does very seldom break his hold if he be once hook'd: but he is so strong, that he will often break both rod or line if he proves to be a big one.

But the *Barbel*, though he be of a fine shape, and looks big, yet he is not accounted the best fish to eat, neither for his wholesomness nor his taste: But the male is reputed much better than the Female, whose Spawn is very hurtful, as I will presently declare to you.

They flock together like sheep, and are at the worst in *April*, about which time they Spawn, but quickly grow to be in season. He is able to live in the strongest swifts of the Water, and in Summer they love the shallowest and sharpest streams; and love to lurk under weeds, and to feed on gravel against a rising ground, and will root and dig in the sands with his nose like a hog, and there nests himself: yet sometimes he retires to deep and swift Bridges, or Flood-gates, or Weires, where he will nest himself amongst piles, or in hollow places, and take such hold of moss or weeds, that be the water never so swift, it is not able to force him from the place that he contends for. This is his constant custom in Summer, when he and most living creatures sport themselves in the Sun: but at the approach of Winter, then he forsakes the swift streams and shallow waters, and by degrees retires to those parts of the River that are quiet and deeper; in which places (and I think about that time) he Spawns, and, as I have formerly told you, with the help of the Melter, hides his Spawn or eggs in holes, which they both dig in the gravel, and then they mutually labour to cover it with the same sand, to prevent it from being devoured by other fish.

There be such store of this fish in the River *Danubie*, that *Rondelitius* says, they may in some places of it, and in some months of the year, be taken by those that dwell near to the River, with their hands, eight or ten load at a time; he says, they begin to be good in *May*, and that they cease to be so in *August*, but it is found to be otherwise in this Nation: but thus far we agree with him, that the Spawn of a *Barbel*, if it be not poison as he says, yet that it is dangerous meat, and especially in the month of *May*; which is so certain, that *Gesner* and *Gasius* declare, it had an ill effect upon them even to the endangering of their lives.

This fish is of a fine cast and handsome shape, with small scales, which are plac'd after a most exact and curious manner, and, as I told you, may be rather

said not to be ill, than to be good meat; the *Chub* and he have (I think) both lost part of their credit by ill cookery, they being reputed the worst or coursest, of fresh-water-fish: but the *Barbel* affords an *Angler* choice sport, being a lusty and a cunning Fish: so lusty and cunning as to endanger the breaking of the Anglers line, by running his head forcibly towards any covert, or hole, or bank: and then striking at the line, to break it off with his tail (as is observed by Plutarch, in his Book *de industria animalium*) and also so cunning to nibble and suck off your worm close to the hook, and yet avoid the letting the hook come into his mouth.

The *Barbel* is also curious for his baits, that is to say, that they be clean and sweet; that is to say, to have your worms well scowred, and not kept in sowre and musty moss, for he is a curious feeder; but at a well-scowred Lob-worm, he will bite as boldly as at any bait, and specially, if the night or two before you fish for him, you shall bait the places where you intend to fish for him, with big worms cut into pieces: and note, that none did ever over-bait the place, nor fish too early or too late for a *Barbel*. And the *Barbel* will bite also at Gentles, which (not being too much scowred, but green) are a choice bait for him; and so is cheese, which is not to be too hard, but kept a day or two in a wet linnen cloth to make it tough: with this you may also bait the water a day or two before you fish for the *Barbel*, and be much the likelier to catch store: and if the cheese were laid in clarified honey a short time before (as namely, an hour or two) you were still the likelier to catch Fish: some have directed to cut the cheese into thin pieces, and toast it, and then tie it on the hook with fine silk: and some advise to fish for the *Barbel* with *sheeps* tallow and soft cheese, beaten or work'd into a Paste, and that it is choicely good in *August*, and I believe it: but doubtless the Lob-worm well scowred, and the Gentle not too much scowred, and cheese ordered as I have directed, are baits enough, and I think will serve in any month; though I shall commend any Angler that tries conclusions, and is industrious to improve the Art. And now, my honest Scholar, the long shower and my tedious discourse are both ended together: and I shall give you but this Observation, that when you fish for a *Barbel*, your Rod and Line be both long, and of good strength, for (as I told you) you will find him a heavy and a dogged fish to be dealt withall; yet he seldom or never breaks his hold, if he be once stucken. And if you would know more of fishing for the *Umber* or *Barbel*, get into favour with Doctor *Sheldon*, whose skill is above others; and of that the Poor that dwell about him have a comfortable experience.

And now lets go and see what interest the *Trouts* will pay us for letting our *Angle-rods* lie so long, and so quietly in the water for their use. Come, Scholar, which will you take up?

Ven. Which you think fit, Master.

Pisc. Why, you shall take up that; for I am certain by viewing the Line, it has a Fish at it. Look you, Scholar: well done. Come now, take up the other too; well, now you may tell my brother *Peter* at night, that you have caught a leash of *Trouts* this day. And now lets move toward our lodging, and drink a draught of *Red-Cows* milk as we go, and give pretty *Maudlin* and her honest mother a brace of *Trouts* for their supper.

Venat. Master, I like your motion very well and I think it is now about milking time, and yonder they be at it.

Pisc. God speed you, good woman, I thank you both for our Songs last night; I and my companion have had such fortune a fishing this day, that we resolve to give you and *Maudlin* a brace of *Trouts* for supper, and we will now taste a draught of your *Red-Cows* milk.

Milkw. Marry, and that you shall with all my heart, and I will be still your debtor when you come this way: if you will but speak the word, I will make you a good *Sillabub*, of new Verjuice; and then you may sit down in a *haycock*, and eat it, and *Maudlin* shall sit by and sing you the good old Song of the *Hunting in Chevy Chase*, or some other good Ballad, for she hath good store of them; *Maudlin*, my honest *Maudlin* hath a notable memory, and she thinks nothing too good for you, because you be such honest men.

Venat. We thank you, and intend once in a month to call upon you again, and give you a little warning, and so, good night: good night *Maudlin*. And now, good Master, lets lose no time; but tell me somewhat more of Fishing, and if you please, first something of Fishing for a *Gudgion*.

Pisc. I will, honest Scholar.

CHAP. XV.

Observations of the Gudgion, *the* Ruffe, *and the* Bleak, *and how to fish for them.*

THE *Gudgion* is reputed a Fish of excellent tast, and to be very wholesom: he is of a fine shape, of a silver colour, and beautified with black spots both on his body and tail. He breeds two or three times in the year, and always in Summer. He is commended for a Fish of excellent nourishment: the *Germans* call him *Groundling*, by reason of his feeding on the ground: and he there feasts himself in sharp streams, and on the gravel, He and the *Barbel* both feed so, and do not hunt for flies at any time, as most other Fishes do: he is an excellent fish to enter a young Angler, being easie to be taken with a small red worm, on or very near to the ground. He is one of those leather-mouthed fish that has his teeth in his throat, and will hardly be lost off from the hook if he be once stucken: they be usually scattered up and down every River in the shallows, in the heat of Summer: but in *Autumn*, when the weeds begin to grow sowr or rot, and the weather colder, then they gather together, and get into the deeper parts of the water: and are to be Fished for there, with your hook always touching the ground, if you Fish for him with a flote, or with a cork: But many will fish for the *Gudgion* by hand, with a running line upon the ground, without a cork, as a *Trout* is fished for, and it is an excellent way, if you have a gentle rod and as gentle a hand.

There is also another Fish called a *Pope*, and by some a *Ruffe*, a Fish that is not known to be in some Rivers: he is much like the *Pearch* for his shape, and taken to be better than the *Pearch*, but will not grow to be bigger than a *Gudgion*; he is an excellent Fish, no fish that swims is of a pleasanter tast, and he is also excellent to enter a young *Angler*, for he is a greedy biter, and they will usually lie abundance of them together in one reserved place where the water is deep and runs quietly; and an easie Angler, if he has found where they lie, may catch forty or fifty, or sometimes twice so many, at a standing.

You must Fish for him with a small red worm, and if you bait the ground with earth, it is excellent.

There is also a *Bleak*, or fresh-water-Sprat, a Fish that is ever in motion, and therefore called by some the *River-Swallow*; for just as you shall observe the *swallow* to be most evenings in Summer, ever in motion, making short and quick turns when he flies to catch Flies in the air (by which he lives) so does the *Bleak* at the top of the water. *Ausonius* would have him called *Bleak* from his whitish colour: his back is of a pleasant sad or Sea-water-green, his belly white and shining as the Mountain-snow: and doubtless though he have the fortune (which virtue has in poor people) to be neglected, yet the *Bleak* ought to be much valued, though we want *Allamot* salt, and the skill that the *Italians* have to turn them into Anchovis. This fish may be caught with a *Pater-noster* line, that is, six or eight very small hooks tyed along the line, one half a foot above the other: I have seen five caught thus at one time, and the bait has been Gentles, than which none is better.

Or this fish may be caught with a fine small artificial flie, which is to be of a very sad, brown colour, and very small, and the hook answerable. There is no better sport than whipping for *Bleaks* in a boat, or on a bank in the swift water in a Summers evening, with a Hazle top about five or six foot long, and a line twice the length of the Rod. I have heard Sir *Henry Wotton* say, that there be many that in *Italy* will catch *Swallows* so, or especially *Martins* (this *Bird-angler* standing on the top of a Steeple to do it, and with a line twice so long as I have spoken of:) And let me tell you, Scholar, that both *Martins* and *Bleaks* be most excellent meat.

And let me tell you, that I have known a *Hern* that did constantly frequent one place, caught with a hook baited with a big Minnow or a small *Gudgion*. The line and hook must be strong, and tied to some loose staff, so big as she cannot fly away with it, a line not exceeding two Yards.

CHAP. XVI.

Is of nothing; or, that which is nothing worth.

M Y purpose was to give you some directions concerning *Roach* and *Dace*, and some other inferiour Fish, which make the Angler excellent sport, for you know there is more pleasure in Hunting the *Hare* than in eating her: but I will forbear at this

time to say any more, because you see yonder come
our brother *Peter* and honest *Coridon*: but I will
promise you, that as you and I fish and walk to
morrow towards *London*, if I have now forgotten
any thing that I can then remember, I will not keep
it from you.

Well met, Gentlemen, this is lucky that we meet
so just together at this very door. Come Hostess,
where are you? is Supper ready? come, first give us
drink, and be as quick as you can, for I believe we are
all very hungry. Well brother *Peter* and *Coridon*, to
you both; come drink; and then tell me *what luck of
fish*: we two have caught but ten Trouts, of which my
Scholar caught three; look here's eight; and a brace we
gave away: we have had a most pleasant day for fishing and talking, and are returned home both weary
and hungry, and now meat and rest will be pleasant.

Pet. and *Coridon* and I have not had an unpleasant
day, and yet I have caught but five Trouts; for indeed we went to a good honest Ale-house, and there
we played at Shovel-board half the day; all the time
that it rained we were there, and as merry as they
that fished, and I am glad we are now with a dry
house over our heads, for hark how it rains and blows.
Come Hostess, give us more Ale, and our supper with
what haste you may: and when we have sup'd let us
have your Song, *Piscator*, and the Catch that your
Scholar promised us, or else *Coridon* will be dogged.

Pisc. Nay, I will not be worse than my word, you shall
not want my Song, and I hope I shall be perfect in it.

Venat. And I hope the like for my Catch, which
I have ready too, and therefore lets go merrily to
supper, and then have a gentle touch at singing and
drinking: but the last with moderation.

Cor. Come, now for your Song, for we have fed heartily. Come Hostess, lay a few more sticks on the fire, and now, sing when you will.

Pisc. Well then, here's to you *Coridon*; and now for my Song.

> *O the gallant Fishers life,*
> *It is the best of any,*
> *'Tis full of pleasure, void of strife,*
> *And 'tis belov'd of many:*
> > *Other joys*
> > *are but toys,*
> > *only this*
> > *lawful is,*
> > *for our skill*
> > *breeds no ill,*
> *but content and pleasure.*
>
> *In a morning up we rise,*
> *Ere* Aurora's *peeping,*
> *Drink a cup to wash our eyes,*
> *Leave the sluggard sleeping:*
> > *Then we go*
> > *to and fro,*
> > *with our knacks*
> > *at our backs,*
> > *to such streams*
> > *as the* Thames,
> *if we have the leasure.*
>
> *When we please to walk abroad*
> *For our recreation,*
> *In the fields is our abode,*
> *Full of delectation.*
> > *Where in a brook*
> > *with a hook,*
> > *or a Lake,*
> > *fish we take:*

> *there we sit,*
> *for a bit,*
> *till we fish entangle.*

We have Gentles in a born,
We have paste and worms too,
We can watch both night and morn,
Suffer rain and storms too:
> *None do here*
> *use to swear,*
> *oaths do fray*
> *Fish away,*
> *we sit still,*
> *and watch our quill;*
fishers must not wrangle.

If the Suns excessive heat
Make our bodies swelter,
To an Osìer *hedge we get*
For a friendly shelter,
> *Where in a dike*
> Pearch *or* Pike.
> Roach *or* Dace.
> *we do chase,*
> Bleak *or* Gudgion
> *without grudging,*
we are still contented.

Or we sometimes pass an hour
Under a green Willow,
That defends us from a showre,
Making earth our pillow,
> *Where we may*
> *think and pray,*
> *before death*
> *stops our breath:*
> *other joys*
> *are but toys,*
and to be lamented,   Jo. Chalkhill.

Venat. Well sung, Master, this days fortune and pleasure, and this nights company and song, do all make me more and more in love with *Angling*. Gentlemen, my Master left me alone for an hour this day, and I verily believe he retired himself from talking with me, that he might be so perfect in this song; was it not, Master?

Pisc. Yes indeed, for it is many years since I learn'd it, and having forgotten a part of it, I was forced to patch it up by the help of mine own Invention, who am not excellent at Poetry, as my part of the song may testifie; But of that I will say no more, lest you should think I mean by discommending it to beg your commendations of it. And therefore without replications let's hear your Catch, Scholar, which I hope will be a good one, for you are both Musical, and have a good fancie to boot.

Venat. Marry and that you shall, and as freely as I would have my honest Master tell me some more secrets of fish and Fishing as we walk and fish towards *London* to morrow. But Master, first let me tell you, that, that very hour which you were absent from me, I sate down under a *Willow-tree* by the water-side, and considered what you had told me of the Owner of that pleasant Meadow in which you then left me; that he had a plentiful estate, and not a heart to think so; that he had at this time many Law-suits depending, and that they both damp'd his mirth, and took up so much of his time and thoughts, that he himself had not leisure to take the sweet content that I (who pretended no title to them,) took in his fields, for I could there sit quietly, and looking on the water, see some Fishes sport themselves in the silver streams, others, leaping at Flies of several shapes and colours; looking on the Hills, I could behold them spotted with Woods and Groves; looking down the Meadows, could see here a Boy gathering *Lillies* and *Lady-smocks*, and there a Girl cropping *Culverkeyes* and *Cow-slips*, all to make Garlands suitable to this present Month of *May*: these and many other Field-flowers, so perfumed the Air, that I thought that very Meadow like that Field in *Sicily* (of which *Diodorus* speaks) where the perfumes arising from the place, make all dogs that hunt in it, to fall off, and to lose their hottest sent. I say, as I thus sate joying in my own happy condition, and pitying this poor rich man, that owned this and many other pleasant Groves and Meadows about me, I did thankfully remember what my Saviour said, that the *meek possess the Earth*; or rather, they enjoy what the others possess and enjoy not, for Anglers and meek quiet-spirited-men, are free from those high, those restless thoughts which corrode the sweets of life; and they, and they only can say as the Poet has happily exprest it.

> *Hail blest estate of lowliness!*
> *Happy enjoyments of such minds,*
> *As rich in self-contentedness,*
> *Can, like the reeds, in roughest winds*
>   *By yielding make that blow but small*
>   *At which proud Oaks and Cedars fall.*

There came also into my mind at that time, certain Verses in praise of a mean estate, and an humble mind, they were written by *Phineas Fletcher*: an excellent Divine, and an excellent Angler, and the Author of excellent piscatory Eclogues, in which you

shall see the picture of this good mans mind, and I
wish mine to be like it.

> No empty hopes, no Courtly fears him fright,
> No begging wants his middle fortune bite:
> But sweet content exiles, both misery and spite.

> His certain life, that never can deceive him,
> Is full of thousand sweets, and rich content;
> The smooth-leav'd beeches in the field receive him,
> With coolest shade, till noon-tides heat be spent:
>   His life, is neither tost in boisterous Seas,
>   Or the vexatious world, or lost in slothful ease;
> Pleas'd & full blest he livse, when he his God can please

> His bed, more safe than soft, yields quiet sleeps,
> While by his side his faithful Spouse hath place,
>   His little son, into his bosom creeps,
>   The lively picture of his fathers face.
> His humble house, or poor state ne're torment him,
> Less he could like, if less his God had lent him
> And when he dies, green turfs do for a tomb content him.

Gentlemen, these were a part of the thoughts that
then possest me, and I there made a conversion of a
piece of an old Catch, and added more to it, fitting
them to be sung by us Anglers: come Master, you
can sing well, you must sing a part of it as it is in
this paper.

> Mans life is but vain: for, 'tis subject to pain
>   And sorrow, and short as a bubble;
> 'Tis a Hodg-poch of business, and mony, and care,
>   And care, and mony, and trouble.
> But we'l take no care when the weather proves fair;
>   Nor will we vex now tho it rain;
> We'l banish all sorrow, and sing till to morrow,
>   And Angle, and Angle again.

The ANGLERS Song.

CANTUS.

a. 2. Voc.　　　　　　　　　　　　　　Set by Mr. Henry Lawes.

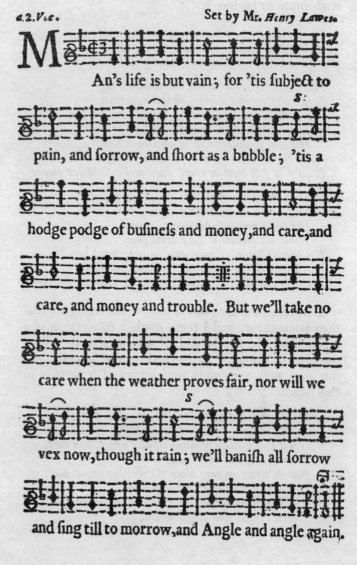

An's life is but vain; for 'tis subject to

pain, and sorrow, and short as a bubble; 'tis a

hodge podge of business and money, and care, and

care, and money and trouble. But we'll take no

care when the weather proves fair, nor will we

vex now, though it rain; we'll banish all sorrow

and sing till to morrow, and Angle and angle again.

The ANGLERS Song.

BASSUS.

Set by Mr. *Henry Lawes*.

a. 2. Voc.

An's life is but vain; for 'tis subject to

pain and sorrow, and short as a bubble; 'tis a

hodge podge of business and money, and care, and

care, and money and trouble. But we'll take no

care when the weather proves fair, nor will we

vex now, though it rain; we'll banish all sorrow

and sing 'till to morrow, and Angle and angle again.

Pet. I marry, Sir, this is Musick indeed, this has cheer'd my heart, and made me to remember six Verses in praise of Musick, which I will speak to you instantly.

> *Musick! miraculous Rhetoric, that speak'st sense*
> *Without a tongue, excelling eloquence;*
> *With what ease might thy errors be excus'd,*
> *Wert thou as truly lov'd as th' art abus'd?.*
> *But though dull souls neglect, & some reprove thee,*
> *I cannot hate thee, 'cause the Angels love thee.*

Ven. And the repetition of these last Verses of musick have called to my memory what Mr. *Ed. Waller* (a Lover of the Angle) says of Love and Musick.

> *Whilst I listen to thy voice*
>   *(Chloris) I feel my heart decay:*
>   *That powerful voice,*
>   *Calls my fleeting soul away;*
>   *Oh! suppress that magick sound,*
>   *Which destroys without a wound.*
>
> *Peace Cloris, peace, or singing die,*
>   *That together you and I*
>   *To Heaven may go:*
>   *For all we know*
>   *Of what the blessed do above*
>   *Is, that they sing, and that they love.*

Pisc. Well remembred, brother *Peter*, these Verses came seasonably, and we thank you heartily. Come, we will all joyn together, my Host and all, and sing my Scholars Catch over again, and then each man drink the tother cup and to bed, and thank God we have a dry house over our heads.

Pisc. Well now, good night to every body.

Pet. And so say I.

Ven. And so say I.

Cor. Good night to you all, and I thank you.

Pisc. Good morrow brother *Peter*, and the like to you, honest *Coridon*: come, my Hostess says there is seven shillings to pay, let's each man drink a pot for his mornings draught, and lay down his two shillings, that so my Hostess may not have occasion to repent her self of being so diligent, and using us so kindly.

Pet. The motion is liked by every body, and so Hostess, here's your money: we Anglers are all beholding to you, it will not be long e're I'll see you again. And now brother *Piscator* I wish you and my brother your Scholar a fair day, and good fortune. Come *Coridon*, this is our way.

CHAP. XVII.

Of Roach *and* Dace, & *how to fish for them*. *And of* Caddis.

VE*n*. Good Master, as we go now towards *London*, be still so courteous as to give me more instructions, for I have several boxes in my memory, in which I will keep them all very safe, there shall not one of them be lost.

Pisc. Well Scholar, that I will, and I will hide nothing from you that I can remember, and can think may help you forward towards a perfection in this Art; and because we have so much time, and I have said so little of *Roach* and *Dace*, I will give you some directions concerning them.

Some say the *Roach* is so called, from *Rutilus*, which they say, signifies red fins: He is a Fish of no great reputation for his dainty taste, and his Spawn is accounted much better than any other part of him. And you may take notice, that as the *Carp* is accounted the *Water-Fox*, for his cunning; so the *Roach* is accounted the *Water-sheep*, for his simplicity or foolishness. It is noted, that the *Roach* and *Dace* recover strength, and grow in season in a fortnight after Spawning, the *Barbel* and *Chub* in a month, the *Trout* in four months, and the *Salmon* in the like time, if he gets into the Sea, and after into fresh water.

Roaches be accounted much better in the River than in a Pond, though ponds usually breed the biggest. But there is a kind of bastard small *Roach* that breeds in ponds with a very forked tail, and of a very small size, which some say is bred by the *Bream* and right *Roach*, and some ponds are stored with these beyond belief; and knowing-men that know their difference, call them *Ruds*; they differ from the true *Roach* as much as a Herring from a Pilchard, and these bastard breed of *Roach* are now scattered in many Rivers, but I think not in *Thames*, which I believe affords the largest and fattest in this Nation, especially below *London-bridg*: the *Roach* is a leather-mouth'd fish, and has a kind of saw-like teeth in his throat. And lastly let me tell you, the *Roach* makes an Angler excellent sport, especially the great Roaches about *London*, where I think there be the best Roach-anglers, and I think the best *Trout-Anglers* be in *Derby-shire*, for the waters there are clear to an extremity.

Next, let me tell you, you shall fish for this *Roach* in Winter with Paste or Gentles, in *April* with worms or Caddis; in the very hot months with little white snails, or with flies under-water, for he seldom takes them at the top, though the Dace will. In many of the hot months, Roaches may also be caught thus:

Take a *May-flie* or *Ant-flie*, sink him with a little lead to the bottom near to the Piles or Posts of a Bridg, or near to any posts of a *Weire*, I mean any deep place where Roaches lie quietly, and then pull your flie up very leisurely, and usually a Roach will follow your bait to the very top of the water and gaze on it there, and run at it, and take it lest the flie should flie away from him.

I have seen this done at *Windsor* and *Henly Bridg*, and great store of *Roach* taken; and sometimes a *Dace* or *Chub*; and in *August* you may fish for them with a Paste made only of the crumbs of Bread, which should be of pure fine Manchet; and that paste must be so tempered betwixt your hands till it be both soft and tough too; a very little water, and time and labour, and clean hands will make it a most excellent paste: But when you fish with it, you must have a small hook, a quick eye, and a nimble hand, or the bait is lost and the fish too (if one may lose that which he never had). With this paste, you may, as I said, take both the Roach and the Dace or Dare, for they be much of a kind, in matter of feeding, cunning, goodness, and usually in size. And therefore take this general direction, for some other baits which may concern you to take notice of. They will bite almost at any flie, but especially at *Antflies*; concerning which, take this direction, for it is very good.

Take the blackish *Ant-flie* out of the Mole-hill or Ant-hill, in which place you shall find them in the month of *June*, or if that be too early in the year, then doubtless you may find them in *July*, *August*, and most of *September*, gather them alive with both their wings, and then put them into a Glass that will hold a quart or a pottle; but first put into the Glass

a handful or more of the moist earth, out of which
you gather them, and as much of the roots of the
grass of the said hillock; and then put in the flies
gently, that they lose not their wings, lay a clod of
earth over it, and then so many as are put into the
glass without bruising, will live there a month or
more, and be always in a readiness for you to fish
with; but if you would have them keep longer, then
get any great earthen pot, or barrel of three or four
gallons (which is better) then wash your barrel with
water and honey; and having put into it a quantity
of earth and grass roots, then put in your flies, and
cover it, and they will live a quarter of a year; these,
in any stream and clear water, are a deadly bait for
Roach or *Dace*, or for a *Chub*; and your rule is, to fish
not less than a handful from the bottom.

I shall next tell you a winter bait for a *Roach*, a
Dace, or *Chub*; and it is choicely good. About *All-
hallantide* (and so till Frost comes) when you see
men ploughing up heath ground, or sandy ground,
or greenswards, then follow the plough, and you
shall find a white worm as big as two Maggots, and
it hath a red head, (you may observe in what ground
most are, for there the Crows will be very watchful
and follow the Plough very close) it is all soft, and
full of whitish guts; a worm that is in *Norfolk* and
some other Counties called a *Grub*, and is bred of
the Spawn or Eggs of a Beetle, which she leaves in
holes that she digs in the ground under Cow or Horse
dung, and there rests all Winter, and in *March* or
April comes to be first a red, and then a black Beetle:
gather a thousand or two of these, and put them with
a peck or two of their own earth into some tub or
firkin, and cover and keep them so warm, that the

frost or cold air, or winds, kill them not; these you may keep all winter, and kill fish with them at any time: and if you put some of them into a little earth and honey a day before you use them, you will find them an excellent bait for *Bream*, *Carp*, or indeed for almost any fish.

And after this manner you may also keep Gentles all winter, which are a good bait then, and much the better for being lively and tough: or you may breed and keep Gentles thus: Take a piece of Beasts liver, and, with a cross stick, hang it in some corner over a pot or barrel half full of dry clay, and as the Gentles grow big, they will fall into the barrel and scowre themselves, and be always ready for use whensoever you incline to fish; and these Gentles may be thus created till after *Michaelmas*. But if you desire to keep Gentles to fish with all the year, then get a dead Cat or a Kite, and let it be fly-blown, and when the Gentles begin to be alive and to stir, then bury it and them in soft, moist earth, but as free from frost as you can, and these you may dig up at any time when you intend to use them, these will last till *March*, and about that time turn to be Flies.

But if you be nice to foul your Fingers, (which good Anglers seldom are) then take this Bait: Get a handful of well-made Malt, and put it into a dish of water, and then wash and rub it betwixt your hands till you make it clean, and as free from husks as you can; then put that water from it, and put a small quantity of fresh water to it, and set it in something that is fit for that purpose over the Fire, where it is not to boil apace, but leasurely and very softly, until it become somewhat soft, which you may try by feeling it betwixt your Finger and Thumb, and when it is soft, then put your water from it, and then take a sharp Knife, and turning the sprout end of the Corn upward, with the point of your Knife take the back part of the husk off from it, and yet leaving a kind of inward husk on the Corn, or else it is marr'd, and then cut off that sprouted end (I mean a little of it) that the white may appear, and so pull off the husk on the cloven side as I directed you, and then cutting off a very little of the other end, that so your hook may enter; and if your hook be small and good, you will find this to be a very choice Bait either for Winter or Summer, you sometimes casting a little of it into the place where your float swims.

And to take the *Roach* and *Dace*, a good Bait is the young brood of Wasps or Bees, if you dip their heads in blood; especially good for *Bream*, if they be baked or hardned in their husks in an Oven, after the bread is taken out of it; or hardned on a Fireshovel; and so also is the thick blood of *Sheep*, being half dried on a Trencher, that so you may cut it into such pieces as may best fit the size of your hook; and a little salt keeps it from growing black, and makes it not the worse but better: This is taken to be a choice Bait if rightly ordered.

There be several Oils of a strong smell that I have been told of, and to be excellent to tempt Fish to bite, of which I could say much, but I remember I once carried a small Bottle from Sir *George Hastings* to Sir *Henry Wotton* (they were both chymical men) as a great Present; it was sent, and receiv'd, and us'd with great confidence; and yet upon enquiry I found it did not answer the expectation of Sir *Henry*, which with the help of this and other circumstances, makes me have little belief in such things as many men talk of: not but that I think Fishes both smell and hear (as I have exprest in my former discourse) but there is a mysterious Knack, which (though it be much easier than the Philosophers Stone, yet) is not attainable by common capacities, or else lies locked up in the brain or breast of some chymical man, that, like the *Rosi-crucians*, will not yet reveal it. But let me nevertheless tell you, that *Camphire* put with moss into your worm-bag with your worms, makes them (if many Anglers be not very much mistaken) a tempting bait, and the Angler more fortunate. But I stepped by chance into this discourse of Oiles and Fishes smelling, and though there might be more said, both of it and of Baits for *Roach* and *Dace*, and other float Fish, yet I will forbear it at this time, and tell you, in the next place, how you are to prepare your Tackling: concerning which I will for sport sake give you an old Rhime out of an old Fish-book, which will prove a part, and but a part of what you are to provide.

> *My Rod and my Line, my Float and my Lead,*
> *My Hook & my Plummet, my whetstone and knife,*
> *My Basket, my Baits both living and dead,*
> *My Net and my Meat, for that is the chief:*
> *Then I must have Thred, & Hairs green and small,*
> *With mine Angling purse, and so you have all.*

But you must have all these Tackling, and twice so many more, with which, if you mean to be a Fisher, you must store your self; and to that purpose I will go with you either to Mr. *Margrave* who dwells amongst the Book-sellers, in St. *Pauls* Church-Yard, or to M. *John Stubs* near to the *Swan* in *Golding-lane*; they be both honest men, and will fit an *Angler* with what *Tackling* he lacks.

I have heard, that the tackling hath been prized at fifty pounds in the Inventory of an Angler.

Venat. Then, good Master, let it be at —————— for
he is nearest to my dwelling, and I pray let's meet
there the ninth of *May* next, about two of the clock,
and I'll want nothing that a Fisher should be furnished with.

Pisc. Well, and I'll not fail you God willing at the
time and place appointed.

Venat. I thank you, good Master, and I will not
fail you: and, good Master, tell me what Baits more
you remember, for it will not now be long ere we
shall be at *Tottenham-high-Cross*, and when we come
thither I will make you some requital of your pains
by repeating as choice a copy of Verses as any we
have heard since we met together; and that is a
proud word for we have heard very good ones.

Pisc. Well, Scholar, and I shall be then right glad
to hear them; and I will as we walk tell you whatsoever comes in my mind, that I think may be worth
your hearing. You may make another choice Bait
thus, Take a handful or two of the best and biggest
Wheat you can get, boil it in a little milk (like as
Frumity is boiled) boil it so till it be soft, and then
fry it very leasurely with Honey and a little beaten
Saffron dissolved in milk, and you will find this a
choice Bait, and good I think for any Fish, especially
for *Roach*, *Dace*, *Chub*, or *Grayling*: I know not but
that it may be as good for a River-*carp*, and especially
if the ground be a little baited with it.

And you may also note, that the spawn of most
Fish is a very tempting bait, being a little hardned on
a warm Tile and cut into fit peices. Nay, Mulberries
and those Black-berries, which grow upon Briers, be
good baits for *Chubs* or *Carps*, with these many have
been taken in Ponds, and in some Rivers where such

Trees have grown near the water and the fruit cus-
tomarily dropt into it, and there be a hundred other
baits more than can be well nam'd, which, by constant baiting the water will become a tempting bait
for any Fish in it.

You are also to know, that there be divers kinds of
Caddis, or *Case-worms*, that are to be found in this
Nation in several distinct Counties, and in several
little Brooks that relate to bigger Rivers; as namely,
one *Cadis* called a *Piper*, whose husk or case is a piece
of reed about an inch long or longer, and as big about
as the compass of a twopence, these worms being
kept three or four days in a woollen bag with sand
at the bottom of it, and the bag wet once a day, will
in three or four days turn to be yellow, and these be
a choice bait for the *Chub* or *Chavender*, or indeed for
any great Fish, for it is a large Bait.

There is also a lesser *Cadis-worm*, called a *Cock-
spur*, being in fashion like the spur of a Cock, sharp
at one end, and the case or house in which this dwells
is made of small husks, and gravel, and slime, most
curiously made of these, even so as to be wondered
at, but not to be made by man no more than a
King-fishers nest can, which is made of little Fishes
bones, and have such a Geometrical inter-weaving
and connexion, as the like is not to be done by the
art of man: This kind of *Cadis* is a choice bait for any
float-Fish; it is much less than the *Piper-Cadis*, and to
be so ordered, and these may be so preserved ten,
fifteen, or twenty days, or it may be longer.

There is also another *Cadis*, called by some a
Straw-worm, and by some a *Ruff-coat*, whose house
or case is made of little pieces of bents, and rushes,
and straws, and water-weeds, and I know not what,

which are so knit together with condensed slime, that
they stick about her husk or case, not unlike the
bristles of a *Hedg-hog*; these three *Cadis's* are commonly taken in the beginning of Summer, and are
good, indeed, to take any kind of fish with float or
otherwise. I might tell you of many more, which as
these do early, so those have their time also of turning to be flies later in Summer; but I might lose
my self, and tire you by such a discourse, I shall therefore but remember you, that to know these, and their
several kinds, and to what flies every particular *Cadis*
turns, and then how to use them first as they be *Cadis*,
and after as they be *flies*, is an art, and an art that every
one that professes to be an Angler has not leisure to
search after, and if he had is not capable of learning.

I'le tell you, Scholar, several Countries have
several kinds of *Caddis's*, that indeed differ as much
as dogs do: That is to say, as much as a very *Cur* and
a *Greyhound* do. These be usually bred in the very
little rills or ditches that run into bigger Rivers, and
I think a more proper bait for those very Rivers, than
any other. I know not how or of what this *Cadis*
receives life, or what coloured flie it turns to; but
doubtless, they are the death of many *Trouts*, and
this is one killing way.

Take one (or more if need be) of these large
yellow *Cadis*, pull off his head, and with it pull out
his black gut, put the body (as little bruised as is
possible) on a very little hook, armed on with a Red
hair (which will shew like the *Caddis-head*) and a
very little thin lead, so put upon the shank of the
hook that it may sink presently; throw this bait thus
ordered (which will look very yellow) into any great
still hole where a Trout is, and he will presently

venture his life for it, 'tis not to be doubted if you be not espyed; and that the bait first touch the water, before the line; and this will do best in the deepest stillest water.

Next let me tell you, I have been much pleased to walk quietly by a Brook with a little stick in my hand, with which I might easily take these, and consider the curiosity of their composure; and if you shall ever like to do so, then note, that your stick must be a little Hasel or Willow cleft, or have a nick at one end of it, by which means you may with ease take many of them in that nick out of the water, before you have any occasion to use them. These, my honest Scholar, are some observations told to you as they now come suddenly into my memory, of which you may make some use: but for the practical part, it is that that makes an Angler: it is diligence, and observation, and practice, and an ambition to be the best in the Art that must do it. I will tell you, Scholar, I once heard one say, *I envy not him that eats better* meat *than I do, nor him that is* richer, *or that wears better* clothes *than I do. I envy no body but him, and him only, that catches more* fish *than I do*. And such a man is like to prove an Angler, and this noble emulation I wish to you and all young Anglers.

CHAP. XVIII.

Of the Minnow *or* Penk, *of the* Loach, *and of the* Bull-head, *or* Millers-thumb.

Pisc. There be also three or four other little fish that I had almost forgot, that are all without scales, and may for excellency of meat be compared to any fish of greatest value, and largest size. They be usually full of eggs or spawn all the months of Summer; for they breed often, as 'tis observed *mice* and many of the smaller four-footed Creatures of the earth do; and as those, so these come quickly to their full growth and perfection. And it is needful that they breed both often and numerously, for they be (besides other accidents of ruine) both a prey, and baits for other fish. And first, I shall tell you of the *Minnow* or *Penk*.

The *Minnow* hath, when he is in perfect season, and not sick (which is only presently after spawning) a kind of dappled or waved colour, like to a *Panther*, on his sides, inclining to a greenish and skie-colour, his belly being milk-white, and his back almost black or blackish. He is a sharp biter at a small worm, and in hot weather makes excellent sport for young Anglers, or boys, or women that love that Recreation, and in the spring they make of them excellent *Minnow-tansies*; for being washed well in salt, and their heads and tails cut off, and their guts taken out, and not washed after, they prove excellent for that use, that is, being *fryd with yolks of eggs, the flowers of* Cowslips, *and of* Primroses, *and a little Tansie* thus us'd they make a dainty dish of meat.

The Loach is, as I told you, a most dainty fish, he breeds and feeds in little and clear swift brooks or rills: and lives there upon the gravel, and in the sharpest streams: He grows not to be above a finger-long, and no thicker than is suitable to that length. This LOACH is not unlike the shape of the Eel: He has a beard or wattels like a *Barbel*. He has two fins at his sides, four at his belly and one at his tail; he is dapled with many black or brown spots; his mouth

is Barbel-like under his nose. This Fish is usually
full of eggs or spawn, and is by *Gesner*, and other
learned Physicians commended for great nourishment, and to be very grateful both to the palate and
stomach of sick persons, he is to be fished for with
a very small worm at the bottom, for he very seldom

or never rises above the Gravel, on which I told you
he usually gets his Living.

The *Millers-thumb*, or *Bull-head*, is a Fish of no
pleasing shape. He is by *Gesner* compared to the
Sea-toad-fish, for his similitude and shape. It has a
head big and flat, much greater than sutable to his
Body; a mouth very wide and usually gaping. He is
without teeth, but his lips are very rough, much like
to a File. He hath two Fins near to his gills, which
be roundish or crested, two Fins also under the Belly,
two on the back, one below the Vent, and the Fin of
his tail is round. Nature hath painted the Body of this
Fish with *whitish*, *blackish*, *brownish* spots. They be
usually full of eggs or spawn all the Summer (I mean
the Females) and those eggs swell their Vents almost
into the form of a dug. They begin to spawn about
April, and (as I told you) spawn several months in
the Summer; and in the winter the Minnow, and
Loach and Bull-head dwell in the mud as the Eel
doth, or we know not where: no more than we know

where the Cuckow and Swallow, and other half year
birds (which first appear to us in *April*) spend their
six cold winter melancholy months. This *Bull-head*
does usually dwell, and hide himself in holes, or
amongst stones in clear water; and in very hot daies
will lie a long time very still, and sun himself, and

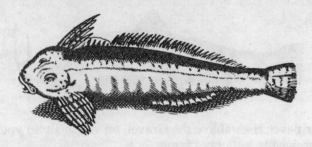

will be easie to be seen upon any flat stone, or any
gravel, at which time, he will suffer an Angler to put
a hook baited with a small worm very near unto his
very mouth and he never refuses to bite, nor indeed
to be caught with the worst of Anglers. *Matthiolus*
commends him much more for his taste and nourishment than for his shape or beauty.

There is also a little Fish called a *Sticklebag*: a Fish
without scales, but hath his body fenc'd with several
prickles. I know not where he dwells in winter, nor
what he is good for in summer, but only to make
sport for boys and women-Anglers, and to feed other
Fish that be Fish of prey, as Trouts in particular,
who will bite at him as at a Penk, and better, if your
hook be rightly baited with him, for he may be so
baited, as his tail turning like the sail of a windmill
will make him turn more quick than any *Penk* or
Minnow can. For note, that the nimble turning of

that or the *Minnow* is the perfection of *Minnow-Fishing*. To which end, if you put your hook into his mouth, and out at his tail, and then having first tied him with white thred a little above his tail, and placed him after such a manner on your hook as he is like to turn, then sow up his mouth to your line, and he is like to turn quick, and tempt any *Trout*: but if he do not turn quick, then turn his tail a little more or less towards the inner part; or towards the side of the hook, or put the *Minnow* or *Sticklebag* a little more crooked or more strait on your hook, until it will turn both true and fast; and then doubt not but to tempt any great *Trout* that lies in a swift stream. And the *Loach* that I told you of will do the like: no bait is more tempting, provided the *Loach* be not too big.

And now *Scholar*, with the help of this fine morning, and your patient attention, I have said all that my present memory will afford me concerning most of the several Fish that are usually fished for in fresh waters.

Venat. But Master, you have by your former civility made me hope that you will make good your promise, and say something of the several Rivers that be of most note in this Nation; and also of *Fish-ponds*, and the ordering of them, and do it I pray good Master, for I love any Discourse of Rivers, and Fish and fishing; the time spent in such discourse passes away very pleasantly.

CHAP. XIX.

Of several Rivers, *and some Observations of Fish.*

PIsc. Well Scholar, since the ways and weather do
both favour us, and that we yet see not *Totten-
ham-Cross*, you shall see my willingness to satisfie
your desire. And, first, for the Rivers of this nation,
there be (as you may note out of Doctor *Heylins
Geography*, and others) in number 325. but those of
chiefest note he reckons and describes as followeth.

The chief is *Thamisis*, compounded of two Rivers,
Thame and *Isis*; whereof the former rising somewhat beyond *Thame* in *Buckinghamshire*, and the later
in *Cyrencester* in *Glocestershire* meet together about
Dorcester in *Oxfordshire*, the issue of which happy
conjunction is the *Thamisis* or *Thames*. Hence it
flyeth betwixt *Berks*, *Buckingham-shire*, *Middlesex*,
Surry, *Kent*, and *Essex*, and so weddeth himself to
the Kentish *Medway* in the very jaws of the Ocean;
this glorious River feeleth the violence and benefit
of the Sea more than any River in *Europe*, ebbing and
flowing twice a day, more than sixty miles: about
whose banks are so many fair Towns, and Princely
Palaces, that a *German Poet* thus truly spake:

> *Tot Campos, &c.*
> *We saw so many* Woods *and Princely* bowers,
> *Sweet* Fields, *brave* Palaces, *and* stately Towers,
> *So many* Gardens *drest with curious care,*
> *That* Thames *with* royal Tyber *may compare.*

2. The second River of note, is *Sabrina* or *Severn*:
it hath its beginning in *Plinilimmon-Hill*, in *Mont-
gomery-shire*, and his end seven miles from *Bristol*,
washing in the mean space the walls of *Shrewsbury*,

Worcester, and *Glocester*, and divers other places and palaces of note.

3. *Trent*, so called for thirty kind of Fishes that are found in it, or for that it receiveth thirty lesser Rivers, who having his fountain in *Staffordshire*, and gliding through the Countries of *Nottingham*, *Lincoln*, *Leicester*, and *York*, augmenteth the turbulent current of *Humber*, the most violent stream of all the Isle. This *Humber* is not, to say truth, a distinct River, having a spring-head of his own, but it is rather the mouth or *Estuarium* of divers Rivers here confluent and meeting together; namely, *Ure*, *Derwent*, and especially of *Ouse* and *Trent*; and (as the *Danow*, having received into its *channel*, the River *Dravus*, *Savus*, *Tibisnus*, and divers others) changeth his name into *Ister*. So also the *Trent*, receiving and meeting the waters above named, changeth his name into this of *Humber*: *Abus* the old Geographers call it.

4. *Medway*, a Kentish River, famous for harbouring the Royal Navy.

5. *Tweed*, the north-east bound of *England*, on whose northern banks is seated the strong and impregnable Town of *Barwick*.

6. *Tine*, famous for *Newcastle*, and her inexhaustible Coal-pits. These and the rest of principal note, are thus comprehended in one of Mr. *Draytons* Sonnets.

> *The floods queen*, Thames, *for ships and swans is crown'd*
> *And stately* Severn *for her shore is prais'd*,
> *The Chrystal* Trent *for fords and fish renown'd*,
> *And* Avons *fame to* Albions *cliffs is rais'd*,
> Carlegion Chester *vaunts her holy* Dee,
> York *many wonders of her* Ouse *can tell*,
> *The* Peak *her* Dove, *whose banks so fertile be*,
> *And* Kent *will say her* Medway *doth excell*.

Cotswool *commends her* Isis *to the* Tame;
Our Northern borders boast of Tweed's *fair flood,*
Our Western parts extoll their Willies *fame,*
And the old Lea *brags of the* Danish *blood.*

These Observations are out of learned Dr. *Heylin,*
and my old deceased friend *Michael Drayton*; and
because you say, you love such discourses as these of
rivers and *fish* and *fishing*, I love you the better, and
love the more to impart them to you: nevertheless,
Scholar, if I should begin but to name the several
sorts of strange Fish that are usually taken in many
of those Rivers that run into the Sea, I might beget
wonder in you, or unbelief, or both; and yet I will
venture to tell you a real truth concerning one lately
dissected by Dr. *Wharton*, a man of great learning
and experience, and of equal freedom to communi-
cate it; one that loves me and my Art, one to whom
I have been beholding for many of the choicest
observations that I have imparted to you. This good
man, that dares to do any thing rather than tell an
untruth, did (I say) tell me he lately dissected one
strange fish and he thus described it to me.

*The Fish was almost a yard broad, and twice that
length; his mouth wide enough to receive or take into it
the head of a man, his stomach seven or eight inches
broad: he is of a slow motion, and usually lyes or lurks
close in the mud, and has a moveable string on his head
about a span, or near unto a quarter of a yard long, by
the moving of which* (which is his natural bait), *when
he lyes close and unseen in the mud, he draws other
smaller fish so close to him, that he can suck them into his
mouth, and so devours and digests them.*

And, Scholar, do not wonder at this, for besides
the credit of the Relator, you are to note, many of

these, and Fishes which are of the like and more
unusual shapes, are very often taken on the mouths
of our Sea-Rivers, and on the Sea-shore; and this will
be no wonder to any that have travelled *Egypt*, where
'tis known the famous river *Nilus* does not only breed
Fishes that yet want names, but, by the overflowing
of that River and the help of the Suns heat on the fat
slime which that River leaves on the Banks (when it
falls back into its natural channel,) such strange fish
and beasts are also bred, that no man can give a
name to, as *Grotius* (in his *Sopham*) and others have
observed.

But whither am I strayed in this discourse? I will
end it by telling you, that at the mouth of some of
these Rivers of ours, Herrings are so plentiful, as
namely, near to *Yarmouth* in *Norfolk*, and in the West-
Country, Pilchers so very plentiful, as you will wonder to read what our learned *Cambden* relates of them
in his *Britannia*, p. 178, 186.

Well, Scholar, I will stop here, and tell you what
by reading and conference I have observed concerning Fish-ponds.

___

CHAP. XX.

Of fish-ponds, and how to order them.

DOctor *Lebault* the learned French man, in his
large discourse of *Mason Rustique*, gives this
direction for making of *Fish-ponds*, I shall refer you
to him to read it at large, but I think I shall contract
it, and yet make it as useful.

He adviseth, that when you have dreined the
ground, and made the earth firm where the head of

the Pond must be, that you must then in that place
drive in two or three rows of Oak or Elme piles, which
should be scorcht in the fire, or half burnt before
they be driven into the earth, (for being thus used it
preserves them much longer from rotting) and having done so, lay Fagots or Bavins of smaller wood
betwixt them, and then earth betwixt and above
them, and then having first very well rammed them
and the earth, use another pile in like manner as the
first were: and note, that the second pile is to be of
or about the height that you intend to make your
Sluce or Flood-gate, or the vent that you intend shall
convey the overflowings of your Pond in any flood
that shall endanger the breaking of the Pond dam.

Then he advises that you plant Willows or Owlers
about it, or both, and then cast in Bavins in some
places not far from the side, and in the most sandy
places, for Fish both to spawn upon, and to defend
them and the young Frie from the many Fish, and
also from Vermin that lie at watch to destroy them,
especially the spawn of the *Carp* and *Tench*, when 'tis
left to the mercy of ducks or Vermin.

He and *Dubravius* and all others advise, that you
make choice of such a place for your Pond, that it
may be refresht with a little rill, or with rain water
running or falling into it; by which Fish are more
inclined both to breed, and are also refresht and fed
the better, and do prove to be of a much sweeter and
more pleasant taste.

To which end it is observed; that such Pools as
be large and have most gravel, and shallows where
fish may sport themselves, do afford Fish of the purest
taste. And note, that in all Pools it is best for fish to
have some retiring place, as namely hollow banks, or

shelves, or roots of trees, to keep them from danger; and, when they think fit from the extream heat of Summer; as also, from the extremity of cold in Winter. And note, that if many trees be growing about your Pond, the leaves thereof falling into the water, make it nauseous to the Fish, and the Fish to be so to the eater of it.

'Tis noted that the *Tench* and *Eel* love mud, and the *Carp* loves gravelly ground, and in the hot months to feed on grass: You are to cleanse your Pond, if you intend either profit or pleasure, once every three or four Years (especially some Ponds) and then let it lye dry six or twelve months, both to kill the water-weeds, as *Water-lilies, Candocks, Reate,* and *Bull-rushes* that breed there; and also that as these die for want of water, so grass may grow in the Ponds bottom, which *Carps* will eat greedily in all the hot months if the Pond be clean. The letting your Pond dry and sowing Oats in the bottom is also good, for the fish feed the faster: and being sometime let dry, you may observe what kind of Fish either increases or thrives best in that water; for they differ much both in their breeding and feeding.

Lebault also advises, that if your Ponds be not very large and roomy, that you often feed your fish by throwing into them chippings of Bread, Curds, Grains, or the entrails of Chickens or of any fowl or beast that you kill to feed your selves; for these afford Fish a great Relief. He says that Frogs and Ducks do much harm, and devour both the Spawn and the young Frie of all Fish, especially of the *Carp.* And I have, besides experience, many testimonies of it. But *Lebault* allows Water-frogs to be good meat, especially in some Months, if they be fat: but you are to note, that he is a *French-man*, and we *English* will hardly believe him, though we know frogs are usually eaten in his Country: however he advises to destroy them and King-fishers out of your ponds; and he advises; not to suffer much shooting at wild fowl, for that (he says) affrightens, and harms, and destroys the Fish.

Note, that Carps and Tench thrive and breed best when no other fish is put with them into the same Pond; for all other fish devour their spawn, or at least the greatest part of it. And note, that clods of grass thrown into any Pond feed any Carps in Summer: and that garden earth and parsley thrown into a Pond, recovers and refreshes the sick fish. And note, that when you store your pond, you are to put into it two or three Melters for one Spawner, if you put them into a breeding Pond: but if into a nurse-pond, or feeding pond, in which they will not breed, then no care is to be taken, whether there be most Male or Female Carps.

It is observed, that the best ponds to breed Carps are those that be stony or sandy, and are warm, and free from wind, and that are not deep, but have willow-trees and grass on their sides, over which the water does sometimes flow: and note, that Carps do more usually breed in marle-pits, or pits that have clean clay bottoms, or in new ponds, or ponds that lie dry a winter season, than in old ponds, that be full of mud and weeds.

Well *Scholar*, I have told you the substance of all that either *observation* or *discourse*, or a diligent *Survey* of *Dubravius* and *Lebault* hath told me, Not that they in their long discourses have not said more, but the most of the rest are so common observations, as if a man should tell a good Arithmetician, that twice two, is four. I will therefore put an end to this discourse, and we will here sit down and rest us.

CHAP. XXI.

Directions for making of a Line, and for the colouring of both Rod and Line.

P*Isc.* Well, Scholar, I have held you too long about these Cadis, and smaller *fish*, and *rivers*, and *Fish-ponds*, and my spirits are almost spent, and so I doubt is your patience; but being we are now almost at *Tottenham*, where I first met you, and where we are to part, I will lose no time, but give you a little direction how to make and order your Lines, and to colour the hair of which you make your Lines, for that is very needful to be known of an Angler; and also how to paint your Rod; especially your top, for a right grown top is a choice Commodity, and should be preserved from the water soaking into it, which makes it in wet weather to be heavy, and fish ill favouredly, and not true, and also it rots quickly for want of painting: and I think a good top is worth preserving, or I had not taken care to keep a top above twenty years.

But first for your line.

First, note, That you are to take care, that your hair be round and clear, and free from galls or scabs, or frets; for a well-chosen, even, clear, round hair, of a kind of glass-colour, will prove as strong as three uneven, scabby hairs, that are ill chosen, and full of galls or unevenness. You shall seldom find a black hair but it is round, but many white are flat and uneven, therefore, if you get a lock of right, round, clear, glass-colour hair make much of it.

And for making your *Line*, observe this rule, First let your hair be clean washt 'ere you go about to twist it: and then chuse not only the clearest hair for it, but hairs that be of an equal bigness, for such do usually stretch all together, and break altogether, which hairs of an unequal bigness never do, but break singly, and so deceive the Angler that trusts to them.

When you have twisted your links, lay them in water for a quarter of an hour, at least, and then twist them over again before you tie them into a Line: for those that do not so, shall usually find their Line to have a hair or two shrink, and be shorter than the rest at the first fishing with it, which is so much of the strength of the Line lost for want of first watering it, and then re-twisting it; and this is most visible in a seven-hair line, one of those which hath always a black hair in the middle.

And for dying of your hairs do it thus:

Take a pint of strong Ale, half a pound of soot, and a little quantity of the juice of *Walnut*-tree leaves, and an equal quantity of Allom, put these together into a pot, pan, or pipkin, and boil them half an hour, and having so done, let it cool; and being cold, put your hair into it, and there let it lie; it will turn your hair to be a kind of water or glass colour, or greenish, and the longer you let it lie, the deeper coloured it will be; you might be taught to make many other colours, but it is to little purpose; for doubtless the water-colour or glass-coloured hair is the most choice and most useful for an *Angler*; but let it not be too green.

But if you desire to colour hair greener; then do it thus: Take a quart of small Ale, half a pound of Allom, then put these into a pan or pipkin; and your hair into it with them; then put it upon a fire, and let it boil softly for half an hour, and then take out your hair, and let it dry, and having so done, then take a pottle of water, and put into it two handful of Marygolds, and cover it with a tile (or what you think fit) and set it again on the Fire, where it is to boil again softly for half an hour, about which time the scum will turn yellow, then put into it half a pound of Copperas beaten small, and with it the hair that you intend to colour, then let the hair be boiled softly till half the liquor be wasted, and then let it cool three or four hours with your hair in it: and you are to observe, that the more Copperas you put into it, the greener it will be, but doubtless the pale green is best; But if you desire yellow hair, (which is only good when the weeds rot) then put in the more *Mary-golds*, and abate most of the Copperas, or leave it quite out, and take a little Verdigrease instead of it.

This for colouring your hair. And as for painting your Rod, which must be in Oil, you must first make a size with glue and water, boiled together, until the glue be dissolved, and the size of a Lie-colour; then strike your size upon the wood with a Bristle, or a Brush, or Pencil, whilst it is hot: that being quite dry, take white Lead, and a little red lead, and a little cole-black, so much as altogether will make an ash-colour; grind these all together with Linseed Oil, let it be thick, and lay it thin upon the wood with a Brush or Pensil, this do for the ground of any colour to lie upon wood.

For a Green.

Take Pink and Verdigreece, and grind them together in Linseed Oil, as thin as you can well
grind it, then lay it smoothly on with your Brush,
and drive it thin; once doing for the most part will
serve, if you lay it well; and if twice be sure your
first colour be throughly dry, before you lay on a
second.

*Well, Scholar; having now taught you to paint your
Rod: and, we having still a mile to* Tottenham High-
Cross, *I will, as we walk towards it, in the cool shade
of this sweet* Hony-suckle-Hedg, *mention to you some
of the thoughts and joys that have possest my Soul since
we two met together. And, these thoughts shall be told
you, that you also may joyn with me in thankfulness to
the giver of every good and perfect gift for our happiness.
And, that our present happiness may apeear to be the
greater, and we the more thankful for it: I will beg you
to consider with me, how many do, even at this very
time, lie under the torment of the* Stone, *the* Gout, *and*
Tooth-ache; *and, this we are free from. And,* every
misery that I miss is a new mercy, *and therefore let us
be thankful. There have been since we met, others, that
have met disasters of broken* Limbs, *some have been
blasted, others* Thunder-strucken; *and we have been freed
from these, and all those many other miseries that
threaten human nature: let us therefore rejoice and be
thankful. Nay, which is a far greater mercy, we are
free from the unsupportable burthen of an accusing, tor-
menting Conscience: a misery that none can bear, and
therefore let us praise him for his preventing grace; and
say,* every misery that I miss, is a new mercy: *Nay,
let me tell you there be many that have forty times our*

*Estates, that would give the greatest part of it to be
healthful and chearful like us; who with the expence of
a little mony, have eat, and drank, and laught, and
Angled, and sung, and slept securely: and rose next day,
and cast away care, and sung, and laught, and Angled
again: which* are *blessings, rich men cannot purchase
with all their money. Let me tell you Scholar: I have
a rich Neighbour that is always so busie, that he has no
leasure to laugh; the whole business of his life is to get
money, and more money, that he may still get more and
more money; he is still drudging on, and says, that*
Solomon *says,* the diligent hand maketh rich: *and 'tis
true indeed: but he considers not that 'tis not in the
power of riches to make a man happy: for it was wisely
said by a man of great observation,* that there be as
many miseries beyond riches as on this side them:
*and yet God deliver us from pinching poverty; and
grant, that having a competency, we may be content and
thankful. Let us not repine, or so much as think the gifts
of God unequally dealt, if we see another abound with
riches, when as God knows, the cares that are the keys
that keep those riches hang often so heavily at the rich
mans girdle, that they clog him with weary days and
restless nights, even when others sleep quietly. We see
but the outside of the rich mans happiness: few consider
him to be like the* Silk-worm, *that, when she seems to
play, is at the very same time spinning her own bowels,
and consuming her self. And this many rich men do;
loading themselves with corroding cares, to keep what
they have (probably) unconscionably got. Let us therefore be thankful for health and a competence; and above
all, for a quiet Conscience.*

Let me tell you, Scholar, that Diogenes *walked on a
day with his friend to see a* Country Fair; *where he saw,*

Ribbins, *and* Looking-glasses, *and* Nut-crackers, *and*
Fiddles, *and* Hobby horses, *and many other* gim-
cracks; *and, having observed them, and, all the other*
finnimbruns *that make a compleat Country fair: he said
to his friend,* Lord! How many things are there in
this world of which *Diogenes* hath no need? *And
truly, it is so, or might be so, with very many who vex
and toyl themselves, to get what they have no need of.
Can any man charge God, that he hath not given him
enough to make his life happy? no doubtless; for, nature
is content with a little: and yet, you shall hardly meet
with a man, that complains not of some want, though
he indeed wants nothing but his will, it may be, nothing
but his will of his poor Neighbour, for not worshipping,
or not flattering him, and thus, when we might be happy
and quiet we create trouble to our selves.   I have heard
of a man, that was angry with himself because he was
no taller, and of a Woman, that broke her* Looking-glass
*because it would not shew her face to be as young and
handsom as her next Neighbours was.   And, I knew
another to whom God had given health, and plenty, but
a Wife that nature had made peevish, and her Husbands
riches had made* Purse-proud, *and must because she was
rich (and for no other vertue) sit in the highest Pew in
the Church: which being denied her, she engag'd her
Husband into a contention for it, and at last, into a
Law-suit with a dogged neighbour who was as rich as
he, and, had a Wife as peevish and* Purse-proud *as the
other: and this Law suit, begot higher oppositions, and
actionable words, and more vexations, and Law-suits;
for you must remember that both were rich and must
therefore have their wills.   Well, this wilful,* Purse-
proud *Law-suit lasted during the life of the first Husband: after which his wife vexed and chid, and chid and*

*vext, till she also chid and vext herself into her grave,
and so the wealth of these poor rich people was curst into
a punishment, because they wanted meek and thankful
hearts; for those only can make us happy.   I knew a man
that had health and riches, and several houses all beautiful and ready furnisht, and would often trouble himself
and Family to be removing from one house to another;
and being ask'd by a friend, why he remov'd so often from
one house to another? replyed,* it was to find content in
some one of them: *but, his friend knowing his temper,
told him, if he would find content in any of his houses?
he must leave himself behind him; for, content will never
dwell but in a meek and quiet soul.   And this may appear
if we read and consider what our Saviour says in St.*
Matthews *Gospel:—for he there says,* Blessed be the
merciful for they shall obtain mercy.—Blessed be the
pure in heart; for they shall see God.—Blessed be
the poor in Spirit; for theirs is the Kingdom of
Heaven.   *And—*Blessed be the meek; for they shall
possess the earth.—*not that the* meek *shall not also
obtain mercy, and see God, and be comforted, and at last
come to the Kingdom of Heaven: but in the mean time
he (and he only) possesses the earth, as he goes toward
that Kingdom of Heaven, by being humble and cheerful,
and content with what his good God has allotted him:
he has no turbulent, repining, vexatious thoughts that he
deserves better: nor is vext when he sees others possesst
of more honour or more riches than his wise God has
allotted for his share; but he possesses what he has
with a meek and contented quietness: such a quietness
as makes his very dreams pleasing both to God and
himself.*

*My honest Scholar, all this is told to incline you to
thankfulness; and to incline you the more, let me tell you*

that though the Prophet David was guilty of Murder and Adultery, and many other of the most deadly sins; yet he was said to be a man after Gods own heart, *because he abounded more with thankfulness than any other that is mentioned in holy Scripture, as may appear in his Book of Psalms; where there is such a Commixture of his confessing of his sins and unworthiness, and such thankfulness for Gods pardon and mercies, as did make him to be accounted, even by God himself, to be* a man after his own heart, *and let us in that, labour to be as like him as we can; let not the blessings we receive daily from God, make us not to value, or not praise him because they be common; let not us forget to praise him for the innocent mirth and pleasure we have met with since we met together, what would a blind man give to see the pleasant Rivers and meadows and flowers and fountains, that we have met with since we met together? I have been told, that if a man that was born blind could obtain to have his sight for but only one hour, during his whole life, and should at the first opening of his eyes, fix his sight upon the Sun when it was in his full glory, either at the rising or setting of it; he would be so transported, and amazed, and so admire the glory of it, that he would not willingly turn his eyes from that first ravishing object, to behold all the other various beauties this world could present to him. And this, and many other like blessings we enjoy daily; and for most of them, because they be so common, most men forget to pay their praises but let not us, because it is a Sacrifice so pleasing to him that made that Sun, and us, and still protects us, and gives us flowers and showers and stomachs and meat and content and leasure to go a fishing.*

Well Scholar, I have almost tir'd my self, and I fear,

more than almost tir'd you: but I now see Tottenham High-Cross; *and our short walk thither shall put a period to my too long discourse, in which, my meaning was, and is, to plant that in your mind, with which I labour to possess my own Soul; that is, a meek and thankful heart. And to that end, I have shew'd you, that riches without them, do not make any man happy. But let me tell you, that riches with them remove many fears, and cares, and therefore my advice is, that you* endeavour to be honestly rich; or contentedly poor: *but be sure that your riches be justly got, or you spoil all. For, it is well said by* Caussin, he that loses his conscience, has nothing left that is worth keeping. *Therefore be sure you look to that. And, in the next place, look to your health: and if you have it praise God, and value it next to a good Conscience; for, health is the second blessing that we Mortals are capable of: a blessing, that money cannot buy, and therefore value it, and be thankful for it. As for money (which may be said to be the third blessing) neglect it not: but note, that there is no necessity of being rich: for I told you,* there be as many miseries beyond riches as on this side them: *and, if you have a competence, enjoy it with a meek, chearful, thankful heart. I will tell you Scholar, I have heard a grave Divine say, that* God has two dwellings; one in Heaven; and the other in a meek and thankful heart. *Which Almighty God grant to me, and to my honest Scholar: and so, you are welcom to* Tottenham High-Cross.

Venat. Well Master, I thank you for all your good directions, but for none more than this last of thankfulness, which I hope I shall never forget. And pray let's now rest our selves in this sweet shady Arbour, which Nature her self has woven with her

own fine fingers; 'tis such a contexture of *Woodbines,
Sweetbrier, Jessamine,* and *Mirtle*; and so interwoven,
as will secure us both from the Suns violent heat; and
from the approaching shower. And being sate down,
I will requite a part of your courtesies with a bottle
of *Sack, Milk, Oranges,* and *Sugar,* which all put
together, make a drink like *Nectar,* indeed too good
for any-body but us *Anglers*: and so Master, here is
a full glass to you of that liquor, and when you have
pledged me, I will repeat the Verses which I promised
you; it is a Copy printed amongst some of Sir *Henry
Wottons,* and doubtless made either by him, or by
a lover of Angling. Come Master, now drink a glass
to me, and then I will pledge you, and fall to my
repetition; it is a description of such *Country-Recrea-
tions* as I have enjoyed since I had the happiness to
fall into your company.

> *Quivering* fears, *heart-tearing* cares,
> *Anxious* sighs, *untimely* tears,
>   *Flye, Flye to* Courts,
>   *Flye to fond worldlings sports,*
> *Where strain'd Sardonick smiles are glosing still,*
> *And* grief *is forc'd to* laugh *against her will.*
>   *Where mirth's but mummery,*
>   *And sorrows only real be.*

> *Fly from our Country-*pastimes, *fly,*
> *Sad troops of humane misery.*
>   *Come serene looks,*
>   *Clear as the Chrystal Brooks,*
> *Or the pure azur'd heaven that smiles to see*
> *The rich attendance on our poverty;*
>   *Peace and a secure mind,*
>   *Which all men seek, we only find.*

Abused Mortals, *did you know*
Where joy, hearts-ease, *and* comforts *grow,*
   You'ld scorn proud Towers,
   And seek them in these Bowers,
Where winds *sometimes, our woods perhaps may shake,*
But blust'ring care *could never tempest make,*
   Nor murmurs e'er come nigh us,
   Saving, of fountains that glide by us.

Here's no fantastick Mask, nor Dance,
But of our *Kids that frisk and prance;*
   Nor wars *are seen,*
   Unless upon the green
Two harmless Lambs *are butting one the other,*
Which done, both bleating run each to his Mother.
   And wounds are never found,
   Save what the plough-share gives the ground.

Here are no entrapping baits
To hasten too, too hasty fates,
   Unless it be
   The fond credulity
Of silly fish, which (worldling like) still look
Upon the bait, but never on the hook:
   Nor envy, 'nless among
   The birds for price of their sweet song.

Go, let the diving Negro *seek*
For Gems *hid in some forlorn creek:*
   We all pearls scorn,
   Save what the dewy morn
Congeals upon each little spire of grass,
Which careless shepherds beat down as they pass:
   And gold ne'er here appears,
   Save what the yellow Ceres *bears.*

Blest silent groves, oh may you be
For ever mirths best nursery;
   May pure contents
   For ever pitch their tents

Upon these downs, *these* meads, *these* rocks, *these* moun-
  tains,
And Peace *still slumber by these purling fountains:*
  Which we may every year
  Meet when we come a fishing here.

Pisc. Trust me (Scholar) I thank you heartily for
these Verses, they be choicely good, and doubtless
made by a lover of Angling: Come, now, drink a glass
to me, and I will requite you with another very good
Copy: it is a Farewell to the vanities of the World,
and some say written by Sir *Harry Wotton*, who I
told you was an excellent Angler. But let them be
writ by whom they will, he that writ them had a
brave soul; and must needs be possest with happy
thoughts at the time of their composure:

Farewell ye gilded follies, pleasing troubles;
Farewell ye honour'd rags, ye glorious bubbles:
Fame's but a hollow eccho, Gold, pure clay;
Honour the darling but of one short day.
Beauty (*th' eye's idol*) *but a damask'd skin*;
State but a golden prison, to live in
And torture free-born minds: embroydred Trains
Meerly but pageants for proud swelling veins:
And Blood Ally'd to Greatness is alone
Inherited, not purchas'd, nor our own.
  Fame, Honour, Beauty, State, Train, Blood, and Birth
  Are but the fading Blossoms of the earth.

I would be great, *but that the Sun doth still*
Level his rayes against the rising hill:
I would be high, *but see the proudest Oak*
Most subject to the rending Thunder-stroak:
I would be rich, *but see men* (*too unkind*)
Dig in the bowels of the richest mind:
I would be wise, but that I often see
The Fox suspected, whilst the Ass goes free:

I would be fair, *but see the fair and proud,*
(*Like the bright Sun*) *oft setting in a cloud:*
I would be poor, *but know the humble grass*
Still trampled on by each unworthy Ass:
Rich *hated:* wise *suspected:* scorn'd *if* poor:
Great *fear'd;* fair *tempted;* high *still envi'd more.*
   I have wish'd all; but now I wisht for neither,
    Great, high, rich, wise, *nor* fair: poor *I'le be rather.*

Would the world now adopt me for her heir?
Would Beauties Queen entitle me the Fair?
Fame speak me Fortunes Minion? *could I vie*
Angels with India, *with a speaking eye*
Command bare heads, bow'd knees, strike Justice dumb
As well as blind and lame, or give a tongue
To stones by Epitaphs: *be call'd* great Master
In the loose Rhimes of every Poetaster?
   Could I be more than any man that lives,
Great, fair, rich, wise all in Superlatives;
Yet I more freely would these gifts resign,
Than ever fortune would have made them mine,
And hold one minute of this holy leasure
Beyond the riches of this empty pleasure.

Welcome pure thoughts, welcome ye silent Groves,
These guests, these courts my soul most dearly loves:
Now the wing'd people of the sky shall sing
My chearful Anthems to the gladsom Spring:
A Pray'r-Book *now, shall be my looking-glass,*
In which I will adore sweet Vertue's face.
Here dwell no hateful looks, no Palace cares,
No broken Vows dwell here, nor pale-fac'd Fears;
Then here I'le sit, and sigh my hot loves folly,
And learn't affect a holy melancholy,
   And if Contentment be a stranger then,
    I'le ne're look for it, but in heaven agen.

Venat. Well Master! these Verses be worthy to
keep a room in every mans memory. I thank you for

them; and I thank you for your many instructions, which (God willing) I will not forget: and as St. *Austin*, in his Confessions (book 4. chap. 3) commemorates the kindness of his friend *Verecundus*, for lending him and his companion a *Country-house* because there they rested and enjoyed themselves free from the troubles of the world; so, having had the like advantage, both by your conversation, and the Art you have taught me, I ought ever to do the like: for indeed, your company and discourse have been so useful and pleasant, that I may truly say, *I have only lived since I enjoyed them, and turned Angler, and not before.* Nevertheless, here I must part with you, here in this now sad place where I was so happy at first to meet you: But I shall long for the ninth of *May*, for then I hope again to enjoy your beloved company at the appointed time and place. And now I wish for some *somniferous potion*, that might force me to sleep away the intermitted time, which will pass away with me as tediously, as it does with men in sorrow; nevertheless I will make it as short as I can by my *hopes* and *wishes*. And, my good Master, I will not forget the doctrine which you told me *Socrates* taught his Scholars, *That they should not think to be honoured so much for being* Philosophers, *as to honour* Philosophy *by their vertuous lives.* You advised me to the like concerning *Angling*, and I will endeavour to do so, and to live like those many *worthy men*, of which you made mention in the former part of your discourse. This is my firm resolution; and as a pious man advised his friend, *That to beget* Mortification *he should frequent* Churches; *and view* Monuments, *and* Charnel-houses, *and then and there consider, how many dead bones time had pil'd up at the gates of death.* So when I would beget *content*, and increase confidence in the *Power*, and *Wisdom*, and *Providence* of Almighty God, I will walk the *Meadows* by some gliding stream, and there contemplate the *Lillies* that take no care, and those very many other various little living *creatures*, that are not only created but fed (man knows not how) by the goodness of the God of *Nature*, and therefore trust in him. This is my purpose: and so, *Let everything that hath breath praise the Lord.* And let the blessing of *St. Peters* Master be with mine.

Pisc. And upon all that are lovers of *Vertue*; and dare trust in his *providence*, and be *quiet*, and go a *Angling.*

       Study to be quiet, 1 Thes. 4. 11.

FINIS.

A SHORT
DISCOURSE
BY WAY OF
POSTSCRIPT,
Touching the
LAWES of ANGLING

My Good Friend,

I cannot but tender my particular thanks to you, for that you have been pleased by three Editions of your Complete Angler, freely to dispence your dear-bought Experiences to all the lovers of that Art, and have thereby so excellently vindicated the Legality thereof, as to divine approbation, that if I should go about to say more in that behalf, it indeed were to light a Candle to the Sun: But since all pleasures (though never so innocent in themselves) lose that stamp, when they are either pursued with inordinate affections, or to the prejudice of another; therefore as to the former, every man ought to endeavour, through a serious consideration of the vanity of worldly contentments, to moderate his affections thereunto, whereby they may be made of excellent use, as some poisons allayed are in Physick: And as to the latter, we are to have recourse to the known Laws, ignorance whereof excuseth no man, and therefore by their directions so to square our actions, that we hurt no man, but keep closs to that golden Rule To do to all men, as we would our-selves be done unto.

Now concerning the Art of Angling, we may conclude, Sir, that as you have proved it to be of great Antiquity; so I find it favoured by the Laws of this kingdom; for where provision is made by our Statutes primo Elizab. cap. 17. against taking Fish by Nets that be not of such and such a size there set down, yet, those Lawmakers had so much respect to Anglers, as to except them; and leave them at liberty to catch as big as they could, and as little as they would catch. And yet though this Apostolical Recreation would be simply in itself lawful, yet no man can go upon another mans ground to fish, without his license, but that he is a Trespasser; but if a man have license to enter into a Close or Ground for such a space of time, there though he practise Angling all that time, he is not a Trespasser, because his fishing is no abuse of his license: but this is to be understood of running Streams, and not of Ponds or standing pools; for in case of a Pond or standing Pool, the owner thereof hath a property in the fish, and they are so far said to be his, that he may have trespass for the fish against any one that shall take them without his license, though it be upon a Common, or adjoyning to the Kings High-way, or adjoyning to another mans ground, who gives license: But in case of a River, where one or more have libera piscaria, only it is otherwise, for there the fishes are said to be feræ naturæ, and the taking of them with an Angle is not Trespass for that no man is said to have a property in them till he have caught them, and then it is a Trespass for any to take them from him: but this is not to be understood of fishes confined to a mans own ground by gates or otherwise, so that they cannot pass away, but may be taken out or put in at pleasure, for in that case the party hath a property in them, as in the case of a standing Pool.

But where any one hath separalis piscaria, as in Child and Greenhills Case in Trin. 15, Car. 1 in the Kings Bench, there it seemeth that the fish may be said to be his, because no man else may take them whilst they are within his several fishing: therefore what is meant by a several fishing is necessary to be considered: and though the difference between a Free-fishing, and a Several fishing be often treated of in the antient books of the Law, and some Opinions will have the difference to be great, and others small or nothing at all; yet the certainest definition of a several fishing is, where one hath the Royalty, and oweth the ground on each side of the water which agreeth with Sir William Calthrops Case, where an Action was brought by him against another for fishing in his several fishing, &c., to which the Defendant pleaded, That the place wherein the Trespass was supposed to be done, contained ten Perches of Land in length, and twenty Perches in breadth, which was his own Free-hold at the time when the Trespass was supposed to be done, and that he fished there as was lawful for him to do, and this was adjudged a good Plea by the whole Court, and upon argument in that very Case it was agreed, that no man could have a several fishing but in his own soil, and that free fishing may be in the soil of another man, which was all agreed unto by Littleton our famous English Lawyer. So that from all this may be drawn this short conclusion, That if the Angler take care that he offend not with his feet, there is no great danger of his hands.

But there are some covetous rigid persons, whose souls hold no sympathy with those of the innocent Anglers, having either got to be Lords of Royalties, or owners of Lands adjoyning to Rivers, and these do, by some apted

Tr. 15.
Car. 1.

Mich. 17.
E. 4. 6. &
Pasc. 18.
E. 4. 4.

clownish nature and education for the purpose, insult and
domineer over the innocent Angler, beating him, breaking
his Rod, or at least taking it from him, and sometimes
imprisoning his person as if he were a Felon, Whereas
a true=bred Gentleman scorns those spider=like attempts,
and will rather refresh a civil stranger at his Table, than
warn him from coming on his ground upon so innocent an
occasion. It would therefore be considered how far such
furious drivers are warranted by the Law and what the
Angler may (in case of such violence) do in defence of
himself: if I come upon another mans ground without his
license, or the license of the Law, I am a Trespasser,
for which the owner may have an Action of Trespass
against me, and if I continue there after warning to depart
by the owner, or his servant thereunto authorised, the
owner, or his servant by his command, may put me off by
force, but not beat me, but in case of resistance by me,
for then I (by resisting) make the assault; but if he beat
me, I not resisting, in that case he makes the assault,
and I may beat him in defence of my self, and to free my
self from his violence: and in case I shall leave my Rod
behind in his ground, he may take it damage feasant,
but he can neither take it from my person by force, nor
break it, but he is a Trespasser to me: Which seems

Mich. 7. clear by the case of Reynell and Champer-
Car. 1. noon, where Reynell brought an Action of
Trespass against Champernoon for taking and cutting
his Nets, the Defendant justified for that he was seised
in fee of a several fishing, and that the Plaintiff with
others endeavoured to row upon his water, and with the
Nets to catch his fish, and that for the safe=guard of his
fishing he took and cut the Nets and Oars; to which plea
the Plaintiff demurred; and there it was adjudged by the
whole Court, that he could not by such colour cut the

Nets and Oars; and judgement was thereupon given for the Plaintiff.

Doubtless our fore-fathers well considered, that man to man was a wolf, and therefore made good laws to keep us from devouring one another, and amongst the rest a very good Statute was made in the three-and-fortieth year of Queen Elizabeth, whereby it is provided, that in personal Actions in the Courts at Westminster, (being not for Land or Battery) when it shall appear to the Judges, (and be so by them signified) that the debt or damages to be recovered amount not to the sum of forty shillings or above, the said Judges shall award to the Plaintiff no more costs than damages, but less at their discretion.

And now with my acknowledgment of the advantage I have had both by your friendship and your book; I wish nothing may ever be that looks like an alteration in the first; nor any thing in the last, unless, by reason of the useful pleasure of it, you had called it The Arcadia of Angling; for it deserves that Title, and I would deserve the continuance of your Friendship.

THE
COMPLEAT ANGLER.

Being Instructions how to angle for a
TROUT or GRAYLING in a clear
Stream.

PART. II.

Qui mihi non credit, faciat licet ipse periclum:
Et fuerit scriptis æquior ille meis.

LONDON,
Printed for *Richard Marriott*, and *Henry Brome*
in St. *Paul*'s Church-yard. MDCLXXVI.

TO
My most Worthy
FATHER and FRIEND,
MR. IZAAK WALTON
The Elder.

SIR,

*Being you were pleased some years past, to grant me
your free leave to do what I have here attempted; and
observing, you never retract any promise when made in
favour even of your meanest friends; I accordingly expect
to see those following particular Directions for the taking of a* Trout, *to wait upon your better and more
general Rules for all sorts of* Angling: *And, though
mine be neither so perfect, so well digested, nor indeed
so handsomely coucht as they might have been, in so long
a time as since your leave was granted; yet, I dare affirm
them to be generally true: And they had appeared too
in something a neater dress, but that I was surpriz'd
with the suddain news of a suddain new Edition of your*
Compleat Angler; *so that, having but a little more than
ten days time to turn me in, and rub up my memory (for
in truth, I have not in all this long time, though I have
often thought on't, and almost as often resolv'd to go
presently about it) I was forc't, upon the instant to
scribble what I here present you: which I have also endeavour'd to accommodate to your own Method. And, if
mine be clear enough for the honest Brothers of the Angle
readily to understand; (which is the only thing I aim*

at) then I have my end; and shall need to make no
further Apology; a writing of this kind, not requiring
(if I were Master of any such thing) any Eloquence to
set it off, or recommend it; so that if you, in your better
Judgment, or kindness rather, can allow it passable for
a thing of this nature; You will then do me honour if
the Cypher *fixt and carv'd in the front of my little*
fishing-house may be here explained: And, to permit me
to attend you in publick, who in private, have ever been,
am, and ever resolve to be

Sir,

Your most affectionate

Son and Servant

Berisford 10th
of *March* 167$\frac{5}{6}$.

Charles Cotton.

THE
COMPLEAT
ANGLER;

OR,

The Contemplative Man's Recreation.

PART. II.

CHAP. I.

Piscator Junior & Viator.

PIsc. You are happily overtaken Sir; may a man be so bold as to enquire how far you travel this way?

Viator. Yes sure Sir very freely; though it be a question I cannot very well resolve you; as not knowing my self how far it is to *Ashborn*, where I intend to night to take up my Inn.

Pisc. Why then Sir, seeing I perceive you to be a Stranger in these parts; I shall take upon me to inform you, that from the Town you last came through, call'd *Brelsford*, it is five miles, and you are not yet above half a mile on this side.

Viat. So much! I was told it was but ten miles from *Derby*, and methinks I have rode almost so far already.

Pisc. O Sir, find no fault with large measure of good Land, which *Derby-shire* abounds in, as much as most Counties of *England*.

Viat. It may be so, and good Land I confess affords a pleasant prospect: but by your good leave Sir, large measure of foul way is not altogether so acceptable.

Piscat. True Sir, but the foul way serves to justify the fertility of the soyl, according to the Proverb: *There is good Land, where there is foul way*; and is of good use to inform you of the Riches of the Country you are come into, and of its continual Travel, and Traffick to the Country Town you came from; which is also very observable by the fullness of its road, and the loaden Horses you meet every where upon the way.

Viat. well Sir, I will be content to think as well of your Country, as you would desire, and I shall have a great deal of reason both to think, and to speak very well of you, If I may obtain the happiness of your company to the forementioned place, provided your affairs lead you that way, and that they will permit you to slack your pace, out of complacency to a Traveller utterly a Stranger in these parts, and who am still to wander further out of my own knowledg.

Piscat. Sir, you invite me to my own advantage, and I am ready to attend you: my way lying through that Town; but my business, that is my home, some miles beyond it: however I shall have time enough to lodg you in your Quarters, and afterwards to perform my own Journey. In the mean time may I be so bold as to enquire the end of your Journey.

Viat. 'Tis into *Lancashire* Sir, and about some business of concern to a near Relation of mine: for I assure you, I do not use to take so long Journeys, as from *Essex* upon the single account of pleasure.

Piscat. From thence Sir! I do not then wonder you should appear dissatisfied with the length of the Miles, and the foulness of the way: though I am sorry you should begin to quarrel with them so soon; for, believe me, Sir, you will find the Miles much longer, and the way much worse before you come to your Journies end.

Viat. Why truly Sir for that, I am prepar'd to expect the worst; but methinks the way is mended since I had the good fortune to fall into your good company.

Piscat. You are not oblig'd to my company for that: but because you are already past the worst, and the greatest part of your way to your Lodging.

Viat. I am very glad to hear it, both for the ease of my self and my Horse; but especially because I may then expect a freer enjoyment of your conversation; though the shortness of the way will, I fear, make me lose it the sooner.

Pisc. That Sir is not worth your care; and I am sure you deserve much better, for being content with so ill company: but we have already talkt away two Miles of your Journey; for from the Brook before us, that runs at the foot of this Sandy Hill, you have but three Miles to *Ashborn.*

Viat. I meet everywhere in this Country with these little Brooks, and they look as if they were full of Fish; have they not Trouts in them?

Pisc. That is a question, which is to be excus'd in a Stranger as you are: otherwise, give me leave to tell you, it would seem a kind of affront to our Country, to make a doubt of what we pretend to be famous for, next, if not before, our Malt, Wool, Lead, and Cole; for you are to understand, that we think we have as many fine Rivers, Rivulets, and Brooks, as any Country whatever, and they are all full of Trouts, and some of them the best (it is said) by many degrees in *England*.

Viat. I was first Sir in love with you, and now shall be so enamour'd of your Country by this account you give me of it, as to wish myself a *Derbyshire* Man, or at least that I might live in it: for you must know I am a pretender to the Angle, and doubtless a Trout affords the most pleasure to the Angler, of any sort of Fish whatever; and the best Trouts must needs make the best sport: But this Brook, and some others I have met with upon this way, are too full of Wood for that recreation.

Pisc. This Sir! why this, and several others like it, which you have past, and some that you are like to pass, have scarce any name amongst us: but we can shew you as fine Rivers, and as clear from wood, or any other encumbrance to hinder an Angler, as any you ever saw; and for clear, beautiful streams, *Hantshire* it self, by Mr. *Izaak Walton's* good leave, can shew none such; nor I think any country in *Europe*.

Viat. You go far Sir, in the praise of your Country Rivers, and I perceive have read Mr *Walton's Compleat Angler*, by your naming of *Hantshire*, and I pray what is your opinion of that Book?

Piscat. My Opinion of Mr. *Walton's* Book is the same with every Man's, that understands any thing of the Art of Angling, that it is an excellent good one, and that the forementioned Gentleman understands as much of Fish, and Fishing as any man living: but I must tell you further, that I have the happiness to know his person, and to be intimately acquainted with him, and in him to know the worthiest Man, and to enjoy the best, and the truest Friend any Man ever had: nay, I shall yet acquaint you further, that he gives me leave to call him Father, and I hope is not yet asham'd to own me for his adopted Son.

Viat. In earnest Sir I am ravisht to meet with a friend of Mr. *Izaak Walton's*, and one that does him so much right in so good and true a Character; for I must boast to you, that I have the good fortune to know him too, and came acquainted with him much after the same manner I do with you; that he was my Master who first taught me to love Angling, and then to become an Angler; and to be plain with you, I am the very man decipher'd in his Book under the name of *Venator*, for I was wholly addicted to the Chace; till he taught me as good, a more quiet, innocent, and less dangerous diversion.

Pisc. Sir, I think my self happy in your acquaintance, and before we part shall entreat leave to embrace you; you have said enough to recommend you to my best opinion; for my Father *Walton* will be seen twice in no Man's company he does not like, and likes none but such as he believes to be very honest men, which is one of the best Arguments, or at least of the best Testimonies I have, that I either am, or that he thinks me one of those, seeing I have not yet found him weary of me

Viat. You speak like a true Friend, and in doing

so render yourself worthy of his friendship. May I
be so bold as to ask your name?

Piscat. Yes surely Sir, and if you please a much
nicer question, my name is ———— and I intend to
stay long enough in your company, if I find you do
not dislike mine, to ask yours too. In the mean time,
because we are now almost at *Ashborn*, I shall freely,
and bluntly tell you, that I am a Brother of the Angle
too, and peradventure can give you some instructions how to Angle for a Trout in a clear River, that
my Father *Walton* himself will not disapprove,
though he did either purposely omit, or did not
remember them, when you, and he sat discoursing
under the *Sycamore Tree*. And being you have already
told me whether your Journey is intended, and that I
am better acquainted with the Country than you are;
I will heartily, and earnestly entreat, you will not
think of staying at this Town: but go on with me six
Miles further to my House, where you shall be ex-
treamly welcom; it is directly in your way, we have
day enough to perform our Journey, & as you like
your entertainment, you may there repose your self
a day or two; or as many more as your occasions will
permit, to recompence the trouble of so much a
longer Journey.

Viat. Sir, you surprise me with so friendly an
invitation upon so short acquaintance: but how advantagious soever it would be to me, and that my
hast perhaps is not so great, but it might dispense
with such a divertisement as I promise my self in
your Company; yet I cannot in modesty accept your
offer, & must therefore beg your pardon: I could
otherwise, I confess be glad to wait upon you, if
upon no other account but to talk of Mr. *I. Walton*,

and to receive those instructions you say you are able to give me for the deceiving a Trout; in which art I will not deny, but that I have an ambition to be one of the greatest deceivers; though I cannot forbear freely to tell you, that I think it hard to say much more than has been read to me upon that subject.

Piscat. well Sir, I grant that too; but you must know that the variety of Rivers, require different ways of Angling: however you shall have the best Rules I am able to give, and I will tell you nothing I have not made my self as certain of, as any Man can be in thirty years experience (for so long I have been a dabler in that art) and that if you please to stay a few days, you shall not in a very great measure see made good to you. But of that hereafter, and now, Sir, if I am not mistaken I have half overcome you; and that I may wholly conquer that modesty of yours, I will take upon me to be so familiar as to say, you must accept my invitation, which that you may the more easily be perswaded to do, I will tell you that my House stands upon the margin of one of the finest Rivers for Trouts and grayling in *England*; that I have lately built a little Fishing House upon it, dedicated to Anglers, over the door of which, you will see the two first letters of my Father *Walton's* name and mine twisted in *Cypher*; that you *as in the Title* shall lye in the same Bed he has some- *page.* times been contented with, and have such Country entertainment, as my Friends sometimes accept, and be as welcome too, as the best Friend of them all.

Viat. No doubt Sir, but my Master *Walton* found good reason to be satisfied with his entertainment in your House; for you who are so friendly to a meer

Stranger who deserves so little, must needs be exceedingly kind and free to him who deserves so much.

Piscat. Believe me, no! and such as are intimately acquainted with that Gentleman, know him to be a Man, who will not endure to be treated like a Stranger. So that his acceptation of my poor entertainments, has ever been a pure effect of his own humility, and good nature, and nothing else. But Sir, we are now going down the Spittle Hill into the Town, and therefore let me importune you suddainly to resolve, and most earnestly not to deny me.

Viat. In truth Sir, I am so overcome by your Bounty, that I find I cannot, but must render my self wholly to be dispos'd by you.

Piscat. Why that's heartily, and kindly spoken, and I as heartily thank you; and being you have abandon'd your self to my conduct, we will only call and drink a glass on Horseback at the *Talbot*, and away.

Viat. I attend you, but what pretty River is this, that runs under this Stone-bridg? has it a name?

Piscat. Yes, 'Tis called *Henmore*, and has in it both Trout and Grayling; but you will meet with one or two better anon. And so soon as we are past through the Town, I will endeavour by such discourse as best likes you to pass away the time, till you come to your ill Quarters.

Viat. We can talk of nothing with which I shall be more delighted than of Rivers and Angling.

Piscat. Let those be the Subjects then, but we are now come to the *Talbot*, what will you drink Sir, Ale, or Wine.

Viat. Nay, I am for the Country liquor, *Derbyshire* Ale, if you please; for a Man should not methinks come from *London* to drink Wine in the Peak.

Piscat. You are in the right; and yet let me tell you, you may drink worse *French-wine* in many Taverns in *London*, than they have sometimes at this House. What hoe! bring us a Flaggon of your best Ale, and now Sir, my service to you, a good health to the honest Gentleman you know of, and you are welcome into the Peak.

Viat. I thank you Sir, and present you my service again, and to all the honest Brothers of the Angle.

Piscat. I'le pledge you Sir, so, there's for your Ale, and farewell. Come Sir, let us be going; for the sun grows low, and I would have you look about you as you ride; for you will see an odd Country, and sights, that will seem strange to you.

CHAP. II.

Piscat. So Sir, now we are got to the top of the Hill out of Town, look about you, and tell me how you like the Country.

Viat. Bless me! what Mountains are here! are we not in *Wales*?

Piscat. No, but in almost as Mountainous a Country, and yet these Hills though high, bleak, and craggy, breed and feed good Beef, and Mutton above ground, and afford good store of Lead within.

Viat. They had need of all those commodities to make amends for the ill Land-schape: But I hope our way does not lye over any of these; for I dread a *precipice*.

Piscat. Believe me but it does, and down one especially, that will appear a little terrible to a

Stranger: though the way is passable enough, and so passable, that we who are Natives of these Mountains, and acquainted with them, disdain to alight.

Viat. I hope though that a Forraigner is priviledged to use his own discretion, and that I may have the liberty to entrust my neck to the fidelity of my own feet, rather than to those of my Horse; for I have no more at home.

Piscat. 'Twere hard else. But in the meantime, I think 'twere best, while this way is pretty even, to mend our pace, that we may be past that Hill I speak of, to the end your apprehension may not be doubled for want of light to discern the easiness of the descent.

Viat. I am willing to put forward as fast as my Beast will give me leave; though I fear nothing in your Company. But what pretty River is this we are going into?

Piscat. Why this Sir is called *Bently* Brook, and is full of very good Trout, and Grayling; but so encumbred with wood in many places, as is troublesom to an Angler.

Viat. Here are the prettiest Rivers, and the most of them in this Country that ever I saw; do you know how many you have in the Country?

Piscat. I know them all, and they were not hard to reckon, were it worth the trouble; but the most considerable of them I will presently name you. And to begin where we now are (for you must know we are now upon the very skirts of *Derby-shire*) we have first the river *Dove*, that we shall come to by and by, which divides the two Counties of *Derby* and *Stafford* for many Miles together, and is so call'd from the swiftness of its current, and that swiftness occasion'd by the declivity of its course, and by being so straitned in that course betwixt the Rocks; by which, and those very high ones, it is hereabout for four, or five Miles confin'd into a very narrow stream. A river that from a contemptible Fountain (which I can cover with my Hat) by the confluence of other Rivers, Rivulets, Brooks, and Rills, is swell'd, before it fall into *Trent* a little below *Egginton*, (where it loses the name,) to such a breadth, and depth, as to be in most places navigable, were not the passage frequently interrupted with Fords and Wires, and has as fertile Bancks as any River in *England*, none excepted. And this River from its head for a Mile or two is a black water (as all the rest of the *Derby-shire* Rivers of note, originally are, for they all spring from the Mosses) but is in a few Miles travel so clarified by the addition of several clear, and very great springs (bigger than it self) which gush out of the Limestone Rocks, that before it comes to my House, which is but six, or seven miles from its source, you will find it one of the purest Chrystalline streams you have seen.

Viat. Does *Trent* spring in these parts?

Piscat. Yes in these parts; not in this County, but somewhere towards the upper end of *Staffordshire*, I think not far from a place call'd *Trentham*, and thence runs down not far from *Stafford* to *Wolsly* Bridg, and washing the skirts and purlews of the Forrest of *Needwood* runs down to *Burton* in the same County; thence it comes into this where we now are, and running by *Swarkston* and *Dunnington*, receives *Derwent* at *Wildon*, and so to *Nottingham*, thence to *Newark*, and by *Gainsborough*, to *Kingston* upon *Hull*, where it takes the name of *Humber*, and thence falls into the Sea: but that the Map will best inform you.

Viat. Know you whence this River *Trent* derives its name?

Piscat. No indeed, and yet I have heard it often discourst upon, when some have given its denomination from the forenamed *Trentham*; though that seems rather a derivative from it; others have said 'tis so called from thirty Rivers that fall into it, and there lose their names, which cannot be neither, because it carries that name from its very Fountain, before any other Rivers fall into it; others derive it from thirty several sorts of Fish that breed there, and that is the most likely derivation: But be it how it will, it is doubtless one of the finest Rivers in the World, and the most abounding with excellent Salmon, and all sorts of delicate Fish.

Viat. Pardon me Sir for tempting you into this digression, and then proceed to your other Rivers; for I am mightily delighted with this discourse.

Piscat. It was no interruption, but a very seasonable question; for *Trent* is not only one of our *Derbyshire* Rivers, but the chief of them, and into which all the rest pay the Tribute of their names; which I had perhaps forgot to insist upon, being got to the other end of the County, had you not awoke my memory. But I will now proceed, and the next River of note (for I will take them as they lye Eastward from us) is the river *Wye*: I say of note, for we have two lesser betwixt us and it, namely *Lathkin*, and *Bradford*, of which *Lathkin* is, by many degrees, the purest, and most transparent stream that I ever yet saw either at home or abroad, and breeds, 'tis said, the reddest, and the best Trouts in *England*; but neither of these are to be reputed Rivers, being no better than great springs. The river *Wye* then, has its source near unto *Buxtons*, a Town some ten Miles from hence, famous for a warm Bath, and which you are to ride through in your way to *Manchester*, a black water too at the Fountain; but, by the same reason with *Dove*, becomes a most delicate clear River, and breeds admirable Trout and Grayling, reputed by those, who, by living upon its Banks, are partial to it, the best of any, and this, running down by *Ashford*, *Bakewell*, and *Haddon*; at a Town a little lower, call'd *Rowsly* falls into *Derwent*, and there loses its name. The next in order is *Derwent* a black water too, and that not only from its Fountain, but quite through its progress, not having these Chrystal springs to wash and cleanse it, which the two forementioned have; but abounds with Trout and Grayling (such as they are) towards its source, and with *Salmon* below; and this River from the upper and utmost part of this Country, where it springs, taking its course by *Chatsworth*, *Darly*, *Matlock*, *Derby*, *Burrow-Ash*, and *Awberson*, falls into *Trent* at a place call'd *Wildon*, and there loses its name. The East side of this County of *Derby* is bounded by little inconsiderable Rivers, as *Awber*, *Eroways*, and the like, scarce worth naming, but Trouty too, and further we are not to enquire. But Sir I have carried you, as a Man may say by water, till we are now come to the descent of the formidable Hill I told you of, at the foot of which runs the River *Dove*, which I cannot but love above all the rest, and therefore prepare your self to be a little frighted.

Viat. Sir, I see you would fortifie me, that I should not shame my self: but I dare follow where you please to lead me, and I see no danger yet; for the descent methinks is thus far green, even, and easy.

Pisc. You will like it worse presently when you come to the brow of the Hill, and now we are there, what think you?

Viat. What do I think? why I think it the strangest place that ever sure Men, and horses went down, and that (if there be any safety at all) the safest way is to alight.

Pisc. I think so too for you, who are mounted upon a Beast not acquainted with these slippery stones; and though I frequently ride down, I will alight too to bear you company, and to lead you the way, and if you please my Man shall lead your Horse.

Viat. Marry Sir! and thank you too, for I am afraid I shall have enough to do to look to my self: and with my Horse in my hand should be in a double fear, both of breaking my neck, and my Horse's falling on me, for it is as steep as a penthouse.

Pisc. To look down from hence it appears so, I confess, but the path winds and turns, and will not be found so troublesom.

Viat. Would I were well down though! Hoist thee! there's one fair scape! these stones are so slippery I cannot stand! yet again! I think I were best lay my heels in my neck, and tumble down.

Pisc. If you think your heels will defend your neck, that is the way to be soon at the bottom; but give me your hand at this broad stone, and then the worst is past.

Viat. I thank you Sir, I am now past it, I can go my self. What's here the sign of a Bridg? Do you use to Travel with wheel-barrows in this Country?

Pisc. Not that I ever saw Sir, why do you ask that question?

Viat. Because this Bridge certainly was made for nothing else; why a mouse can hardly go over it: 'Tis not two fingers broad.

Pisc. You are pleasant, and I am glad to see you so: but I have rid over the Bridg many a dark night.

Viat. Why according to the *French* proverb, and 'tis a good one among a great many of worse sense and sound that language abounds in, *Ce que Diu garde est bien gardé*. They, whom God takes care of are in safe protection: but, let me tell you, I would not ride over it for a thousand pounds, nor fall off it for two; and yet I think I dare venture on foot, though if you were not by to laugh at me: I should do it on all four.

Pisc. Well Sir, your mirth becomes you, and I am glad to see you safe over, and now you are welcome into *Stafford-shire*.

Viat. How *Stafford-shire*! What do I there trow! there is not a word of *Stafford-shire* in all my direction.

Pisc. You see you are betray'd into it, but it shall be in order to something that will make amends; and 'tis but an ill Mile or two out of your way.

Viat. I believe all things Sir, and doubt nothing. Is this your beloved River *Dove*? 'Tis clear, and swift, indeed, but a very little one.

Pisc. You see it here at the worst; we shall come to it anon again after two Miles riding, and so near as to lye upon the very Banks.

Viat. Would we were there once; but I hope we have no more of these Alpes to pass over.

Pisc. No, no Sir, only this ascent before you, which

you see is not very uneasy, and then you will no more quarrel with your way.

Viator. Well, if ever I come to *London* (of which many a Man there, if he were in my place would make a question;) I will sit down and write my Travels, and, like *Tom Coriate* print them at my own charge. Pray what do you call this Hill we come down?

Pisc. We call it *Hanson Toot*.

Viat. Well farewell *Hanson Toot*, I'le no more on thee; I'le go twenty Miles about first: Puh. I sweat, that my shirt sticks to my back.

Pisc. Come Sir, now we are up the Hill, and now how do you?

Viat. Why very well I humbly thank you Sir and warm enough I assure you. What have we here, a Church! As I'm an honest Man a very pretty Church! Have you Churches in this Country Sir?

Pisc. You see we have: but had you seen none, why should you make that doubt Sir?

Viat. Why, if you will not be angry, I'le tell you, I thought my self a Stage, or two beyond *Christendom*.

Pisc. Come, come, wee'l reconcile you to our Country before we part with you; if shewing you good sport with Angling will do't.

Viat. My respect to you, and that together may do much, Sir: otherwise, to be plain with you, I do not find myself much inclin'd that way.

Pisc. Well Sir, your raillery upon our Mountains has brought us almost home; and look you where the same River of *Dove* has again met us to bid you welcome, and to invite you to a dish of Trouts to morrow.

Viat. Is this the same we saw at the foot of *Penmen-Maure*? It is much a finer River here.

Pisc. It will appear yet much finer to morrow. But look you Sir here appears the House, that is now like to be your Inn, for want of a better.

Viat. It appears on a suddain, but not before 'twas lookt for, it stands prettily, and here's wood about it too, but so young, as appears to be of your own planting.

Pisc. It is so, will it please you to alight Sir; and now permit me after all your pains and dangers to take you in my arms, and to assure you, that you are infinitely welcome.

Viat. I thank you Sir, and am glad with all my heart I am here, for, in down right truth, I am exceeding weary.

Pisc. You will sleep so much the better; you shall presently have a light supper, and to bed. Come, Sirs, lay the Cloth, and bring what you have presently, and let the Gentleman's Bed be made ready in the mean time in my Father *Waltons* Chamber; and now Sir here is my service to you, and once more welcome.

Viat. I marry Sir this glass of good Sack has refresht me, and I'le make as bold with your meat; for the Trot has got me a good stomach.

Pisc. Come Sir fall to then, you see my little supper is always ready when I come home, and I'le make no Stranger of you.

Viat. That your Meal is so soon ready is a sign your Servants know your certain hours, Sir; I confess I did not expect it so soon; but now 'tis here, you shall see I will make my self no Stranger.

Pisc. Much good do your heart, and I thank you for that friendly word: and now Sir my service to you in a Cup of *More-Lands* Ale: for you are now in the

More-Lands, but within a spit, and a stride of the peak: fill my Friend his Glass.

Viat. Believe me you have good Ale in the *More-Lands*; far better than that at *Ashborn*.

Pisc. That it may soon be; for *Ashborn* has (which is a kind of a Riddle) always in it the best Mault, and the worst Ale in *England*. Come take away, and bring us some pipes, and a bottle of Ale, and go to your own Suppers. Are you for this diet Sir?

Viat. Yes Sir, I am for one pipe of Tobacco; and I perceive yours is very good by the smell.

Pisc. The best I can get in *London*, I assure you: But Sir, now you have thus far comply'd with my designs, as to take a troublesom Journey into an ill Country, only to satisfie me; how long may I hope to enjoy you?

Viat. Why truly Sir, as long as I conveniently can; and longer I think you would not have me.

Pisc. Not to your inconvenience by any means Sir, but I see you are weary, and therefore I will presently wait on you to your Chamber, where take Counsel of your pillow, and to morrow resolve me. Here take the lights, and pray follow them, Sir; Here you are like to lye, and now I have shew'd you your Lodging, I beseech you command any thing you want, and so I wish you good rest.

Viat. Good night *Sir*.

CHAP. III.

Pisc. Good morrow *Sir*, what up and drest so early?

Viat. Yes *Sir*, I have been drest this half hour;

for I rested so well, and have so great a mind either to take, or to see a Trout taken in your fine River, that I could no longer lye a bed.

Pisc. I am glad to see you so brisk this morning, and so eager of sport; though I must tell you, this day proves so calm, and the Sun rises so bright, as promises no great success to the Angler: but however we'l try, and one way or other we shall sure do something. What will you have to your breakfast, or what will you drink this Morning.

Viat. For breakfast I never eat any, and for Drink am very indifferent; but if you please to call for a Glass of Ale, I'me for you; and let it be quickly if you please: for I long to see the little Fishing-house you spoke of, and to be at my Lesson.

Pisc. Well *Sir*, You see the Ale is come without Calling; for though I do not know yours, my people know my diet, which is always one glass so soon as I am drest, and no more till Dinner, and so my Servants have served you.

Viat. My thanks, and now if you please let us look out this fine morning.

Pisc. With all my heart, Boy take the Key of my Fishing-house, and carry down those two Angle-Rods in the Hall window thither, with my Fish-pannier, Pouch, and landing Net, and stay you there till we come. Come *Sir* we'l walk after, where by the way I expect you should raise all the exceptions against our Country you can.

Viat. Nay *Sir*, do not think me so ill natur'd, nor so uncivil, I only made a little bold with it last night to divert you, and was only in jeast.

[*Piscator.*] You were then in as good earnest as I am now with you: but had you been really angry at it, I could not blame you: For, to say the truth, it is not very taking at first sight: But look you, *Sir*, now you are abroad, does not the Sun shine as bright here as in *Essex*, *Middlesex*, or *Kent*, or any of your Southern Countries?

Viat. 'Tis a delicate Morning indeed, and I now think this a marvellous pretty place.

Pisc. Whether you think so or no, you cannot oblige me more than to say so; and those of my friends who know my humour, and are so kind as to comply with it, usually flatter me that way. But look you *Sir*, now you are at the brink of the Hill, how do you like my River, the Vale it winds through like a Snake, and the scituation of my little Fishing-house?

Viat. Trust me 'tis all very fine, and the house seems at this distance a neat building.

Pisc. Good enough for that purpose; and here is a bowling Green too, close by it, so though I am my self no very good bowler, I am not totally devoted to my own pleasure; but that I have also some regard to other men's. And now *Sir*, you are come to the door, pray walk in, and there we will sit, and talk as long as you please.

There is under this Motto, the Cifer *mentioned in the Title Page and some part of the* Fishing-house *has been* describ'd; *but the pleasantness of the River, Mountains, and Meadows about it, cannot; unless Sir* Philip Sidney, *or* Mr. Cotton's Father, *were again alive to do it.*

Viat. Stay, what's here over the door? *Piscatoribus sacrum.* Why then, I perceive I have some Title here, for I am one of them, though one of the worst, and here below it is the Cifer too you spoke of, and 'tis prettily contriv'd. Has my master *Walton* ever been here to see it; for it seems new built?

Pisc. Yes he saw it cut in the stone before it was set up; but never in the posture it now stands: for the house was but building, when he was last here, and not rais'd so high as the Arch of the dore, and I am afraid he will not see it yet; for he has lately writ me word he doubts his coming down this Summer, which I do assure you was the worst news he could possibly have sent me.

Viat. Men must sometimes mind their affairs to make more room for their pleasures; and 'tis odds he is as much displeas'd with the business, that keeps him from you, as you are that he comes not. But I am the most pleased with this little house of anything I ever saw: It stands in a kind of *Peninsula* too, with a delicate clear River about it. I dare hardly go in, lest I should not like it so well within as without; but by your leave, I'le try. Why, this is better and better, fine lights, finely wainscoted, and all exceeding neat, with a Marble Table and all in the middle!

Pisc. Enough, *Sir*, enough, I have laid open to you the part where I can worst defend my self, and now you attaque me there. Come Boy set two Chairs, and whilst I am taking a Pipe of Tobacco, which is alwaies my Breakfast, we will, if you please, talk of some other Subject.

Viat. None fitter then *Sir* for the time and place, than those Instructions you promis'd.

Pisc. I begin to doubt, by something I discover in you, whether I am able to instruct you, or no; though, if you are really a stranger to our clear *Northern* Rivers I still think I can; and therefore, since it is yet too early in the morning at this time of the year, to day being but the seventh of *March*, to cast a Flie upon the water, if you will direct me what kind of Fishing for a Trout I shall read you a Lecture on, I am willing and ready to obey you.

Viat. Why *Sir*, if you will so far oblige me, and that it may not be too troublesome to you, I would entreat you would run through the whole body of it; and I will not conceal from you, that I am so far in love with you, your courtesie, and pretty Moreland Seat, as to resolve to stay with you long enough by Intervals (for I will not oppress you) to hear all you can say upon that Subject.

Pisc. You cannot oblige me more than by such a promise, and therefore without more Ceremony, I will begin to tell you; that my father *Walton* having read to you before, it would look like a presumption in me, and peradventure would do so in any other man, to pretend to give Lessons for angling after him, who I do really believe understands as much of it, at least as any man in *England*, did I not preacquaint you, that I am not tempted to it by any vain opinion of my self, that I am able to give you better directions; but having from my Childhood pursued the recreation of angling in very clear Rivers (truly I think by much (some of them at least) the clearest in this Kingdom) and the manner of Angling here with us by reason of that exceeding clearness, being something different from the method commonly us'd in others, which by being not near so bright, admit of stronger tackle, and allow a nearer approach to the stream; I may peradventure give you some Instructions, that may be of use even in your own Rivers, and shall bring you acquainted with more Flies and show you how to make them, and with what dubbing too, than he has taken notice of in his *Compleat Angler*.

[*Viator.*] I beseech you *Sir* do, and if you will lend me your Steel, I will light a Pipe the while, for that is commonly my Breakfast in a morning too.

CHAP. IV.

P*Isc.* Why then *Sir*, to begin methodically, as a Master in any art should do (and I will not deny, but that I think my self a Master in this) I shall divide Angling for Trout or Grayling into these three ways,

> *At the Top,*
> *At the bottom, and*
> *In the Middle.*

Which three ways, though they are all of them (as I shall hereafter endeavour to make it appear) in some sort common to both those kinds of Fish; yet are they not so generally and absolutely so, but that they will necessarily require a distinction, which in due place I will also give you.

That which we call Angling at the top, is with a Flie;
At the bottom with a ground-bait.
In the middle with a Minnow, or Ground-bait.

Angling at the Top is of two sorts,

> *With a quick Flie:*
> or,
> *With an artificial Flie.*

That we call Angling at the bottom is also of two sorts,

> *By hand:*
> or,
> *With a Cork, or Float.*

That we call Angling in the middle is also of two sorts.

> *With a Minnow for a Trout:*
> or,
> *With a Ground-bait for a Grayling.*

Of all which several sorts of Angling, I will, if you can have the patience to hear me, give you the best account I can.

Viat. The trouble will be yours, and mine the pleasure and the obligation: I beseech you therefore to proceed.

Pisc. Why then first of Flie-Fishing.

CHAP. V.

Of Flie-Fishing.

P*Isc.* Flie-Fishing or Fishing at the top, is, as I said before, of two sorts,

With a natural and living Flie:

or,

With an artificial and made Flie.

First then of the natural Flie; of which we generally use but two sorts, and those but in the two months of *May* and *June* only, namely the *Green Drake*, and the *Stone-Flie*; though I have made use of a third that way, called the *Chamblet-Flie* with very good success for *Grayling*, but never saw it angled with by any other after this manner, my Master only excepted, who did many years ago, and was one of the best Anglers, that ever I knew.

These are to be angled with, with a short Line, not much more than half the length of your Rod, if the air be still; or with a longer very near, or all out as long as your Rod, if you have any wind to carry it from you, and this way of Fishing we call *Daping*, *Dabbing* or *Dibling*, wherein you are always to have your Line flying before you up or down the River as the wind serves, and to angle as near as you can

to the bank of the same side whereon you stand,
though where you see a Fish rise near you, you may
guide your quick Flie over him, whether in the
middle, or on the contrary side, and if you are pretty
well out of sight, either by kneeling, or the Inter-
position of a bank, or bush, you may almost be sure
to raise, and take him too, if it be presently done; the
Fish will otherwise peradventure be remov'd to some
other place, if it be in the still deeps, where he is
always in motion, and roving up and down to look
for prey, though, in a stream, you may alwaies
almost, especially if there be a good stone near, find
him in the same place. Your Line ought in this Case
to be three good hairs next the hook, both by reason
you are in this kind of angling, to expect the biggest
Fish and also that wanting length to give him Line
after he is struck, you must be forc't to tugg for 't; to
which I will also add, that not an Inch of your Line
being to be suffered to touch the water in dibbling;
it may be allow'd to be the stronger. I should now
give you a Description of those Flies, their shape and
colour, and then give you an account of their breeding, and withal shew you how to keep and use them;
but shall defer that to their proper place and season.

Viat. In earnest, Sir, you discourse very rationally
of this affair, and I am glad to find my self mistaken
in you; for in plain truth, I did not expect so much
from you.

Pisc. Nay Sir, I can tell you a great deal more
than this, and will conceal nothing from you. But
I must now come to the second way of angling at the
top, which is with an artificial Flie, which also I will
shew you how to make before I have done, but first
shall acquaint you, that with this you are to angle

with a Line longer by a yard and a half, or sometimes two yards than your Rod, and with both this, and the other in a still day in the streams, in a breeze, that curles the water in the still deeps, where (excepting in *May* and *June*, that the best Trouts will lye in shallow streams to watch for prey, and even then too) you are like to hit the best Fish.

For the length of your Rod, you are always to be govern'd by the breadth of the River you shall chuse to angle at; and for a Trout River, one of five or six yards long is commonly enough, and longer (though never so neatly and artificially made) it ought not to be, if you intend to Fish at ease, and if otherwise, where lies the sport?

Of these, the best that ever I saw are made in *York-shire*, which are all of one piece; that is to say, of several, six, eight, ten or twelve pieces, so neatly piec't, and ty'd together with fine thred below, and Silk above, as to make it taper, like a switch, and to ply with a true bent to your hand; and these are too light, being made of Fir wood, for two or three lengths, nearest to the hand, and of other wood nearer to the top, that a Man might very easily manage the longest of them that ever I saw, with one hand; and these when you have given over Angling for a season, being taken to pieces, and laid up in some dry place, may afterwards be set together again in their former postures, and will be as strait, sound, and good as the first hour they were made, and being laid in Oyl and colour according to your Master *Waltons* direction, will last many years.

The length of your line, to a Man that knows how to handle his Rod, and to cast it, is no manner of encumbrance, excepting in woody places, and in landing of a Fish, which every one that can afford to Angle for pleasure, has some body to do for him, and the length of line is a mighty advantage to the fishing at distance; and to fish *fine, and far off* is the first and principal Rule for Trout Angling.

Your Line in this case should never be less, nor ever exceed two hairs next to the hook, for one (though some I know will pretend to more Art, than their fellows) is indeed too few, the least accident, with the finest hand being sufficient to break it: but he that cannot kill a Trout of twenty inches long with two, in a River clear of wood and weeds, as this and some others of ours are, deserves not the name of an Angler.

Now to have your whole line as it ought to be, two of the first lengths, nearest the hook, should be of two hairs a piece, the next three lengths above them of three, the next three above them of four, and so of five, and six, and seven, to the very top: by which means your Rod and tackle will in a manner be taper from your very hand to your hook; your line will fall much better and straiter, and cast your Flie to any certain place to which the hand and eye shall direct it, with less weight and violence, that would otherwise circle the water, and fright away the fish.

In casting your line, do it always before you, and so that your flie may first fall upon the water, and as little of your line with it as is possible, though if the wind be stiff, you will then of necessity be compell'd to drown a good part of your line to keep your flie in the water: and in casting your flie, you must aim at the further, or nearer Bank, as the wind serves your turn, which also will be with, and against you on the same side several times in an hour, as the River winds in its course, and you will be forc't to Angle up and down by turns accordingly; but are to endeavour, as much as you can, to have the wind evermore on your back, and always be sure to stand as far off the Bank as your length will give you leave when you throw to the contrary side, though when the wind will not permit you so to do, and that you are constrain'd to Angle on the same side whereon you stand, you must then stand on the very brink of the River, and cast your Flie at the utmost length of your Rod and Line, up or down the River as the gale serves.

It only remains, touching your Line, to enquire whether your two hairs next to the hook, are better twisted, or open; and for that, I should declare that I think the open way the better, because it makes less shew in the water, but that I have found an inconvenience, or two, or three, that have made me almost weary of that way; of which one is, that without dispute they are not so strong twisted, as open; another, that they are not easily to be fastned of so exact an equal length in the arming, that the one will not cause the other to bagge, by which means a Man has but one hair, upon the matter, to trust to; and the last is; that these loose flying hairs are not only more apt to catch upon every twig, or bent they meet with; but moreover the hook, in falling upon the water, will very often rebound, and fly back betwixt the hairs, and there stick (which in a rough water especially, is not presently to be discern'd by the Angler) so as the point of the hook shall stand revers't, by which means your Flie swims backward, makes a much greater circle in the water, and till taken home to you, and set right, will never raise any Fish, or if it should, I am sure, but by a very extraordinary chance, can hit none.

Having done with both these ways of fishing at the top; the length of your Rod, and Line and all: I am next to teach you how to make a Flie; and afterwards of what dubbing you are to make the several Flies I shall hereafter name to you.

In making a Flie then (which is not a Hackle or Palmer-Flie for of those, and their several kinds we shall have occasion to speak every Month in the Year) you are first to hold your hook fast betwixt the fore finger and thumb of your left hand, with the back of the shanck upwards, and the point towards your fingers end; then take a strong small silk of the colour of the Flie you intend to make, wax it well with wax of the same colour too (to which end you are always (by the way) to have wax of all colours about you) and draw it betwixt your finger and thumb, to the head of the shanck, and then whip it twice or thrice about the bare hook, which, you must know, is done, both to prevent slipping, and also that the shanck of the hook may not cut the hairs of your Towght, (which sometimes it will otherwise do) which being done, take your Line, and draw it likewise betwixt your finger and thumb, holding the Hook so fast, as only to suffer it to pass by, untill you have the knot of your Towght almost to the middle of the shanck of your hook, on the inside of it, then whip your silk twice or thrice about both hook and Line, as hard as the strength of the silk will permit, which being done, strip the feather for the wings proportionable to the bigness of your Flie, placing that side downwards, which grew uppermost before,

upon the back of the hook, leaving so much only as to
serve for the length of the wing of the point of the
plume, lying revers't from the end of the shanck upwards, then whip your silk twice, or thrice about the
root end of the feather, hook, and towght, which
being done clip off the root end of the feather close
by the arming, and then whip the silk fast and firm
about the hook, and tought untill you come to the
bend of the hook: but not further (as you do at
London; and so make a very unhandsom, and, in
plain *English*, a very unnatural and shapeless Flie)
which being done, cut away the end of your tought,
and fasten it, and then take your dubbing which is to
make the body of your Flie, as much as you think
convenient, and holding it lightly, with your hook,
betwixt the finger, and thumb of your left hand, take
your silk with the right, and twisting it betwixt the
finger and thumb of that hand, the dubbing will spin
it self about the silk, which when it has done, whip
it about the arm'd hook backward, till you come to
the setting on of the wings; and then take the feather
for the wings; and divide it equally into two parts,
and turn them back towards the bend of the Hook,
the one on the one side, and the other on the other
of the shanck; holding them fast in that posture betwixt the fore finger, and thumb of your left hand,
which done, warp them so down, as to stand, and
slope towards the bend of the hook, and having
warpt up to the end of the shanck, hold the Flie fast
betwixt the finger and thumb of your left hand, and
then take the silk betwixt the finger, and thumb oɪ
your right hand, and where the warping ends, pinch
or nip it with your thumb nail, against your finger,
and strip away the remainder of your dubbing from

the silk, and then with the bare silk whip it once or twice about; make the wings to stand in due order, fasten, and cut it off; after which with the point of a needle raise up the dubbing gently from the warp, Twitch off the superfluous hairs of your dubbing, leave the wings of an equal length (your Flie will never else swim true) and the work is done. And this way of making a Flie (which is certainly the best of all other) was taught me by a Kinsman of mine, one Captain *Henry Jackson*, a near neighbour, an admirable Flie Angler, by many degrees the best Flie maker, that ever I yet met with. And now that I have told you how a Flie is to be made, you shall presently see me make one, with which you may peradventure take a Trout this morning, notwithstanding the unlikeliness of the day; for it is now nine of the Clock, and Fish will begin to rise, if they will rise to day; I will walk along by you, and look on, and after dinner I will proceed in my lecture of Flie-Fishing.

Viat. I confess I long to be at the River, and yet I could sit here all day to hear you: but some of the one, and some of the other will do well: and I have a mighty ambition to take a Trout in your River *Dove.*

Pisc. I warrant you shall: I would not for more, than I will speak of but you should, seeing I have so extoll'd my River to you: nay I will keep you here a Month, but you shall have one good day of sport before you go.

Viat. You will find me I doubt too tractable that way; for in good earnest, if business would give me leave, and that if it were fit, I could find in my heart to stay with you for ever.

Pisc. I thank you *Sir*, for that kind expression, and now let me look out my things to make this flie.

CHAP. VI.

PIsc. Boy, come give me my dubbing bagg here presently; and now Sir, since I find you so honest a man, I will make no scruple to lay open my Treasure before you.

Viat. Did ever any one see the like! What a heap of Trumpery is here! certainly never an Angler in *Europe* has his shop half so well furnisht, as you have.

Pisc. You perhaps may think now, that I rake together this Trumpery, as you call it, for shew only, to the end that such as see it (which are not many I assure you) may think me a great Master in the Art of angling: but let me tell you here are some colours (as contemptible as they seem here) that are very hard to be got, and scarce any one of them, which if it should be lost, I should not miss, and be concern'd about the loss of it too, once in the year; but look you, Sir, amongst all these I will chuse out these two colours only, of which this is Bears-hair, this darker no great matter what; but I am sure I have kill'd a great deal of Fish with it; and with one or both of these you shall take Trout or Grayling this very day, notwithstanding all disadvantages, or my Art shall fail me.

Viat. You promise comfortably, and I have a great deal of reason to believe every thing you say; but I wish the Flie were made, that we were at it.

Pisc. That will not be long in doing: and pray

observe then. You see first how I hold my hook, and thus I begin. Look you here are my first two or three whips about the bare hook, thus I joyn hook and line, thus I put on my wings, thus I twirle and lap on my dubbing, thus I work it up towards the head, thus I part my wings, thus I nip my super-fluous dubbing from my silk, thus fasten, thus trim and adjust my Flie, and there's a Flie made, and now how do you like it?

Viat. In earnest, admirably well, and it perfectly resembles a Flie: but we about *London* make the bodies of our Flies both much bigger and longer, so long as even almost to the very beard of the Hook.

Pisc. I know it very well, and had one of those Flies given me by an honest Gentleman, who came with my Father *Walton* to give me a Visit, which (to tell you the truth) I hung in my parlour Window to laugh at: but *Sir*, you know the Proverb, *They who go to* Rome, *must do as they at* Rome *do*; and believe me you must here make your Flies after this fashion, or you will take no Fish. Come I will look you out a Line, and you shall put it on, and try it. There *Sir*, now I think you are fitted, and now beyond the farther end of the walk you shall begin, I see at that bend of the water above, the air crisps the water a little, knit your Line first here, and then go up thither, and see what you can do.

Viat. Did you see that, *Sir*?

Pisc. Yes, I saw the Fish, and he saw you too, which made him turn short, you must fish further off, if you intend to have any sport here, this is no *New-River* let me tell you. That was a good Trout believe me, did you touch him?

Viat. No, I would I had, we would not have parted

so. Look you there was another; this is an excellent Flie.

Pisc. That Flie I am sure would kill Fish, if the day were right; but they only chew at it I see, and will not take it. Come *Sir*, let us return back to the Fishing-house; this still water I see will not do our business to day; you shall now, if you please, make a Flie your self, and try what you can do in the streams with that, and I know a Trout taken with a Flie of your own making will please you better than twenty with one of mine. Give me that Bag again, *Sirrah*; look you *Sir*, there is a hook, tought, silk, and a feather for the wings, be doing with those, and I will look you out a Dubbing, that I think will do.

Viat. This is a very little hook.

Pisc. That may serve to inform you, that it is for a very little Flie, and you must make your wings accordingly; for as the case stands it must be a little Flie, and a very little one too, that must do your business. Well said! believe me you shift your fingers very handsomely; I doubt I have taken upon me to teach my Master. So here's your dubbing now.

Viat. This dubbing is very black.

Pisc. It appears so in hand; but step to the doors and hold it up betwixt your eye and the Sun, and it will appear a shining red; let me tell you never a man in *England* can discern the true colour of a dubbing any way but that, and therefore chuse always to make your Flies on such a bright Sun-shine day as this, which also you may the better do, because it is worth nothing to fish in, here put it on, and be sure to make the body of your Flie as slender as you can. Very good! Upon my word you have made a marvellous handsom Flie.

Viat. I am very glad to hear it; 'tis the first that ever I made of this kind in my life.

Pisc. Away, away! You are a Doctor at it! but I will not commend you too much, lest I make you proud. Come put it on, and you shall now go downward to some streams betwixt the rocks below the little foot bridg you see there, and try your Fortune. Take heed of slipping into the water as you follow me under this rock: So now you are over, and now throw in.

Viat. This is a fine stream indeed: There's one! I have him!

Pisc. And a precious catch you have of him; pull him out! I see you have a tender hand: This is a diminutive Gentleman, e'en throw him in again, and let him grow till he be more worthy your anger.

Viat. Pardon me, *Sir*, all's Fish that comes to' th' hook with me now. Another!

Pisc. And of the same standing.

Viat. I see I shall have good sport now: Another! and a Grayling. Why you have Fish here at will.

Pisc. Come, come, cross the Bridge, and go down the other side lower, where you will find finer streams, and better sport I hope than this. Look you *Sir*, here is a fine stream now, you have length enough, stand a little further off, let me entreat you, and do but Fish this stream like an Artist, and peradventure a good Fish may fall to your share. How now! what is all gone?

Viat. No, I but touch't him; but that was a Fish worth taking.

Pisc. Why now let me tell you, you lost that Fish by your own fault, and through your own eagerness and haste; for you are never to offer to strike a good

Fish, if he do not strike himself, till first you see him turn his head after he has taken your Flie, and then you can never strain your tackle in the striking, if you strike with any manner of moderation. Come throw in one again, and fish me this stream by inches; for I assure you here are very good Fish, both Trout and Grayling, lie here; and at that great stone on the other side, 'tis ten to one a good Trout gives you the meeting.

Viat. I have him now, but he is gone down towards the bottom, I cannot see what he is; yet he should be a good Fish by his weight; but he makes no great stir.

Pisc. Why then, by what you say, I dare venture to assure you, 'tis a Grayling, who is one of the deadest hearted Fishes in the world, and the bigger he is the more easily taken. Look you, now you see him plain; I told you what he was, bring hither that landing net, Boy, and now *Sir*, he is your own; and believe me a good one, sixteen Inches long I warrant him, I have taken none such this year.

Viat. I never saw a Grayling before look so black.

Pisc. Did you not? Why then let me tell you, that you never saw one before in right season: for then a Grayling is very black about his head, guills, and down his back, and has his Belly of a dark grey, dappled with black spots, as you see this is, and I am apt to conclude, that from thence he derives his name of *Umber*. Though I must tell you this Fish is past his prime, and begins to decline, and was in better season at Christmas than he is now. But move on, for it grows towards dinner-time, and there is a very great and fine stream below, under that Rock, that fills the deepest pool in all the River, where you are almost sure of a good Fish.

Viat. Let him come, I'le try a fall with him; but I had thought, that the Grayling had been always in season with the Trout, and had come in, and gone out with him.

[*Piscator.*] Oh no! assure your self a Grayling is a winter-fish: but such a one as would deceive any but such as know him very well indeed; for his flesh, even in his worst season, is so firm, and will so easily calver, that in plain truth he is very good meat at all times; but in his perfect season (which, by the way, none but an overgrown Grayling will ever be) I think him so good a fish, as to be little inferiour to the best Trout that ever I tasted in my life.

Viat. Here's another skip-jack, and I have rais'd five or six more at least whilst you were speaking: Well, go thy way, little *Dove*! thou art the finest River, that ever I saw, and the fullest of fish. Indeed, *Sir*, I like it so well, that I am afraid you will be troubled with me once a year, so long as we two live.

Pisc. I am afraid I shall not *Sir*; but were you once here a *May* or a *June*, if good sport would tempt you, I should then expect you would sometimes see me; for you would then say it were a fine River indeed, if you had once seen the sport at the height.

Viat. Which I will do, if I live, and that you please to give me leave, there was one, and there another.

Pisc. And all this in a strange River, and with a Flie of your own making! why what a dangerous man are you!

Viat. I, *Sir*, but who taught me? and as *Dametas* says by his man *Dorus*, so you may say by me,

> *If my man such praises have,*
> *What then have I, that taught the Knave?*

But what have we got here? A Rock springing up in the middle of the River! this is one of the oddest sights, that ever I saw.

Pisc. Why, *Sir*, from that *Pike*, that you see standing up there distant from the rock, this is call'd *Pike-Pool*: and young Mr. *Izaac Walton* was so pleas'd with it, as to draw it in Landschape in black and white, in a blank Book I have at home,

'Tis a Rock, in the fashion of a Spire-steeple; *and almost as big. It stands in the midst of the River* Dove; *and not far from Mr.* Cotton's *house, below which place this delicate River takes a swift* Carere *betwixt many mighty Rocks, much higher and bigger than St.* Pauls Church, *before 'twas burnt. And this* Dove *being oppos'd by one of the highest of them, has at last, forc't it self a way through it; and after a miles concealment, appears again with more glory and beauty than before that opposition; running through the most pleasant Valleys and most fruitful Meadows, that this Nation can justly boast of.*

as he has done several prospects of my house also, which I keep for a memorial of his favour, and will shew you, when we come up to dinner.

Viat. Has young Master *Izaak Walton* been here too?

Pisc. Yes marry has he Sir, and that again, and again too, and in *France* since, and at *Rome*, and at *Venice*, and I can't tell where: but I intend to ask him a great many hard questions so soon as I can see him, which will be, God willing, next Month. In the mean time, Sir, to come to this fine stream at the head of this great Pool, you must venture over these slippery cobling stones; believe me, Sir, there you were nimble or else you had been down; but now you are got over, look to your self; for on my word if a Fish rise here, he is like to be such a one, as will endanger your tackle: How now!

Viat. I think you have such command here over the Fishes, that you can raise them by your word, as they say Conjurers can do Spirits, and afterward make them do what you bid them: for here's a Trout has taken my Flie, I had rather have lost a Crown. What luck's this! He was a lovely Fish, and turn'd up a side like a Salmon.

Pisc. O Sir, this is a War where you sometimes win, and must sometimes expect to loose. Never concern your self for the loss of your Flie; for ten to one I teach you to make a better. Who's that calls?

Serv. Sir, Will it please you to come to dinner?

Pisc. We come. You hear Sir we are call'd, and now take your choice, whether you will climb this steep Hill before you, from the top of which you will go directly into the House, or back again over these stepping stones, and about by the Bridg.

Viat. Nay, sure the nearest way is best; at least my stomach tells me so; and I am now so well acquainted with your Rocks, that I fear them not.

Pisc. Come then, follow me, and so soon as we have din'd; we will down again to the little House; where I will begin at the place I left off about Fliefishing, and read you another Lecture; for I have a great deal more to say upon that Subject.

Viat. The more the better; I could never have met with a more obliging Master, my first excepted; nor such sport can all the Rivers about *London* ever afford, as is to be found in this pretty River.

Pisc. You deserve to have better, both because I see you are willing to take pains, and for liking this little so well; and better I hope to shew you before we part.

CHAP. VII.

Viat. Come Sir, having now well din'd, and being again set in your little House; I will now challenge your promise, and entreat you to proceed in your instruction for Flie-fishing, which, that you may be the better encourag'd to do, I will assure you, that I have not lost, I think, one syllable of what you have told me; but very well retain all your directions both for the Rod, Line, and making a Flie, and now desire an account of the Flies themselves.

Pisc. Why Sir, I am ready to give it you, and shall have the whole afternoon to do it in, if no body come in to interrupt us; for you must know (besides the unfitness of the day) that the afternoons so early in *March* signifie very little to Angling with a Flie, though with a Minnow, or a Worm something might (I confess) be done.

To begin then where I left off, my father *Walton* tells us but of 12 Artificial flies only, to Angle with at the top, and gives their names; of which some are common with us here; and I think I guess at most of them by his description, and I believe they all breed, and are taken in our Rivers, though we do not make them either of the same Dubbing, or fashion. And it may be in the Rivers about *London*, which I presume he has most frequented, and where 'tis likely he has done most execution, there is not much notice taken of many more: but we are acquainted with several others here (though perhaps I may reckon

some of his by other names too) but if I do, I shall
make you amends by an addition to his Catalogue.
And although the forenamed great Master in the Art
of Angling (for so in truth he is) tells you that no
man should in honesty catch a Trout till the middle
of *March*, yet I hope he will give a man leave sooner
to take a Grayling, which, as I told you, is in the
dead Months in his best season; and do assure you
(which I remember by a very remarkable token) I
did once take upon the sixt day of December one,
and only one, of the biggest Graylings and the best
in season, that ever I yet saw, or tasted; and do
usually take Trouts too, and with a Flie, not only
before the middle of this Month, but almost every
year in *February*, unless it be a very ill spring indeed,
and have sometimes in *January*, so early as New-
years-tide, and in frost and snow taken Grayling in
a warm sunshine day for an hour or two about Noon;
and to fish for him with a Grub it is then the best
time of all.

I shall therefore begin my Flie-fishing with that
Month (though I confess very few begin so soon,
and that such as are so fond of the sport as to embrace all opportunities, can rarely in that Month find
a day fit for their purpose) and tell you, that upon
my knowledg these Flies in a warm sun, for an hour
or two in the day, are certainly taken.

January

1. A red-brown with wings of the Male of a
Malard almost white: the dubbing of the tail of a
black long coated Cur, such as they commonly make
muffs of; for the hair on the tail of such a Dog dies,
and turns to a red Brown, but the hair of a smoth

coated Dog of the same colour will not do, because
it will not dye, but retains its natural colour, and this
flie is taken in a warm sun, this whole Month
thorough.

2. There is also a very little bright Dun Gnat, as
little as can possibly be made, so little as never to be
fisht with, with above one hair next the hook, and
this is to be made of a mixt dubbing of Martins fur,
and the white of a Hares scut; with a very white, and
small wing; and 'tis no great matter how fine you
fish, for nothing will rise in this Month but a Grayling, and of them I never at this season saw any taken
with a Flie, of above a foot long in my life: but of
little ones about the bigness of a smelt in a warm day,
and a glowing Sun, you may take enough with these
two flies, and they are both taken the whole North
through.

February

1. Where the Red-brown of the last Month ends,
another almost of the same colour begins with this,
saving that the dubbing of this must be of something
a blacker colour, and both of them warpt on with red
silk; the dubbing that should make this Flie, and that
is the truest colour, is to be got of the black spot of
a Hog's ear: not that a black spot in any part of the
Hog will not afford the same colour; but that the hair
in that place is by many degrees softer, and more fit
for the purpose: his wing must be as the other, and
this kills all this Month, and is call'd the lesser Red-
brown.

2. This Month also a plain Hackle, or palmer-
Flie, made with a rough black body, either of black
Spaniels furr, or the whirl of an *Estridg* feather, and

the red Hackle of a Capon over all, will kill, and if the weather be right make very good sport.

3. Also a lesser Hackle with a black body also, silver twist over that, and a red feather over all, will fill your pannier if the Month be open, and not bound up in Ice, and snow, with very good Fish; but in case of a frost and snow, you are to Angle only with the smallest Gnats, Browns and Duns you can make, and with those are only to expect Graylings no bigger, than sprats.

4. In this Month, upon a whirling round water, we have a great Hackle, the body black, and wrapped with a red feather of a Capon untrim'd; that is, the whole length of the Hackle staring out for we sometimes barb the Hackle feather short all over; sometimes barb it only a little, and sometimes barb it close underneath, leaving the whole length of the feather on the top, or back of the Flie which makes it swim better, and as occasion serves kills very great Fish.

5. We make use also in this Month of another great Hackle the body black, and rib'd over with Gold twist, and a red feather over all, which also does great execution.

6. Also a great Dun, made with Dun Bears Hair, and the wings of the grey feather of a Mallard near unto his tail, which is absolutely the best Flie can be thrown upon a River this Month, and with which an Angler shall have admirable sport.

7. We have also this Month the great blew Dun, the dubbing of the bottom of Bears hair next to the roots, mixt with a little blue Camlet, the wings of the dark grey feather of a Mallard.

8. We have also this Month a Dark-Brown, the

dubbing of the brown hair of the Flanck of a brended
Cow, and the wings of the grey-Drakes feather.

And note, that these several Hackels, or Palmer
Flies, are some for one Water, and one Skye, and
some for another, and according to the change of
those, we alter their size, and colour, and note also,
that both in this, and all other Months of the Year,
when you do not certainly know what Flie is taken;
or cannot see any Fish to rise, you are then to put
on a small Hackle, if the Water be clear, or a bigger
if something dark, untill you have taken one, and
then thrusting your finger thorough his Guills, to
pull out his Gorge, which being opened with your
knife, you will then discover what Flie is taken, and
may fit your self accordingly.

For the making of a Hackle, or Palmer Flie, my
father *Walton* has already given you sufficient
direction.

March

For this Month you are to use all the same
Hackels, and Flies with the other, but you are to
make them less.

1. We have besides, for this Month a little Dun
call'd a whirling Dun (though it is not the whirling
Dun, indeed, which is one of the best flies we have)
and for this the dubbing must be of the bottom fur
of a Squirrels tail and the wing of the grey feather
of a Drake.

2. Also a bright brown, the dubbing either of the
brown of a Spaniel, or that of a Cows flanck, with a
grey wing.

3. Also a whitish Dun made of the roots of Camels
hair, and the wings of the grey feather of a Mallard.

4. There is also for this Month a Flie, call'd the Thorn Tree Flie; the dubbing an absolute black mixt with eight or ten hairs of *Isabella* coloured Mohair, the body as little as can be made, and the wings of a bright Malards feather, an admirable Flie, and in great repute amongst us for a killer.

5. There is besides this another blew Dun, the dubbing of which it is made being thus to be got. Take a small tooth comb, and with it comb the neck of a black Grey hound, and the down that sticks in the teeth, will be the finest blew, that ever you saw. The wings of this Flie can hardly be too white, and he is taken about the tenth of this Month, and lasteth till the four and twentieth.

6. From the tenth of this Month also till towards the end, is taken a little black Gnat; the dubbing either of the fur of a black water-Dog, or the down of a young black water-Coot; the wings of the Male of a Mallard as white as may be, the body as little as you can possibly make it, and the wings as short as his body.

7. From the Sixteenth of this Month also to the end of it, we use a bright brown, the dubbing for which, is to be had out of a Skinners Lime-pits, and of the hair of an abortive Calf, which the lime will turn to be so bright, as to shine like Gold, for the wings of this Flie, the feather of a brown Hen is best; which Flie is also taken till the tenth of *April*.

April

All the same Hackles, and Flies that were taken in *March* will be taken in this Month also, with this distinction only concerning the Flies, that all the browns be lapt with red silk, and the Duns with yellow.

1. To these a small bright-brown, made of Spaniels fur, with a light grey wing; in a bright day, and a clear water is very well taken.

2. We have too a little dark brown, the dubbing of that colour, and some violet Camlet mixt, and the wing of the grey feather of a Mallard.

3. From the sixth of this Month to the tenth, we have also a Flie called the violet Flie, made of a dark violet stuff, with the wings of the grey feather of a Mallard.

4. About the twelfth of this Month comes in the Flie call'd the whirling Dun, which is taken every day about the mid time of day all this Month through, and by fits from thence to the end of *June*, and is commonly made of the down of a Fox Cub, which is of an Ash colour at the roots, next the skin, and ribb'd about with yellow silk, the wings of the pale grey feather of a Mallard.

5. There is also a yellow Dun, the dubbing of Camels hair, and yellow Camlet, or wool mixt, and a white grey wing.

6. There is also this Month another little brown, besides that mention'd before, made with a very slender body, the dubbing of dark brown, and violet Camlet mixt, and a grey wing; which though the direction for the making be near the other, is yet another Flie, and will take when the other will not, especially in a bright day, and a clear water.

7. About the twentieth of this Month comes in a Flie call'd the Horse-flesh Flie, the dubbing of which is a blew Mohair, with pink colour'd, and red Tammy mixt, a light coloured wing, and a dark brown head. This flie is taken best in an Evening, and kills from two hours before Sun set till twilight, and is taken the Month thorough.

May

And now Sir, that we are entring into the Month of *May*, I think it requisite to beg not only your attention; but also your best patience; for I must now be a little tedious with you, and dwell upon this Month longer than ordinary; which that you may the better endure, I must tell you, this Month deserves, and requires to be insisted on, for as much as it alone, and the next following afford more pleasure to the Flie-Angler than all the rest; and here it is that you are to expect an account of the Green Drake and stone-flie, promis'd you so long ago, and some others that are peculiar to this Month, and part of the month following, and that (though not so great either in bulk, or name) do yet stand in competition with the two before named, and so, that it is yet undecided amongst the Anglers to which of the pretenders to the Title of the May-flie, it does properly, and duly belong, neither dare I (where so many of the learned in this Art of Angling are got in dispute about the controversie) take upon me to determine; but I think I ought to have a vote amongst them, and according to that priviledg shall give you my free opinion, and peradventure when I have told you all, you may incline to think me in the right.

Viat. I have so great a deference to your judgment in these matters, that I must always be of your opinion; and the more you speak, the faster I grow to my attention, for I can never be weary of hearing you upon this Subject.

Pisc. Why that's encouragement enough; and now prepare your self for a tedious Lecture; but I will first begin with the flies of less esteem (though almost any thing will take a Trout in *May*) that I may afterwards insist the longer upon those of greater note and reputation; know therefore that the first flie we take notice of in this Month, is call'd the Turky-Flie.

1. The dubbing ravell'd out of some blew stuff, and lapt about with yellow silk, the wings of a grey Mallards feather.

2. Next a great Hackle; or Palmer-flie, with a yellow body ribb'd with Gold twist, and large wings of a Mallards feather dyed yellow, with a red Capons Hackle over all,

3. Then a black flie, the dubbing of a black Spaniels fur, and the wings of a grey Mallards feather.

4. After that a light brown with a slender body, the dubbing twirl'd upon small red silk, and rais'd with the point of a needle, that the ribs or rows of silk may appear through the wings of the grey feather of a Mallard.

5. Next a little Dun, the dubbing of a Bears dun whirl'd upon yellow silk, the wings of the grey feather of a Mallard.

6. Then a white Gnat, with a pale wing, and a black head.

7. There is also this Month a flie called the Peacock-flie, the body made of a whirl of a Peacocks feather, with a red head, and wings of a Mallards feather.

8. We have then another very killing flie, known by the name of the Dun-Cut, the dubbing of which is a Bears dun, with a little blew, and yellow mixt with it, a large dun wing, and two horns at the head, made of the hairs of a Squirrels tail.

9. The next is the Cow-Lady, a little flie, the body of a Peacocks feather, the wing of a red feather, or strips of the red hackle of a Cock.

10. We have then the Cow-turd flie; the dubbing light brown, and yellow mixt, the wing the dark grey feather of a Mallard. And note that besides these abovementioned, all the same Hackles and Flies, the Hackles only brighter, and the Flies smaller, that are taken in *April*, will also be taken this Month, as also all Browns and Duns; and now I come to my Stone-flie, and Green-Drake, which are the Matadores for Trout and Grayling, and in their season kill more fish in our *Derbyshire* Rivers, than all the rest past, and to come, in the whole year besides.

But first I am to tell you, that we have four several flies which contend for the Title of the May-Flie, namely,

> *The Green-Drake,*
> *The Stone-Flie,*
> *The Black-Flie, and*
> *The little yellow May-Flie.*

And all these have their Champions and Advocates to dispute, and plead their priority; though I do not understand why the two last named should; the first two having so manifestly the advantage, both in their beauty, and the wonderful execution they do in their season.

11. Of these the Green-Drake comes in about the twentieth of this Month, or betwixt that, and the latter end (for they are sometimes sooner, and sometimes later according to the quality of the Year) but never well taken till towards the end of this Month, and the beginning of *June*. The Stone-Flie comes much sooner, so early as the middle of *April*; but is

never well taken till towards the middle of *May*, and continues to kill much longer than the Green-Drake stays with us, so long as to the end almost of *June*; and indeed, so long as there are any of them to be seen upon the water; and sometimes in an Artificial Flie, and late at night, or before Sun rise in a morning, longer.

Now both these Flies (and I believe many others, though I think not all) are certainly, and demonstratively bred in the very Rivers where they are taken, our Caddis or Cod-bait which lye under stones in the bottom of the water, most of them turning into those two Flies, and being gather'd in the husk, or crust, near the time of their maturity, are very easily known, and distinguisht, and are of all other the most remarkable, both for their size, as being of all other the biggest (the shortest of them being a full inch long, or more) and for the execution they do, the Trout and Grayling being much more greedy of them, than of any others; and indeed the Trout never feeds fat, nor comes into his perfect season, till these Flies come in.

Of these the Green-Drake never discloses from his husk, till he be first there grown to full maturity, body, wings, and all, and then he creeps out of his cell, but with his wings so crimpt, and ruffled, by being prest together in that narrow room, that they are for some hours totally useless to him, by which means he is compelled either to creep upon the flags, sedges, and blades of grass (if his first rising from the bottom of the water be near the banks of the River) till the Air, and Sun, stiffen and smooth them! or if his first appearance above water happen to be in the middle, he then lies upon the surface of the water like a Ship at Hull (for his feet are totally useless to him there, and he cannot creep upon the water as the Stone-Flie can) untill his wings have got stiffness to fly with, if by some Trout, or Grayling he be not taken in the interim (which ten to one he is) and then his wings stand high, and clos'd exact upon his back, like the Butterfly, and his motion in flying is the same. His body is in some of a paler, in others of a darker yellow (for they are not all exactly of a colour) rib'd with rows of green, long, slender, and growing sharp towards the tail, at the end of which he has three long small whisks of a very dark colour, almost black, and his tail turns up towards his back like a Mallard, from whence questionless he has his name of the green-Drake. These (as I think I told you before) we commonly dape, or dibble with, and having gathered great store of them into a long draw box, with holes in the Cover to give them Air (where also they will continue fresh, and vigorous a night or more) we take them out thence by the wings, and bait them thus upon the Hook. We first take one (for we commonly fish with two of them at a time) and putting the point of the Hook into the thickest part of his Body under one of his wings, run it directly through and out at the other side, leaving him spitted cross upon the Hook, and then taking the other, put him on after the same manner, but with his head the contrary way, in which posture they will live upon the Hook, and play with their wings for a quarter of an hour, or more: but you must have a care to keep their wings dry, both from the water, and also that your fingers be not wet when you take them out to bait them; for then your bait is spoil'd.

Having now told you how to Angle with this Flie
alive; I am now to tell you next, how to make an
Artificial Flie, that will so perfectly resemble him, as
to be taken in a rough windy day, when no Flies can
lye upon the water; nor are to be found about the
Banks and sides of the River, to a wonder, and with
which you shall certainly kill the best Trout, and
Grayling in the River.

The Artificial Green-Drake then is made upon a
large Hook, the Dubbing, Camels hair, bright Bears
hair, the soft down that is comb'd from a Hogs
bristles, and yellow Camlet, well mixt together, the
body long, and ribb'd about with green silk, or
rather yellow waxt with green-wax, the whisks of
the tail of the long hairs of sables, or fitchet, and the
wings of the white grey feather of a Mallard dyed
yellow, which also is to be dyed thus.

*Take the root of a Barbary Tree, and shave it, and
put to it Woody viss, with as much Alum as a Walnut,
and boyl your feathers in it with Rain water; and they
will be of a very fine yellow.*

I have now done with the Green-drake, excepting
to tell you, that he is taken at all hours during his
season, whilst there is any day upon the Sky; and
with a made Flie, I once took, ten days after he was
absolutely gone, in a Cloudy day, after a showr, and
in a whistling wind, five and thirty very great
Trouts, and Graylings betwixt five, and eight of
the Clock in the Evening, and had no less than five,
or six Flies with three good hairs a piece taken from
me in despite of my heart, besides.

12. I should now come next to the Stone-Flie,
but there is another Gentleman in my way: that
must of necessity come in between, and that is the

Grey-Drake, which in all shapes, and dimensions is perfectly the same with the other, but quite almost of another colour, being of a paler, and more livid yellow, and green, and ribb'd with black quite down his body, with black shining wings, and so diaphanous and tender, cob-web like, that they are of no manner of use for Daping; but come in, and are taken after the Green-Drake, and in an Artificial Flie kill very well, which Flie is thus made, the Dubbing of the down of a Hogs bristles, and black Spaniels fur mixt, and ribb'd down the body with black silk, the whisks of the hairs of the beard of a black Cat, and the wings of the black grey feather of a Mallard.

And now I come to the Stone-Flie, but am afraid I have already wearied your patience, which if I have, I beseech you freely tell me so, and I will defer the remaining instructions for Flie-Angling till some other time.

Viat. No truly Sir, I can never be weary of hearing you: but if you think fit, because I am afraid I am too troublesom, to refresh your self with a glass, and a pipe; and may afterwards proceed, and I shall be exceedingly pleas'd to hear you.

Pisc. I thank you *Sir* for that motion; for believe me I am dry with talking, Here Boy, give us here a Bottle, and a Glass; and *Sir*, my service to you, and to all our friends in the South.

Viat. Your Servant *Sir*, and I'le pledg you as heartily; for the good powder'd beef I eat at Dinner, or something else, has made me thirsty.

CHAP. VIII.

Viat. So, *Sir*, I am now ready for another Lesson so soon as you please to give it me.

Pisc. And I, *Sir*, as ready to give you the best I can. Having told you the time of the Stone-Flie's coming in, and that he is bred of a Caddis in the very River where he is taken, I am next to tell you, that

13. This same Stone-Flie has not the patience to continue in his Crust, or Husk, till his wings be full grown; but so soon as ever they begin to put out, that he feels himself strong (at which time we call him a Jack) squeezes himself out of Prison, and crawls to the top of some stone, where if he can find a chink that will receive him, or can creep betwixt two stones, the one lying hollow upon the other (which, by the way, we also lay so purposely to find them) he there lurks till his wings be full grown, and there is your only place to find him (and from thence doubtless he derives his name) though, for want of such convenience, he will make shift with the hollow of a Bank, or any other place where the wind cannot come to fetch him off. His body is long, and pretty thick, and as broad at the tail almost, as in the middle; his colour a very fine brown, ribbed with yellow, and much yellower on the belly than the back, he has two or three whisks also at the tag of his tail, and two little horns upon his head, his wings, when full grown, are double, and flat down his back of the same colour, but rather darker than his body, and longer than it; though he makes but little use of them, for you shall rarely see him flying, though often swimming, and padling with several feet he has under his belly upon the water, without stirring a

wing: but the Drake will mount Steeple height into
the Air, though he is to be found upon flags and
grass too, and indeed every where high and low,
near the River; there being so many of them in their
season as, were they not a very inoffensive insect,
would look like a Plague; and these Drakes (since I
forgot to tell you before, I will tell you here) are
taken by the Fish to that incredible degree, that upon
a calm day you shall see the still deeps continually
all over circles by the Fishes rising, who will gorge
themselves with those Flies, till they purge again
out of their Guills; and the Trouts are at that time
so lusty and strong, that one of eight, or ten inches
long, will then more struggle, and tug, and more
endanger your Tackle, than one twice as big in
winter: but pardon this digression.

This Stone-flie then we dape or dibble with as
with the Drake, but with this difference, that whereas
the green-Drake is common both to stream and still,
and to all hours of the day, we seldom dape with this
but in the streams, for in a whistling wind a made
Flie in the deep is better, and rarely, but early and
late, it not being so proper for the mid-time of the
day; though a great *Grayling* will then take it very
well in a sharp stream, and here and there a Trout
too: but much better toward 8, 9, 10, or eleven of the
clock at night, at which time also the best Fish rise,
and the later the better, provided you can see your
Flie, and when you cannot, a made Flie will murder,
which is to be made thus: The dubbing of bears dun
with a little brown and yellow Camlet very well
mixt, but so plac'd that your Flie may be more yellow
on the belly and towards the tail underneath than in
any other part, and you are to place two or three

hairs of a black Cats beard on the top of the hook in
your arming, so as to be turn'd up when you warp
on your dubbing, and to stand almost upright, and
staring one from another, and note that your Flie is
to be ribb'd with yellow silk, and the wings long, and
very large, of the dark grey feather of a Mallard.

14. The next *May-Flie* is the black Flie, made with
a black body of the whirle of an Ostridg-feather,
rib'd with silver twist, and the black hackle of a
Cock over all; and is a killing Flie, but not to be
nam'd with either of the other.

15. The last *May-Flie* (that is of the four pretenders) is the little yellow *May-Flie*, in shape exactly the same with the green-Drake, but a very little
one, and of as bright a yellow as can be seen; which
is made of a bright yellow Camlet, and the wings of
a white grey feather died yellow.

16. The last Flie for this month (and which continues all *June*, though it comes in the middle of
May) is the Flie called the Camlet-Flie, in shape like
a moth with fine diapred, or water-wings, and with
which (as I told you before) I sometimes used to
dibble; and Grayling will rise mightily at it. But the
artificial Flie (which is only in use amongst our
Anglers) is made of a dark-brown shining Camlet,
rib'd over with a very small light green silk, the
wings of the double grey feather of a Mallard;
and 'tis a killing Flie for small Fish, and so much
for *May*.

June.

From the first to the four and twentieth, the
green-Drake and Stone-Flie are taken (as I told you
before.)

1. From the twelfth to the four and twentieth late at night is taken a flie, called the Owl-Flie; the dubbing of a white Weesel's tail, and a white Grey wing.

2. We have then another *Dunne,* call'd the *Barm-Flie,* from it's yesty colour, the dubbing of the fur of a yellow dun Cat, and a grey wing of a Mallards feather.

3. We have also a hackle with a purple body, whipt about with a red Capons feather.

4. As also a gold twist Hackle with a purple body, whipt about with a red Capons feather.

5. To these we have this month a Flesh-flie, the dubbing of a black Spaniels furre, and blew wool mixt, and a grey wing.

6. Also another little flesh-flie, the body made of the whirle of a Peacocks feather, and the wings of the grey feather of a Drake.

7. We have then the Peacock-flie, the body and wing both made of the feather of that bird.

8. There is also the flying Ant, or Ant-flie, the dubbing of brown and red Camlet mixt, with a light grey wing.

9. We have likewise a brown Gnat, with a very slender body of brown and violet Camlet well mixt, and a light grey wing.

10. And another little black Gnat, the dubbing of black mohair, and a white Grey wing.

11. As also a green Grasshopper, the dubbing of green and yellow Wool mixed, rib'd over with green Silk, and a red Capons feather over all.

12. And lastly a little dun Grasshopper, the body slender made of a dun Camlet, and a dun hackle at the top.

July.

First all the small flies that were taken in *June*, are also taken in this month.

1. We have then the Orange Flie, the dubbing of Orange Wool, and the wing of a black feather.

2. Also a little white dun, the body made of white Mohair, and the wings, blew of a Herons feather.

3. We have likewise this month a Wasp-flie, made either of a dark brown dubbing, or else the furre of a black Cats tail, ribb'd about with yellow silk, and the wing of the grey feather of a Mallard.

4. Another flie taken this month is a black Hackle, the body made of the whirle of a Peacock's feather, and a black hackle feather on the top.

5. We have also another made of a Peacocks whirle without wings.

6. Another flie also is taken this month call'd the shel-flie, the dubbing of yellow-green Jersey Wool, and a little white Hoggs hair mixt, which I call the Palm-flie, and do believe it is taken for a Palm, that drops off the willows into the water; for this flie I have seen Trouts take little pieces of moss, as they have swam down the River, by which I conclude that the best way to hit the right colour is to compare your dubbing with the Moss, and mix the colours as near as you can.

7. There is also taken this month a black blew Dun, the dubbing of the furre of a black Rabbet mixt with a little yellow, the wings of the Feather of a blew Pigeons wing.

August.

The same Flies with *July.*

1. Then another Art-flie, the dubbing of the black

brown hair of a Cow, some red warpt in for the Tagg of his tail, and a dark wing, a killing flie.

2. Next a fly call'd the Fern-flie, the dubbing of the fur of a Hares neck, that is of the colour of Fearn or Brackin, with a darkish grey wing of a Mallards feather, a killer too.

3. Besides these we have a white Hackle, the body of white Mo-hair, and wrapped about with a white Hackle Feather, and this is assuredly taken for Thistle-down.

4. We have also this month a Harry-long-leggs, the body made of Bears dun, and blew wool mixt, and a brown hackle Feather over all.

Lastly in this month all the same browns and duns are taken, that were taken in *May*.

September.

This month· the same Flies are taken, that are taken in *April*.

1. To which I shall only add a Camel-brown Flie, the dubbing pull'd out of the lime of a Wall whipt about with red Silk, and a darkish grey Mallards feather for the wing.

2. And one other for which we have no name; but it is made of the black hair of a Badgers skin mixt with the yellow softest down of a sanded Hog.

October.

The same Flies are taken this month, that were taken in *March*.

Novemb.

The same Flies that were taken in *February*, are taken this month also.

December.

Few men angle with the Flie this month, no more than they do in *January*: but yet if the weather be warm (as I have known it sometimes in my life to be, even in this cold Country where it is least expected) then a brown that looks red in the hand, and yellow-ish betwixt your eye and the Sun, will both raise and kill in a clear water, and free from snow-broth: but at the best, 'tis hardly worth a man's labour.

And now, *Sir*, I have done with Flie-fishing, or angling at the top, excepting once more to tell you, that of all these (and I have named you a great many very killing flies) none are fit to be compared with the Drake and Stone-flie, both for many and very great fish; and yet there are some daies, that are by no means proper for the sport, and in a calm you shall not have near so much sport even with daping, as in a whistling gale of wind, for two reasons, both because you are not then so easily discovered by the fish, and also because there are then but few flies can lye upon the water; for where they have so much choice, you may easily imagine they will not be so eager and forward to rise at a bait, that both the shadow of your body, and that of your Rod, nay of your very line, in a hot calm day will, in spite of your best caution, render suspected to them: but even then, in swift streams, or by sitting down patiently behind a willow bush, you shall do more execution than at almost any other time of the year with any other flie, though one may sometimes hit of a day, when he shall come home very well satisfied with sport with several other Flies: but with these two, the green Drake and the Stone-flie, I do verily believe I could some daies in my life, had I not been weary of slaughter, have loaden a lusty boy, and have sometimes, I do honestly assure you, given over upon the meer account of satiety of sport; which will be no hard matter to believe, when I likewise assure you, that with this very flie, I have in this very River that runs by us in three or four hours taken thirty, five and thirty, and forty of the best Trouts in the River. What shame and pity is it then, that such a River should be destroyed by the basest sort of people, by those unlawful ways of fire and netting in the night, and of damming, groping, spearing, hanging and hooking by day, which are now grown so common, that, though we have very good Laws to punish such Offenders, every Rascal does it, for ought I see, *impunè*.

To conclude, I cannot now in honesty but frankly tell you, that many of these flies I have nam'd, at least so made as we make them here, will peradventure do you no great service in your Southern Rivers, and will not conceal from you, but that I have sent flies to several friends in *London*, that for ought I could ever hear, never did any great feats with them, and therefore if you intend to profit by my instructions, you must come to angle with me here in the Peak; and so, if you please, let us walk up to Supper, and to morrow, if the day be windy, as our daies here commonly are, 'tis ten to one but we shall take a good dish of fish for dinner.

CHAP. IX.

P*Isc.* A good day to you, *Sir*; I see you will alwaies be stirring before me.

Viat. Why, to tell you the truth, I am so allur'd

with the sport I had yesterday, that I long to be at the River again, and when I heard the wind sing in my Chamber window, could forbear no longer, but leap out of bed, and had just made an end of dressing my self as you came in.

Pisc. Well, I am both glad you are so ready for the day, and that the day is so fit for you, and look you I have made you three or four flies this morning, this silver twist hackle, this bears dun, this light brown and this dark brown, any of which I dare say will do; but you may try them all, and see which does best, only I must ask your pardon that I cannot wait upon you this Morning, a little business being fal'n out, that for two or three hours, will deprive me of your Company: but I'le come call you home to dinner, and my man shall attend you.

Viat. Oh, *Sir*, mind your affairs by all means, do but lend me a little of your skill to these fine flies, and, unless it have forsaken me since yesterday, I shall find luck of my own I hope to do something.

Pisc. The best Instruction I can give you, is, that, seeing the wind curles the water, and blows the right way, you would now angle up the still deep to day; for betwixt the Rocks where the streams are, you would find it now too brisk, and besides I would have you take fish in both Waters.

Viat. I'le obey your Direction, and so a good morning to you. Come young man, let you and I walk together. But heark you, *Sir*, I have not done with you yet; I expect another lesson for angling at the bottom, in the afternoon.

Pisc. Well, Sir, I'le be ready for you.

CHAP. X.

PIsc. Oh *Sir*, are you return'd? you have but just prevented me. I was coming to call you.

Viat. I am glad then I have sav'd you the labour.

Pisc. And how have you sped?

Viat. You shall see that, *Sir*, presently, look you *Sir*, here are three* brace of Trouts, one of them the biggest but one, that ever I killed with a flie in my life, and yet I   ** Spoke like a South-Country man.* lost a bigger than that, with my Flie to boot, and here are three Graylings, and one of them longer by some inches than that I took yesterday, and yet I thought that a good one too.

Pisc. Why you have made a pretty good mornings work on't; and now *Sir*, what think you of our River *Dove*?

Viat. I think it to be the best Trout River in *England*; and am so far in love with it, that if it were mine, and that I could keep it to my self, I would not exchange that water, for all the Land it runs over; to be totally debarr'd from't.

Pisc. That Complement to the River, speaks you a true lover of the Art of angling: And now, *Sir*, to make part of amends for sending you so uncivilly out alone this Morning, I will my self dress you this dish of fish for your dinner, walk but into the parlour, you will find one Book or other in the window, to entertain you the while, and you shall have it presently.

Viat. Well *Sir*, I obey you.

Pisc. Look you *Sir*, have I not made haste?

Viat. Believe me *Sir*, that you have, and it looks so well, I long to be at it.

Pisc. Fall to, then; now *Sir*, what say you! am I a tolerable Cook or no?

Viat. So good a one, that I did never eat so good Fish in my life. This Fish is infinitely better, than any I ever tasted of the kind in my life. 'Tis quite another thing, than our Trouts about *London*.

Pisc. You would say so, if that Trout you eat of were in right season: but pray eat of the Grayling, which, upon my word at this time, is by much the better Fish.

Viat. In earnest, and so it is: and I have one request to make to you, which is, that as you have taught me to catch Trout and Grayling, you will now teach me how to dress them as these are drest, which, questionless is of all other the best way.

Pisc. That I will *Sir*, with all my heart, and am glad you like them so well, as to make that request, and they are drest thus.

Take your Trout, wash, and dry him with a clean Napkin; then open him, and having taken out his guts and all the blood, wipe him very clean within, but wash him not, and give him three scotches with a Knife to the bone on one side only. After which take a clean Kettle, and put in as much hard stale Beer (but it must not be dead) Vinegar, and a little Whitewine, and Water, as will cover the Fish you intend to boyl: then throw into the Liquor a good quantity of Salt, the Rind of a Lemon, a handful of slic't Horse-Radish root, with a handsom little fagot of Rosemary, Time, and Winter-Savory. Then set your Kettle upon a quick fire of wood, and let your Liquor boyl up to the height before you put in your Fish, and then, if there be many, put them in one by one, that they may not so cool the Liquor, as to make it fall; and whilst your Fish is boyling, beat up the

Butter for your Sawce with a Ladle full or two of the Liquor it is boyling in, and being boyled enough, immediately pour the Liquor from the Fish, and being laid in a Dish, pour your Butter upon it, and strewing it plentifully over with shav'd Horse-Raddish, and a little pounded Ginger, garnish your sides of your Dish, and the Fish it self, with a slic't Lemon or two, and serve it up. A Grayling is also to be drest exactly after the same manner, saving that he is to be scal'd, which a Trout never is: and that must be done either with ones nails, or very lightly and carefully with a Knife for [fear of] bruising the Fish. And note, that these kinds of Fish, a Trout especially, if he is not eaten within four, or five hours after he be taken, is worth nothing.

But come *Sir,* I see you have din'd; and therefore if you please, we will walk down again to the little House, and there I will read you a Lecture of Angling at the bottom.

CHAP. XI.

Viat. So *Sir,* now we are here, and set: let me have my instructions for Angling for Trout, and Grayling at the bottom; which though not so easy, so cleanly, nor (as 'tis said) so Gentile a way of Fishing, as with a Flie; is yet (if I mistake not) a good holding way and takes Fish when nothing else will.

Pisc. You are in the right, it does so: and a worm is so sure a bait at all times, that, excepting in a Flood, I would I had laid [a] thousand pounds that I kill'd Fish more, or less with it, Winter or Summer every day throughout the Year; those days always excepted, that, upon a more serious account always ought so to be. But not longer to delay you, I will begin, and tell you, that Angling at the bottom is also commonly of two sorts (and yet there is a third way of Angling with a Ground-bait, and to very great effect too, as shall be said hereafter) namely.

By Hand:
or,
With a Cork, or Float.

That we call Angling by hand, is of three sorts.

The first with a line about half the length of the Rod, a good weighty plum, and three hairs next the Hook, which we call a running Line, and with one large Brandling, or a dew-worm of a moderate size, or two small ones of the first, or any other sort, proper for a Trout, of which my father *Walton* has already given you the names, and sav'd me a labour; or indeed almost any worm whatever; for if a Trout be in the humour to bite, it must be such a worm as I never yet saw, that he will refuse; and if you fish with two, you are then to bait your hook thus. You are first to run the point of your hook in at the very head of your first worm, and so down through his body till it be past the knot, and then let it out, and strip the worm above the arming (that you may not bruise it with your fingers) till you have put on the other by running the point of the Hook in below the knot, and upwards through his body towards his head till it be just cover'd with the head, which being done, you are then to slip the first worm down over the arming again, till the knots of both worms meet together.

The second way of Angling by hand, and with a running Line, is with a Line something longer than the former, and with Tackle made after this same manner. At the utmost extremity of your line, where the Hook is always placed in all other ways of angling, you are to have a large Pistol or Carabine Bullet, into which the end of your Line is to be fastned with a Peg or Pin, even and close with the Bullet, and about half a foot above that, a branch of Line, of two, or three handfuls long; or more, for a swift stream, with a Hook at the end thereof, baited with some of the forenamed worms, and another half foot above that, another arm'd and baited after the same manner; but with another sort of worm, without any lead at all above: by which means you will always certainly find the true bottom in all depths, which with the Plums upon your line above you can never do, but that your bait must always drag whilst you are sounding (which in this way of Angling must be continually) by which means you are like to have more trouble, and peradventure worse success. And both these ways of Angling at the bottom are most proper for a dark, and muddy water, by reason that in such a condition of the stream, a Man may stand as near as he will, and neither his own shadow; nor the roundness of his Tackle will hinder his sport.

The third way of Angling by hand with a Groundbait, and by much the best of all other, is, with a Line full as long, or a yard and half longer than your Rod, with no more than one hair next the hook, and for two or three lengths above it, and no more than one small pellet of shot for your plum, your Hook little, your worms of the smaller Brandlings very well scour'd; and only one upon your hook at a time, which is thus to be baited. The point of your hook is to be put in at the very tagg of his tail, and run up

his body quite over all the arming, and still stript on
an inch at least upon the hair, the head and remaining part hanging downward; and with this line and
hook thus baited you are evermore to angle in the
streams, always in a clear rather than a troubled
water, and always up the River, still casting out your
worm before you with a light one-handed Rod, like
an artificial Flie, where it will be taken, sometimes
at the top, or within a very little of the *Superficies* of
the water, and almost always before that light plumb
can sink it to the bottom, both by reason of the stream,
and also that you must always keep your worm in
motion by drawing still back towards you, as if you
were angling with a flie; and believe me, whoever
will try it, shall find this the best way of all other to
angle with a worm, in a bright water especially; but
then his rod must be very light and pliant, and very
true and finely made, which, with a skilful hand will
do wonders, and in a clear stream is undoubtedly
the best way of angling for a Trout, or Grayling
with a worm, by many degrees, that any man can
make choice of, and of most ease and delight to the
Angler. To which let me add, that if the Angler be
of a constitution that will suffer him to wade, and will
slip into the tail of a shallow stream, to the Calf of
the leg or the knee, and so keep off the bank, he
shall almost take what fish he pleases.

The second way of angling at the bottom is with
a Cork or float; and that is also of two sorts.

With a worm:
or,
With a Grub *or* Caddis.

With a worm you are to have your line within.

a foot, or a foot and half as long as your rod, in a
dark water with two, or if you will with three; but
in a clear water never with above one hair next the
hook, and two or three for four or five lengths above
it, and a worm of what size you please, your plums
fitted to your Cork, your Cork to the condition of the
River (that is to the swiftness or slowness of it) and
both, when the water is very clear, as fine as you can,
and then you are never to bait with above one of the
lesser sort of Brandlings; or, if they are very little
ones indeed, you may then bait with two after the
manner before directed.

When you angle for a Trout, you are to do it as
deep, that is, as near the bottom as you can, provided
your bait do not drag, or if it do, a Trout will sometimes take it in that posture: if for a Grayling, you
are then to fish further from the bottom, he being a
fish that usually swims nearer to the middle of the
water, and lyes alwaies loose; or however is more
apt to rise than a Trout, and more inclin'd to rise
than to descend even to a Ground-bait.

With a Grub or Caddis, you are to angle with the
same length of Line; or if it be all out as long as your
Rod, 'tis not the worse, with never above one hair
for two or three lengths next the hook, and with the
smallest Cork, or float, and the least weight of plumb
you can that will but sink, and that the swiftness of
your stream will allow; which also you may help,
and avoid the violence of the Current, by angling in
the returnes of a stream, or the Eddies betwixt two
streams, which also are the most likely places wherein to kill a Fish in a stream, either at the top or
bottom.

Of Grubs for a Grayling, the Ash-Grub, which is

plump, milk-white, bent round from head to tail, and exceeding tender with a red head; or the Dock worm, or Grub of a pale yellow, longer, lanker, and tougher than the other, with rows of feet all down his belly, and a red head also are the best, I say for a Grayling, because, although a Trout will take both these (the Ash-Grub especially) yet he does not do it so freely as the other, and I have usually taken ten Graylings for one Trout with that bait, though if a Trout come, I have observed, that he is commonly a very good one.

These baits we usually keep in Bran, in which an Ash-Grub commonly grows tougher, and will better endure baiting, though he is yet so tender, that it will be necessary to warp in a piece of a stiff hair with your arming, leaving it standing out about a straw breadth at the head of your hook, so as to keep the Grub either from slipping totally off when baited, or at least down to the point of the hook, by which means your arming will be left wholly naked and bare, which is neither so sightly, nor so likely to be taken; though to help that (which will however very oft fall out) I always arm the hook I design for this Bait with the whitest horse-hair I can chuse, which it self, will resemble, and shine like that bait, and consequently will do more good, or less harm than an arming of any other colour. These Grubs are to be baited thus, the hook is to be put in under the head or Chaps of the bait, and guided down the middle of the belly without suffering it to peep out by the way (for then (the Ash-Grub especially) will issue out water and milk, till nothing but the skin shall remain, and the bend of the hook will appear black through it) till the point of your hook come so low, that the head of your bait may rest, and stick upon the hair that stands out to hold it, by which means it can neither slip of it self; neither will the force of the stream nor quick pulling out, upon any mistake, strip it off.

Now the Caddis, or Cod-bait, (which is a sure killing bait, and for the most part, by much, surer, than either of the other) may be put upon the Hook, two or three together, and is sometimes (to very great effect) joyn'd to a worm, and sometimes to an Artificial Flie to cover the point of the Hook; but is always to be Angled with at the bottom (when by itself especially) with the finest Tackle; and is for all times of the year, the most holding bait of all other whatever, both for Trout, and Grayling.

There are several other baits besides these few I have nam'd you, which also do very great execution at the bottom, and some that are peculiar to certain Countries, and Rivers, of which every Angler may in his own place, make his own observation: and some others that I do not think fit to put you in mind of, because I would not corrupt you, and would have you, as in all things else I observe you to be a very honest Gentleman, a fair Angler. And so much for the second sort of Angling for a Trout at the bottom.

Viat. But Sir, I beseech you give me leave to ask you one question. Is there no art to be us'd to worms to make them allure the Fish, and in a manner compel them to bite at the bait?

Pisc. Not that I know of; or did I know any such secret, I would not use it my self, and therefore would not teach it you. Though I will not deny to you, that in my younger days, I have made trial of Oyl of Ospray, Oyl of Ivy, Camphire, Assa-faetida,

juice of Nettles, and several other devices that I was
taught by several Anglers I met with, but could
never find any advantage by them; and can scarce
believe there is anything to be done that way, though
I must tell you I have seen some men who I thought
went to work no more artificially than I, and have
yet with the same kind of worms I had, in my own
sight taken five, and sometimes ten for one. But
we'l let that business alone if you please; and because
we have time enough, and that I would deliver you
from the trouble of any more Lectures, I will, if you
please, proceed to the last way of angling for a Trout
or Grayling, which is in the middle; after which I
shall have no more to trouble you with.

Viat. 'Tis no trouble, *Sir*, but the greatest satis-
faction that can be, and I attend you.

CHAP. XII.

P*Isc*. Angling in the middle then for a Trout or
Grayling is of two sorts.

With a Pink or Minnow for a Trout:
or,
With a Worm, Grub or Caddis for a Grayling.

For the first, it is with a Minnow, half a foot, or
a foot within the *Superficies* of the water, and as to
the rest that concerns this sort of angling, I shall
wholly refer you to Mr. *Walton*'s direction, who is
undoubtedly the best Angler with a Minnow in *England*; only in plain truth I do not approve of those
baits he keeps in salt, unless where the Living ones

are not possibly to be had (though I know he
frequently kills with them, and peradventure more,
than with any other, nay I have seen him refuse a
living one for one of them) and much less of his
artificial one; for though we do it with a counterfeit
flie, me thinks it should hardly be expected, that a
man should deceive a fish with a counterfeit fish.
Which having said, I shall only add, and that out of
my own experience, that I do believe a Bull-head,
with his Guill-fins cut off (at some times of the year
especially) to be a much better bait for a Trout, than
a Minnow, and a Loach much better than that, to
prove which I shall only tell you, that I have much
oftner taken Trouts with a Bull-head or a Loach in
their Throats (for there a Trout has questionless his
first digestion) than a Minnow; and that one day
especially, having Angled a good part of the day
with a Minnow, and that in as hopeful a day, and as
fit a water, as could be wisht for that purpose, without raising any one Fish; I at last fell to't with the
worm, and with that took fourteen in a very short
space, amongst all which there was not to my remembrance, so much as one, that had not a Loach
or two, and some of them three, four, five, and six
Loaches, in his throat and stomach; from whence I
concluded, that had I Angled with that bait, I had
made a notable days work of't.

But after all, there is a better way of Angling with
a Minnow than perhaps is fit either to teach or to
practice; to which I shall only add, that a Grayling
will certainly rise at, and sometimes take a Minnow,
though it will be hard to be believ'd by any one, who
shall consider the littleness of that Fishes mouth,
very unfit to take so great a bait: but is affirm'd by

many, that he will sometimes do it, and I my self know it to be true; for though I never took a Grayling so, yet a Man of mine once did, and within so few paces of me, that I am as certain of it, as I can be of anything I did not see, and (which made it appear the more strange) the Grayling was not above eleven inches long.

I must here also beg leave of your Master, and mine, not to controvert, but to tell him, that I cannot consent to his way of throwing in his Rod to an overgrown Trout, and afterwards recovering his Fish with his Tackle. For though I am satisfied he has sometimes done it, because he says so; yet I have found it quite otherwise, and though I have taken with the Angle, I may safely say, some thousands of Trouts in my life, my top never snapt, though my Line still continued fast to the remaining part of my Rod (by some lengths of Line curl'd round about my top, and there fastened, with waxt silk against such an accident) nor my hand never slackt, or slipped by any other chance, but I almost always infallibly lost my Fish, whether great, or little, though my Hook came home again. And I have often wondred how a Trout should so suddainly disengage himself from so great a Hook as that we bait with a Minnow, and so deep bearded, as those Hooks commonly are, when I have seen by the forenam'd accidents, or the slipping of a knot in the upper part of the Line, by suddain, and hard striking, that though the Line has immediately been recover'd, almost before it could be all drawn into the water, the Fish clear'd, and gone in a moment. And yet to justifie what he says, I have sometimes known a Trout, having carried away a whole Line, found dead three, or four days

after with the Hook fast sticking in him: but then it
is to be suppos'd he had gorg'd it, which a Trout
will do, if you be not too quick with him when he
comes at a Minnow, as sure and much sooner than a
Pike; and I my self have also, once or twice in my
life, taken the same Fish with my own flie sticking
in his Chaps, that he had taken from me the day
before, by the slipping of a Hook in the arming: but
I am very confident a Trout will not be troubled two
hours with any Hook that has so much as one handful
of Line left behind with it, or that is not struck through
a bone, if it be in any part of his mouth only; nay, I do
certainly know, that a Trout so soon as ever he feels
himself prickt, if he carries away the Hook, goes
immediately to the bottom, and will there root like a
Hog upon the Gravel, till he either rub out, or break
the Hook in the middle. And so much for this first
sort of Angling in the middle for a Trout.

The second way of Angling in the middle, is with
a Worm, Grub, Caddis, or any other Ground-bait
for a Grayling, and that is with a Cork, and a foot
from the bottom, a Grayling taking it much better
there, than at the bottom, as has been said before;
and this always in a clear water, and with the finest
Tackle.

To which we may also, and with very good reason,
add the third way of Angling by hand with a Ground-
bait, as a third way of Fishing in the middle, which is
common to both Trout and Grayling, and (as I said
before) the best way of Angling with a Worm, of
all other I ever try'd whatever.

And now Sir, I have said all I can at present think
of concerning Angling for a Trout and Grayling;
and I doubt not have tir'd you sufficiently: but I will

give you no more trouble of this kind, whilst you stay; which I hope will be a good while longer.

Viat. That will not be above a day longer; but if I live till *May* come twelve Month, you are sure of me again, either with my master *Walton*, or without him, and in the mean time shall acquaint him how much you have made of me for his sake, and I hope he loves me well enough, to thank you for it.

Pisc. I shall be glad *Sir*, of your good Company at the time you speak of and shall be loath to part with you now; but when you tell me you must go, I will then wait upon you more Miles on your way, than I have tempted you out of it, and heartily wish you a good Journey.

FINIS

To my most Honoured Friend, Charles Cotton, Esq;

Sir,

You Now see, I have return'd you your very pleasant, and useful discourse of the Art of *Flie-Fishing*, Printed, just as 'twas sent me: for I have been so obedient to your desires, as to endure all the praises you have ventur'd to fix upon me in it. And, when I have thankt you for them, as the effects of an undissembled love: then, let me tell you, *Sir*, that I will really endeavour to live up to the Character you have given of me, if there were no other reason; yet for this alone, that you, that love me so well; and always think what you speak, may not, for my sake, suffer by a mistake in your Judgment.

And *Sir*, I have ventur'd to fill a part of your Margin, by way of Paraphrase, for the Readers clearer understanding the situation both of your *Fishing-House*, and the pleasantness of that you dwell in. And I have ventur'd also to give him a Copy of Verses, that, you were pleas'd to send me, now some Years past; in which, he may see a good Picture of both; and, so much of your own mind too, as will make any Reader that is blest with a Generous Soul, to love you the better. I confess, that for doing this, you may justly Judg me too bold: if you do, I will say so too: and so far commute for my offence, that, though I be more than a hundred Miles from you, and in the eighty third Year of my Age, yet I will forget both, and next Month begin a Pilgrimage to beg your pardon, for, I would dye in your favour: and till then will live.

Sir,

Your most affectionate

Father and Friend,

Izaak Walton.

London, *April.*
29*th.* 1676

THE
RETIREMENT.

Stanzes Irreguliers
TO
Mr. *IZAAK WALTON.*

Farewell thou busie World, and, may
  We never meet again:
Here I can eat, and sleep, and pray,
And do more good in one short day,
Than he, who his whole Age out wears
Upon the most conspicuous Theaters,
Where nought, but vanity and vice appears.

2.

Good God! how sweet are all things here!
How beautiful the Fields appear!
How cleanly, do we feed and lye!
Lord! what good hours do we keep!
  How quietly we sleep!
What peace, what unanimity!
How innocent from the lewd fashion,
Is all our business, all our recreation!

3.

Oh, how happy here's our leisure!
Oh, how innocent our pleasure!
Oh, ye Valleys, Oh, ye Mountains!
Oh, ye Groves, and Chrystal Fountains,
  How I love at liberty,
By turns, to come and visit ye!

4.

Dear solitude, the Souls best friend,
That Man, acquainted with himself dost make,
And, all his maker's wonders to intend,
    With thee, I here converse at will,
    And would be glad to do so still,
For, it is thou alone, that keep'st the Soul awake.

5.

How Calm, and quiet a delight,
        Is it, alone
To read, and meditate, and write;
By none offended, and, offending none?
To walk, ride, sit, or sleep at ones own ease!
And, pleasing a Mans self, none other to displease.

6.

Oh my beloved Nymph fair Dove;
Princess of rivers, how I love
    Upon thy flowry banks to lye,
      And view thy silver stream,
When guilded by a Summers beam!
And in it, all thy wanton fry
      Playing at liberty:
And, with my Angle upon them
      The all of treachery
I ever learnt industriously to try.

7.

Such streams, Romes yellow Tyber cannot show,
The Iberian Tagus or Ligurian Po;
      The Mause, the Danube, and the Rhine
Are puddle water all, compar'd with thine:
And Loyres pure streams yet too polluted are
      With thine much purer to compare;

The rapid Garonne, *and the winding* Seine,
> *Are both too mean*
>> *Beloved* Dove, *with thee*
>> *To vie priority;*
Nay, Tame *and* Isis, *when conjoyn'd submit,*
And lay their Trophies at thy silver feet.

8.

> *Oh my beloved* Rocks *that rise*
> *To awe the Earth, and brave the Skies:*
> *From some aspiring Mountains crown,*
>> *How dearly do I love,*
> *Giddy with pleasure, to look down.*
And from the vales, to view the noble heights above!

9.

> *Oh my beloved Caves! from dog-star's heat,*
> *And all anxieties, my safe retreat:*
> *What safety, privacy, what true delight,*
>> *In th' artificial night,*
>> *Your gloomy entrals make,*
>> *Have I taken, do I take!*
> *How oft when grief has made me fly*
> *To hide me from society,*
> *Even, of my dearest friends, have I*
>> *In your recesses friendly shade;*
>> *All my sorrows open laid,*
And, my most secret woes, entrusted to your privacy!

10.

> *Lord! would men let me alone;*
> *What an over happy one*
> *Should I think my self to be!*
> *Might I in this desart place*
> (*Which most Men in discourse disgrace*)

Live but undisturb'd and free!
Here, in this despis'd recess
Would I, maugre Winters cold,
And the Summers worst excess,
Try, to live out to sixty full years old!
And, all the while
Without an envious eye,
On any thriving under fortunes smile,
Contented live, and then, contented dye.

C. C.

FINIS.

NOTES

These notes are revised and abbreviated from those by T. Balston in the Clarendon Press edition of 1915.

p. 3 l. 3 *John Offley* (d. 1658). Grandson or great-grandson of Sir Thomas Offley, Lord Mayor of London in 1557. Walton himself was born at Stafford, but moved to London some time before 1610; about 1646, 'finding it dangerous for honest men to be there', he left that city and lived sometimes at Stafford and elsewhere.

p. 4 l. 5 *curiosity*. Hobby.

l. 10 *Sir Henry Wotton* (1568–1639). Ambassador at Venice and at the Hague, and Provost of Eton, where he was frequently visited by Walton. His fame rests chiefly on *Reliquiae Wottonianae* (1651), to which Walton prefixed a memoir, and more especially on the two poems 'The Character of a Happy Life' and 'On his Mistress, the Queen of Bohemia'. Donne addressed poems to him, and Milton printed a letter from him with the first edition of *Comus*. He was also a notable connoisseur of Venetian painting.

p. 5 l. 6 *own*: i.e. put his name to the book.

l. 27 *sowre-complexion'd*. Complexion has here its earlier sense of 'disposition'.

p. 6 l. 6 *Nat. and R. Roe*. Presumably relatives of Walton. Hawkins states that there was a copy of Walton's *Lives* with the inscription in the author's handwriting, 'For my cousin Roe'.

l. 10 *the excellent picture*. The pictures appeared in the first edition. It is not known by whom they were drawn or engraved.

l. 23 *Cambden*. See *Britannia*, Monmouthshire, William Camden (1551–1623), head master of Westminster, published his *Britannia* in Latin in 1586. The first English translation, by Philemon Holland, appeared in 1610.

l. 31 *Mr. Hales*. George Hale, whose *The Private schoole of defence* was published in 1614.

p. 7 l. 21 *conference*. Collection.

l. 22 *censure*. Judgement.

l. 26 *12 several flies*. See Ch. V.

p. 8 l. 13 *this fifth impression*. The *Compleat Angler* was first published in 1653, and the fifth edition (here reprinted) in 1676; being the last during the author's lifetime.

p. 9 l. 21 *Jo. Floud*. Perhaps of St. John's College, Cambridge. See note under Rob. Floud, p. 14. Probably both men were related to Walton's first wife.

p. 10 l. 25 *Ch. Harvie*. Probably Christopher Harvey, born 1597, educated at Brasenose College, Oxford, and author of two anti-Puritan books: *The Right Rebel*, 1661, and *Faction Supplanted*, 1663.

p. 13 l. 13 *Tho. Weaver*. His verses are dated earliest. He was born 1616 and died 1664. Educated at Christ Church, Oxford, of which he became a minor Canon but was ejected 1648. Author of *Songs and Poems of Love and Drollery*, 1654.

p. 14 l. 17 *Edv. Powel*. Perhaps the Edward Powell who was born 1614 and went up to Balliol, Oxford, 1632, and was surmaster of St. Paul's 1641–7; but there are several others of this name.

l. 24 *Rob. Floud, C.* If 'C' means Cambridge, this may be the Robert Flood (or Floyd, or Lloyd) who was born 1621 and went up to St. John's College, 1637, and was contemporary there with John Floud, born 1619. But there are several other possibilities.

p. 15 l. 7 *Henry Bayley*. No graduate of this name and date can be traced.

p. 17 l. 18 *Jaco. Dup. D.D.* James Duport, 1606–79, son of John Duport D.D., Master of Jesus College, Cambridge, who entered Trinity College as a Westminster Scholar in 1622. Fellow of Trinity College, 1627, Regius Professor of Greek, 1639, from which he was ejected 1654 as a Royalist. In 1655 elected Vice Master of Trinity and in 1668 appointed Master of Magdalene College. He was created D.D. by royal mandate 1660.

p. 19 l. 11 *Piscator, Venator, Auceps.* Lat. for Angler, Hunter, and Falconer.

p. 20 l. 1 *Hodsden.* Hoddesdon.

l. 9 *Theobalds.* Lord Burghley built a magnificent palace there, which his son, the first Earl of Salisbury, exchanged in 1607 for Hatfield House with James I. James died there in 1625. The palace was demolished by order of Parliament during the Commonwealth, and its materials sold for the benefit of the army.

l. 10 *mews.* To 'mew' is to take care of a hawk, usually when in moult, which it could not have been in May.

l. 17 *as the Italians say.* Sir Harris Nicolas gives 'Compagno allegro per camino ti serve per ronzino', 'A gay companion on the road is as good as a pony.' This is taken from the *Sententiae* of Publilius Syrus (fl. 45 B.C.), 'Comes facundus in via pro vehiculo.'

p. 21 l. 5 *Mr Sadler's.* Ralph Sadler (d. 1660) lived at Standon, a village 5 miles NE of Ware. His grandfather was Sir Ralph Sadler, Henry VIII's Secretary of State, and Lord Burghley's chief agent in the matter of Mary, Queen of Scots.

l. 6 *prevent.* Anticipate.

p. 22 l. 5 *Lucian.* Greek author (*c.* A.D. 120–200) of satirical dialogues. The following epigram is adapted from lines by T. H. (Thomas Hickes) among the prefatory matter in 'Certaine Select Dialogues of Lucian. . . . By Mr. Francis Hickes . . . Oxford, 1634.'

l. 10 *what Solomon says of Scoffers.* Proverbs xxiv. 9.

p. 23 l. 9 *Mountaigne*. Michel de Montaigne (1533–92) published two books of his *Essais* in 1580 and a third in 1588. John Florio's English translation appeared in 1603, and Charles Cotton's in 1685. This is presumably Walton's own version.

p. 24 l. 24 *testifie*. Prove.

l. 26 *use*. Am accustomed.

p. 25 l. 5 *Joves servant in Ordinary*. The Eagle, in Greek and Roman mythology, was the armour-bearer of Zeus. 'In ordinary' is an expansion of *ordinary* (adj.): 'belonging to the regular staff.'

l. 8 *the son of Dædalus*. Icarus, who flew with his father from Crete, but the sun melted the wax with which his wings were fastened, and he fell into the sea and was drowned.

l. 28 *witness the not breaking of Ice*. A concise way of saying 'as is seen if ice is not broken for them'.

p. 26 l. 1 *wants*. Lacks.

l. 12 *excrements*. Outgrowths, especially of hair, nails, or, as here, feathers.

l. 15 *curious*. Skilful, clever.

l. 24 *Thrassel*. Song-thrush.

l. 29 *Leverock*. The lark mentioned above is the skylark, and here perhaps the woodlark is intended.

Tit-lark. Meadow-pipit.

l. 30 *both alive and dead*. There was a belief that robins would cover unburied corpses with leaves: cf. Webster, *The White Devil*, v. iv, Shakespeare, *Cymbeline*, IV. ii. 221–9, and the story of 'The Babes in the Wood'.

p. 27 l. 10 *Varro his Aviarie*. Marcus Terentius Varro (116–27 B.C.) describes his aviary in *De Re Rustica*, iii. 5, where it is said to be 'sub Casino', under Monte Cassino in Campania. There are no such ruins known at Rome.

l. 20 *when the Turks besieged Malta or Rhodes*. In 1480 the Turks, under Mahomet II, besieged the Knights Hospitallers of St. John of Jerusalem in Rhodes and were

repulsed with great loss. In 1522 the Knights evacuated
Rhodes and were given Malta by the Emperor Charles V
as a reward for their long resistance. The Turks followed,
and in 1565, after one of the greatest sieges in history, were
repulsed with heavy loss.

l. 23 *Mr. G. Sandis, in his* Travels. See p. 209 of *A
relation of a journey begun An. Dom. 1610* (1615), by
George Sandys (1578–1644).

l. 26 *the Dove.* Genesis viii. 8–12.

l. 29 *for the sacrifices of the Law,* etc. Leviticus xii. 6, 8;
Luke ii. 24.

l. 32 *when God would feed.* 1 Kings xvii. 4–6.

p. 28 l. 3 *the shape of a Dove.* Luke iii. 22 seems to mean
that the Holy Ghost descended in the bodily shape of a
dove. Matthew iii. 16, Mark i. 10, and John i. 32 say
that its descent was like the descent of a dove.

l. 9 *the laborious Bee.* Walton had no doubt read 'The
Feminine Monarchie, or the Historie of Bees' by Charles
Butler (1623).

l. 21 *the long-winged and the short-winged Hawk.*
Falconidae and *Accipitridae.*

l. 24 *The Gerfalcon and Jerkin.* These are the female
and male of the same species, as also are the six following
couples.

l. 25 *Tassel-gentel.* Tiercel-gentle.

l. 27 *Bockerel.* First here, unidentified.

l. 31. *Stelletto.* Unidentified.

l. 32 *The Bloud red Rook.* Perhaps from Arabic *rukh,*
represented in English by the mythical roc.

l. 33 *The Waskite.* Possibly the swallow-tailed kite.

p. 29 l. 4 *The French Pye.* One of the grey shrikes.

l. 12 *Eires.* Any young hawk whose training is not
completed.

      Brancher. Young hawk when it first leaves the
nest.

      Ramish Hawk. Young hawk.

l. 13 *Haggard.* Peregrine.

Lentner. Perhaps lanner.

l. 14 *Ayries.* Aeries. Nesting-places.

Mewings. Moultings.

l. 15 *rare order of casting.* Hawks *cast* up fur and feathers with the indigestible portions of their food. *Rare order =* peculiar practice.

l. 16 *their reclaiming.* Taming.

p. 30 l. 10 *the Fichat, the Fulimart.* Names of the polecat. The ferret is a domesticated polecat.

l. 11 *Mouldwarp.* Mole.

l. 18 *Cleopatra.* Plutarch, *Antony,* xxviii. Eight boars were roasted whole for a supper of twelve people.

l. 25 *Pismire.* Ant.

p. 31 l. 7 *Xenophon. Cyropaedia,* I. iv. 5.

l. 25 *Rascal game.* The young lean or inferior deer of a herd.

p. 32 l. 2 *Moses in the Law permitted.* Leviticus xi. 3, Deuteronomy xiv. 6.

l. 26 *the eldest daughter.* Genesis i. 2.

l. 33 *skilled in all the learning.* Acts vii. 22.

l. 34 *the friend of God.* In the Bible Abraham alone is called 'the friend of God', James ii. 23 (see also 2 Chronicles xx. 7, Isaiah xli. 8); but 'The Lord spake unto Moses face to face, as a man speaketh unto his friend', Exodus xxxiii. 11.

p. 33 l. 4 *many Philosophers.* Thales of Miletus (*c.* 640–550 B.C.) taught that water is the primal substance, out of which all things are composed, and to which they revert. It is improbable that 'many philosophers' accepted Thales's solution, however flattering to anglers.

p. 34 l. 1 *increase.* The plural verb shows that 'offspring' is here the meaning.

l. 6 *the casting off of Lent.* The laws commanding a Lenten fast were not repealed till 1863, but after the Reformation there was considerable laxity in observing them.

l. 7 *given the Lie to*: i.e. 'gone contrary to', but I can find no parallel of this use.

l. 10 *many putrid, shaking, intermitting Agues*. In Walton's time, and (*pace* Walton) for centuries before, London had been a hot-bed of exotic diseases, which culminated in the Great Plague of 1665. Walton, as a member of the Established Church and a friend of many bishops, hardly shrinks from suggesting that the Puritans are the culprits.

l. 14 *in Story*. In history, including contemporary history and books of travel.

l. 16 *the chief diet*. Leviticus xi. 9 and Deuteronomy xiv. 9 ordain that the Israelites may eat all things in the waters that have fins and scales. It is a fisherman's exaggeration to say that fish was to be their chief diet.

l. 19 *the Whale* is not a fish, but a warm-blooded mammal.

l. 21 *The Romans*. Fortunes were squandered in building and maintaining fish-ponds from which to supply their tables. Athenaeus (vii, p. 294 c) tells how the sturgeon was brought in to music by garlanded servants. Enormous sums were paid for single fish. See also Seneca, *Ep.* 95. 42; Juvenal, iv. 15; Macrobius, *Sat.* iii. 16. 9; Pliny, ix. 66–7.

Ambrosius Theodosius Macrobius (fifth century A.D.) wrote *Saturnaliorum Conviviorum Libri Septem*.

For Varro see note to p. 27 l. 10. The reference here is to *De Re Rustica*, iii. 17.

l. 34 *Dr. Wharton*. Thomas Wharton, M.D. (1614–73) discovered the sub-maxillary (Wharton's) gland. As physician to St. Thomas's Hospital, he was one of the few doctors who remained at their posts during the Plague of 1665.

p. 35 l. 19 *St. Jerome* (345 ?–420). Author of the Latin translation of the Bible known as the Vulgate.

l. 23 *the Monuments*. No such monument is known in Rome. At Padua there is a tomb which was long honoured as Livy's, until the progress of scholarship corrected an error in deciphering the inscription.

l. 26 *of Virgil*. Virgil was buried not in Rome, but on the road from Naples to Pozzuoli: a grotto has been shown for more than six centuries as the tomb, but its authenticity is uncertain.

l. 28 *the humble house*. Under the Church of Santa Maria in Via Lata in Rome is a crypt which tradition asserts to have been part of St. Paul's 'own hired house'.

l. 32 *lie buried together*. The body of St. Paul is possibly under the High Altar of the Basilica of St. Paul without the Walls, and his head may be in the Basilica of St. John Lateran, while the tomb of St. Peter is under the High Altar of St. Peter's.

p. 36 l. 4 *the very Sepulchre*. Macarius, a bishop, was commissioned by the Emperor Constantine to find the Holy Sepulchre. For some unknown reason, perhaps a tradition, he decided that it was under a temple of Aphrodite erected in Jerusalem by Hadrian. The temple was removed and a rock-cut Jewish sepulchre was discovered. A magnificent church was built over it, since destroyed by the Turks and built again. The authenticity, however, of the tomb is very doubtful.

l. 14 *to have spoken to a fish*. Jonah ii. 10.

l. 15 *made a whale a ship*. Jonah i. and ii. But 'the great fish' is not said to have been a whale.

l. 22 *except against*. Take exception to.

p. 37 l. 22 *any Hawk you have named*. Auceps, who has now left them, not Venator, gave the list of hawks. See p. 28.

l. 29 *like poetry, men are to be born so*. 'Poeta nascitur, non fit' (proverbial).

l. 33 *wit*. In original sense of 'intellect'.

p. 38 l. 8 *first, for the antiquity*. In the first edition there is a marginal note, 'J. Da. Jer. Mar.,' i.e. John Davors, Jervis (Gervase) Markham.

In *The Secrets of Angling*, by J. D. Esqre (London, 1613), Bk. i, there is a chapter headed 'The Author of Angling',

which describes how, after the great flood, Deucalion and
Pyrrha, his wife, re-peopled the earth by throwing stones
over their shoulders, which immediately became men and
women, and how, to feed this sudden family, Deucalion
was inspired with the idea of angling. The previous
chapter contains the verses on p. 55, which are attributed
by Walton to John Davors. The author's real name was
John Dennys. Nothing is known of him.

The reference to Markham is to *The Pleasures of Princes
or Good Men's Recreations, containing a Discourse of the
generall art of Fishing*, etc. London, 1635, chap. i, § 3,
'The Antiquity of Angling', where Markham reconciles
the various traditions, 'for it is most certaine that both
Ducallion, Saturne and Bellus are taken for figures of
Noah and his family, and the invention of the Art of
Angling is truely sayd to come from the sonnes of Seth,
of which Noah was most principall.'

l. 10 *Belus*. Son of Poseidon, and father of Aegyptus
and Danaus. Markham calls him 'the son of Nimrod'.

l. 14 *Seth*. The son born to Adam after the death of
Abel. Josephus, *Ant.* I. ii. 3, says that the descendants
of Seth inscribed their discoveries on two pillars, one of
which survived in his time.

l. 28 *in the Prophet Amos*, etc. Amos iv. 2 and Job xli. 1.
There are other references to angles and fish-hooks in the
Bible. See Isaiah xix. 8 and Habakkuk i. 15. The Book of
Job has seldom been claimed for Moses.

p. 40 l. 18 *Pet. du Moulin* (1568–1658). Peter du Moulin,
French Protestant divine, who received from James I a
prebend at Canterbury for assisting him in his religious
controversies. His son of the same name was chaplain to
Charles II. Walton refers to a passage in the preface
to *The accomplishment of the Prophecies, Translated out of
the French by J. Heath* (Oxford, 1613).

l. 34 *an ingenuous Spaniard*. Moses Browne, who edited
The Compleat Angler (1750) at Dr. Johnson's suggestion,
says that the reference is to *The Hundred and Ten Con-
siderations of Signor Valdesso*, of which an English

translation by Nicholas Farrar, junior, was published in
1638: but the passage does not appear there.

p. 41 l. 18 *a river in Epirus*. Pliny, *Nat. Hist.* ii. 228,
relates that Jove's fountain at Dodona in Epirus performs
this feat.

l. 20 *Some waters*. Lyncestis causes drunkenness,
Pliny, *Nat. Hist.* ii. 230; but I cannot trace the others.

l. 22 *Selarus*. The Silarus, which forms the boundary of
Campania and Lucania in South Italy. For its petrifying
power, see Pliny, *Nat. Hist.* ii. 226; Strabo, v. 251;
Sil. Ital. viii. 582.

l. 23 *Cambden*. See note to p. 6, l. 23. The English well
is at Knaresborough; there is no mention of a Lochmere in
Camden, but the petrifying properties of Lough Neagh are
mentioned.

l. 25 *river in Arabia*. Lucian, *De Syria Dea*, viii, tells of
a river Adonis rising in Mt Libanus, which turns blood-red
every spring.

l. 27 *Aristotle* (384–322 B.C.). Greek philosopher.
The first edition of *The Compleat Angler* has a marginal
note, 'In his wonders of Nature'. I cannot trace either the
passage in Aristotle or the river.

p. 42 l. 1 *Mole*. It rises near Horley and joins the Thames
at Hampton Court. In dry seasons it disappears for nearly
3 miles, from Burford Bridge to near Leatherhead, being
drained by 2 swallows into an underground course, which,
except in dry seasons, is already full of water.

l. 5 *Anus*. Camden rightly has 'Anas', the ancient name
of the Guadiana, a corruption of Wadi Anas. The Guadiana Alto shortly after leaving the last of the Lagunas de
Ruidera disappears into the ground. The subterranean
course is between 20 and 30 miles long.

l. 8 *Josephus* (A.D. 37–100 ?). *The Jewish War*, vii. 5.

l. 15 *Pliny the philosopher*. C. Plinius Secundus (23–79),
author of the *Natural History*.

l. 17 *Balaena*. Pliny (§ 4) talks of 'ballaenae quaternum
jugerum', 'whales of four acres each'. Walton means

'Whirlpool' as a translation of *Ballaena*. Cf. Job xli. 1, marginal note on Leviathan, 'a whale or a whirlpool;' and in a list of sea-monsters in *The Faerie Queene* (II. xii. 23) comes, 'Great whirlpooles which all fishes make to flee.'

l. 26 *Cadara, an island near this place*. Cadara, says Pliny, is a large peninsula in the Red Sea: 'this place' is the Indian Sea.

p. 43 l. 2 *Dr. Casaubon*. Meric Casaubon (1599–1671), son of Isaac Casaubon, was educated at Eton and Christ Church by command of James I and afterwards took orders. *Of Credulity and Incredulity* (London, 1668), pp. 235–47, relates many tales of dolphins, which the author thinks not improbable.

l. 6 *John Tredescant*. There were two of this name, father and son. The father (d. 1637 ?), a traveller and naturalist, introduced the apricot, and established at Lambeth the first physic garden in England. His son (1608–62) made in Virginia a collection of flowers, plants, and shells, which he kept at Lambeth, and published a catalogue of it called *Museum Tradescantium* (1656). He gave his collection to Elias Ashmole (1617–92), who subsequently presented it to Oxford University as the nucleus of the Ashmolean Museum.

l. 14 *the Hog-fish*. This list of curiosities is presumably drawn from the *Museum Tradescantium*. Hog-fish = scorpion-fish.

l. 15 *Cony-fish*. Burbot. *Parrot-fish*. One of the tropical *Scaridae*.

l. 29 *Mr. George Herbert* (1593–1633). Prebendary of Lincoln and author of *The Temple: Sacred Poems and Private Ejaculations* (1633). These stanzas are 36, 8, and 7, from a poem entitled 'Providence'. Walton, as usual, makes some alterations in the text, of which the chief are l. 7, 'strangely 'for 'strongly', and l. 8, 'end' for 'will'.

l. 34 *ows*. Owns.

p. 44 l. 15 *Pliny says*. *Nat. Hist.* xxxi. 1.

l. 20 *Gesner*   Conrad von Gesner (1516–65) wrote

many works on Natural History, of which *Historia Animalium* was the chief.

Rondelitius. Guillaume Rondelet (1507–66), French naturalist, wrote *De Piscibus Marinis* (1554) and *Universae Aquatilium Historiae pars altera* (1555).

Ausonius. Decimus Magnus Ausonius, a fourth-century poet. His tenth Idyll, 'Mosella', is a *locus classicus* on fishes.

l. 23 *divine Dubartas.* Guillaume de Salluste du Bartas (1544?–90), a Gascon poet. His poem in seven books on the Creation was translated by Joshua Sylvester as *Du Bartas his Divine Weekes and Workes.* His fish lore is largely drawn from the *Halieutica* of Oppian (second century A.D.). The present extract is adapted from The fifth Day of the first Week, ll. 30–48.

l. 26 *we may see all creatures.* Many of these marine counterparts of things in heaven and on earth are well known (e.g. stars and horses), but some of them (e.g. Rooks, Stares, Roses and Vines) do not appear to be known to modern naturalists.

l. 30 *Stares.* Starlings.

p. 45 l. 4 *the mitred Bishop.* Rondeletius, *De Piscibus Marinis*, xvi, ch. 21, tells how in 1531 a marine monster resembling a bishop was caught in Poland and taken to the King; and in xvi, ch. 20, how a monster 'humana facie, sed rustica et agresti, capite raso et levi', and with something like a monk's cowl on its shoulders, was caught in Norway, as was proved by a picture of it given to the author by Queen Margaret of Navarre.

l. 6 *Polonian.* Polish.

l. 14 *The Cuttle-fish will cast a long gut.* From Montaigne's 'An Apologie of Raymond Sebond' (*Essayes*, Bk. II, ch. xii), where Aristotle is given as the authority, but the true reference is Plutarch, *De Sollertia Animalium*, ch. xxvi. It is not the cuttle-fish, but the angler-fish or sea-devil (*Lophius piscatorius*) which has this gift.

l. 25 *a Hermit.* See Du Bartas, *ubi supra*, ll. 388 sqq.

l. 31 *Aelian.* A Roman writer of the third century A.D.

His *De Animalium Natura*, written in Greek, is a collection of anecdotes about animals, drawn from various authors. His account of the Adonis is in Bk. ix, ch. 36.

p. 46 l. 7 *the Sargus*. A sea-bream. See Du Bartas, *ubi supra*, ll. 195–200.

l. 22 *the Cantharus*. The black sea-bream. See Du Bartas, *ubi supra*, ll. 201–4.

p. 47 l. 1 *the Thracian women*. Du Bartas (*ubi supra*, ll. 209–12) has this simile of the mullets:

> As yerst those famous, loving Thracian Dames
> That leapt alive into the funerall flames
> Of their dead Husbands; who deceast and gone,
> Those loyal wives hated to live alone.

See also Montaigne's 'An Apologie of Raymond Sebond' (*Essayes*, Bk. II, ch. xii).

l. 18 *But for chaste love*. Du Bartas, *ubi supra*, ll. 205–8. *Pheer* = fere = mate; *prest* = ready (Fr. *prêt*).

l. 26 *senseless*. Without sense, i.e. feeling.

l. 34 *as his Father had done Job*. I cannot find that God ever quoted Job as a pattern of patience. Walton probably had in mind James v. 11, where St. James takes him 'for an example of patience'.

p. 48 l. 2 *flags*. Flat stones, suitable for paving.

l. 8 *the Spawner and the Melter*. The female and male fish. The spawner lays her spawn or eggs, and the melter (more generally 'milter') drops his milt upon them and fertilizes them.

l. 18 *They that occupy*. Psalm cvii. 23, 24.

l. 30 *a power to speak all languages*. Walton refers to the miracle of Pentecost, Acts ii.

p. 49 l. 5 *as he did the Scribes*. Luke xi. 44.

l. 6 *and the Mony-changers*. Matthew xxi. 13; Mark xi. 17.

l. 19 *the Catalogue of his twelve Apostles*. Matthew x. 2–4.

l. 25 *at his Transfiguration*. Matthew xvii. 1–8; Mark

ix. 2–8; Luke ix. 28–36. The three were Peter, James, and John.

p. 50 l. 11 *his beloved had Eyes*. Song of Solomon vii. 4.

l. 16 *who was a shepherd*. Amos i. 1.

l. 18 *fish-hooks*. See note to p. 38, l. 28.

l. 19 *meek Moses*. Numbers xii. 3. For *friend of God*, see note to p. 32, l. 34.

l. 34 *our Saviour's bidding*. Matthew xvii. 27.

p. 51 l. 4 *the Voyages of Ferdinand Mendez Pinto*. Pinto (1510–83), a Portuguese by birth, spent most of his life in China, Japan, etc., as soldier, sailor, merchant, doctor, missionary, and ambassador. For a year he was a member of the Society of Jesus. His *Peregrination* (1614: first complete English translation 1663) was once proverbial for mendacity, but it is now known for a careful and truthful narrative.

l. 10 *used Angling as a principal recreation*. Plutarch's *Antony* in the *Parallel Lives*. Antony went fishing with Cleopatra and, ashamed of catching nothing, secretly ordered fishermen to dive and put fresh-taken fishes on his hook. Cleopatra, detecting the deceit, invited a large company to the next day's fishing and instructed a servant to fix a salted fish upon the hook.

l. 15 *Ecclesiastical Canons*. The laws of the Church, especially the decrees of Popes and statutes of Councils. The Canon referred to is found in the *Corpus Iuris Canonici* of Gregory XIII (1682), Dist. lxxxvi, ch. 11 (American Editor).

l. 22 *Perkins*. William Perkins (1558–1602), an eminent Puritan theologian. I cannot find among his works his commendation of angling.

l. 24 *Dr. Whitaker*. William Whitaker (1548–95), Regius Professor of Divinity at Cambridge. See Fuller's *Holy State*, iii. 13: 'Fishing with an angle is to some rather a torture than a pleasure, to stand an hour as mute as the fish thev mean to take: yet herewithal Dr. Whitaker was much delighted.'

l. 29 *Dr. Nowel.* Alexander Nowell, D.D. (1507–1602), became a Fellow of Brasenose College, Oxford, in 1526, Principal in 1555, and Dean of St. Paul's in 1560. His monument was destroyed in the burning of old St. Paul's in the Great Fire of London (1666), but the picture of which Walton speaks is still at Brasenose, and a replica is at Westminster School, of which he was a master in 1543.

p. 52 l. 2 *a Catechism.* Nowell published A Catechism, A Middle Catechism, and a Small Catechism. 'It seems clear that Nowell was the author of the first part of the Church Catechism now in use, which was first published in the Prayer Book of 1549, the later portion on the Sacraments afterwards (1604) added, as is generally held, by Bishop Overall, having been reduced and altered from Nowell's' (*Dict. Nat. Biog.*).

p. 53 l. 11 *Sir Henry Wotton.* See note to p. 4, l. 10.
l. 17 *censurer.* See note to p. 7, l. 22.

p. 54 l. 7 *This day dame Nature.* Slightly adapted from a poem which appears in the *Reliquiae Wottonianae* (see note to p. 4, l. 10) under the title, 'On a Banck as I sate a fishing, A description of the spring.'
l. 10 *valentines.* Sweethearts chosen on February 14 (St. Valentine's Day). Cf. Chaucer, *Parliament of Fowls*, 310.
l. 14 *his trembling quill*: i.e. the float of his fishing line, generally made of a quill.
l. 16 *the swift Pilgrim.* The house-martin.
l. 18 *Philomel.* Nightingale.
l. 23 *foot-ball swain.* Football has been a popular English game for five centuries. Walton no doubt knew of the Shrove Tuesday game in Ashbourne.
l. 24 *strokes a syllabub.* A dish made by mixing wine or cider with cream or milk and thus forming a soft curd. 'Strokes' presumably means that she whips the mixture with her own hand.
l. 35 *Jo. Davors, Esq.* See note to p. 38, l. 8. Walton has made considerable alterations in the poem.

p. 55 l. 16 *gander-grass.* A corruption of 'gandergoose':

the ragwort or *Senecio jacobaea.*

culver-keys. In the seventeenth century the bluebell, now generally the cowslip or oxlip.

l. 23–4. *Aurora ... Tithonus.* Aurora, the Dawn-Goddess, was the wife of Tithonus. Every morning she rose from his couch and drove her chariot to heaven to announce the coming of the light.

l. 28 *veins.* Watersheds.

p. 56 l. 1 *Flora.* Goddess of flowers in Latin mythology.

p. 57 l. 19 *Lady-smocks.* Cuckoo-flowers.

l. 25 *compliment.* Exchange compliments.

p. 58 l. 16 *a beast or a fish.* Topsell decides that the otter is all flesh, while the beaver is flesh except its tail, which is fish. See p. 572 of his *Historie of Foure-footed Beastes*, (*1607*).

l. 18 *the Colledge of Carthusians.* According to Gesner, *Hist. An.* I. 777 (quoted by Topsell), they eat otter, although forbidden to eat all manner of flesh.

l. 30 *dog-fisher.* The Latin names are *Lutra* and *Fluviatilis Canicula*, 'Dog of the Waters' (Topsell, p. 572).

l. 32 *Gesner.* See note to p. 44, l. 15. This is not in Gesner's account of the otter (Bk. i, pp. 775–7), though Topsell (*l.c.*, p. 574) gives him as his authority for saying that an otter can smell a fish 'a mile or two off'.

l. 33 *falling sickness.* Epilepsy.

l. 34 *Benione.* Benzoin (popularly, Benjamin), a resinous substance, with a fragrant odour and slightly aromatic taste, obtained from the *Styrax benzoin*, a tree of Sumatra, Java.

p. 59 l. 6 *Ottersey.* The Ottery, in Devonshire.

l. 10 *at vent.* Risen to the surface to take air.

p. 60 l. 5 *Mr. Nich. Seagrave.* Nothing is known of him.

l. 12 *Old Rose.* The song alluded to was the following. It was inserted in Dr Harrington's *Collection* from a publication *temp.* Charles I:

Now we're met like jovial fellows,

>   Let us do as wise men tell us,
>   Sing Old Rose and burn the bellows;
>   Let us do as wise men tell us,
>   Sing, etc.
>
>   When the jowl with claret glows,
>   And wisdom shines upon the nose,
>   O then's the time to sing Old Rose,
>   And burn, burn, the bellows,
>   The bellows, and burn, burn, the bellows, the bellows.
>   Sir Harris Nicolas.

p. 61 l. 2 *the fence-months*. Months in which rivers are in fence – under a prohibition. See below, ll. 10 sqq.

l. 5 *make conscience of*. Make it a matter of conscience to keep. See note to p. 34, l. 6.

l. 19 *13th of Edward the First*. 'That the waters of Humber, Owse, Trent, Done, Arre, Derwent, Wherfe, Nid, Yore, Swale, Tese, Tine, Eden, and other waters (wherein Salmons be taken within the kingdom) shall be in defence for taking Salmons from the Nativity of Our Lady unto St. Martin's Day; and that likewise young Salmons shall not be taken nor destroyed by nets, nor by other engines, at mill-pools, from the midst of April unto the Nativity of St. John the Baptist.' 13th Edw. I, stat. 1, cap. 47.

l. 20 *Rich. the II*. 13 Rich. II, stat. 1, cap. 19, rehearses and confirms the earlier statute.

l. 28 *conservators*. Persons having charge of a river and supervision of its fisheries, navigation, water-mills, etc. The best known are the Conservators of the Thames, called as a body the Thames Conservancy.

l. 34 *in the Levitical law*. Deuteronomy xxii. 6.

p. 62 l. 4 *the Gorrara*. Unidentified. Caracara?

l. 5 *the Puet*. The Peewit or Lapwing.

the Craber. Water-rat. The word is only found in this passage.

l. 22 *Trout Hall*. They did not sleep at Trout Hall, but returned to the ale-house where they dined, which we are told later was Bleak Hall (p. 80, l. 15). Trout Hall cannot be identified.

p. 63 l. 3 *Many a one.* I cannot trace this quotation.

p. 65 l. 25 *eat.* Intrans.: now a conscious archaism.

l. 30 *short.* Crumbling bread.

l. 31 *Un Villain.* So Rondeletius, *Univ. Aquat. Hist. pars alt.* (1555), p. 190.

p. 66 l. 11 *verjuice.* An acid liquor pressed out of crab-apples, unripe grapes, etc.

p. 68 l. 11 *leather-mouth'd.* Explained at p. 69, ll. 18–19.

l. 24 *towardly.* Apt.

l. 34 *Bob.* The grub or larva of a beetle.

p. 69 l. 2 *a Gentle.* A maggot, the larva of the blue-bottle.

l. 3 *cod-worm . . . case-worm.* Both = Caddis-worm, the larva of the caddis fly.

p. 70 l. 25 *Penk.* Now survives as 'pink' in some dialects.

l. 32 *his spawn.* The soft roe of the male.

p. 71 l. 7 *Seneca.* The passage is in *Natural Questions,* iii. 17, which Walton found in Hakewill's *Apologie of the power and providence of God in the Government of the World* (3rd ed., 1635), Bk. iv, p. 433.

l. 28 *generous.* Of good stock; Lat. *generosus.*

l. 31 *Gesner. Hist. Anim.* iv, De piscium et Aquatilium natura (1558), p. 1203, l. 62.

p. 72 l. 19 *three Cubits.* Gesner (*ubi supra,* p. 1201) says two cubits.

l. 21 *Mercator* (1512–94). The Dutch geographer who first constructed marine charts on the system known as Mercator's Projection.

l. 26 *a little Brook in Kent.* Perhaps the Cray, which is famous for small trout.

l. 29 *about the size of a Gudgeon.* The gudgeon is rarely more than eight inches long.

l. 30 *as Winchester*: i.e. as the Itchen at Winchester.

l. 32 *Samlet*. A contracted diminutive of 'salmon'. The samlet or skegger is a young salmon that has not gone down to the sea.

p. 73 l. 4 *a Fordidge Trout*. Fordwich, a village in Kent upon the river Stour, 2 miles ENE of Canterbury.

l. 10 *Sir George Hastings* (d. 1657). Son of Henry Hastings, the Dorsetshire sporting squire. His odd old-fashioned ways were described by the first Earl of Shaftesbury, whose account of him was first printed 1753, reprinted in *The Connoisseur*, No. 81, 1755.

l. 26 *in the Psalms*. Psalm cxlvii. 9.

l. 31 *the Stork . . . knows his season*. Jeremiah viii. 7.

p. 74 l. 6 *Shelsey*. Now Selsey: i.e. of Selsey Bill.

l. 8 *Amerly*. Now Amberley.

l. 12 *Swallows and Bats*. Walton's own note refers to his *Natural History*.

l. 21 *Albertus*. Albertus Magnus (1193?–1280), a learned student of Theology and Physics; his works fill twenty-one volumes. Quoted by Topsell (*Hist. of Serpents*, 1608, p. 180), he says that the common frogs 'in the month of August, never open their mouthes, either to take in meate or drinke, or to utter any voyce, and their chaps are so fast joyned or closed together, that you can hardly open them with your finger, or with a sticke'.

l. 32 *birds of Paradise, and the Camelion*. See Du Bartas, I. vi. Sir Thos. Browne, in his *Vulgar Errors*, has a chapter on this alleged peculiarity of the chameleon; the belief arose from the fact that it can go as much as four months without food, and that it has the power of inflating not merely its lungs, but its whole body, including its tail and feet.

p. 75 l. 14 *Sir Francis Bacon* (1561–1626). The most learned English philosopher of his time. The reference is to his *History of Life and Death* (Bacon's *Works*, ed. Spedding, vol. ii, p. 128, § 47).

p. 76 l. 32 *hogback*. The ideal hog's back rises gradually

from the head to a point in its middle and then falls as gradually towards the tail, the flanks falling away sharply on either side of the line.

p. 77 l. 12 *Helmits*. The helmet pigeon has the plumage of its head of a different colour from that of its body.

l. 13 *Croper*. More properly 'cropper', the pouter pigeon.

l. 14 *the Royal Society*. Founded in 1660. The publication referred to is 'A Table of Spiders found in England by Dr. M. Lister' (*Philosophical Transactions*, vi, 2170–6, 1671).

p. 78 l. 9 *the sleight*. The feat of skill.

l. 23 *a Catch*. A short composition for three or more voices, which sing the same melody, the second singer beginning the first line as the first goes on to the second line, and so with each successive singer. 'Three Blind Mice' is the best known today.

l. 26 *A match*. Agreed.

p. 79 l. 2 *have with you*. It apparently means 'Lend a hand here'.

l. 3 *loggerheaded*: i.e. with head out of proportion to its body.

l. 21 *securely*. Without care.

l. 28 *I was for that time*. I cannot trace this quotation.

p. 80 l. 4 *that smooth song*. Stanzas 1, 2, 3, and 5 of the Milk-maid's Song first appeared in the *Passionate Pilgrim* (1599); and with the addition of stanzas 4 and 7 in *England's Helicon* (1600) with the author's initials. The sixth stanza first appeared in the second edition of *The Compleat Angler* (1655).

l. 6 *sung an answer*. 'The Milk-maid's Mother's Answer' was in the same collection, but is by an unknown writer. Raleigh (1552–1618) wrote a response to Marlowe's poem, in *England's Helicon*.

l. 15 *Bleak-Hall*. A rural inn on the banks of the river Lea, about a mile from Edmonton.

l. 22 *a Sillybub of new Verjuice*. See notes to p. 54, l. 24, and p. 66, l. 11.

l. 34 *Come, Shepherds*. A copy of this song was sold among the collection of Richard Heber in 1834, and was afterwards printed by Pickering. – Jesse. A song 'Come shepherds deck your heads' is in MS. Ashmole 38, in the Bodleian Library.

p. 81 l. 1 *As at noon*. An early seventeenth-century song: see Percy's *Reliques*, Vol. III, book ii, No. 21.

l. 2 *Phillida flouts me*. Ritson's *Ancient Songs* (1792), p. 235.

Chevy Chase. Not the old historical ballad, but a modernized and popular version of James I's reign. Percy's *Reliques*, Vol. I, book iii, No. 1 and Child's *English and Scottish Popular Ballads*, No. 162.

Johnny Armstrong. Child, No. 169.

l. 3 *Troy Town*. A sixteenth-century ballad in Percy's *Reliques*, Vol. III, book ii, No. 22.

l. 27 *Kirtle*. A skirt or outer petticoat.

p. 82 l. 15 *our good Queen Elizabeth*. 'She hearing upon a time out of hir garden at Woodstocke, a certeine milk-maid singing pleasantlie, wished hir selfe to be a milke-maid as she was, saieng that hir case was better, and life more merier than was hirs in that state as she was.' Holin-shed's *Chronicles of England* (new edn., 1808), vol. iv, p. 133. This was during Elizabeth's imprisonment at Woodstock in the last year of Queen Mary's reign.

l. 20 *Sir Thomas Overbury* (1581–1613). Friend and adviser of James I's favourite, Robert Carr, afterwards Earl of Somerset. The Countess of Essex, whose marriage with Carr he opposed, contrived to have him imprisoned in the Tower, and there slowly poisoned. Two years later the plot was discovered, and she and Carr were tried and convicted (1616), but pardoned in 1621. This wish occurs at the end of a 'Fair and Happy Milkmaid' in Overbury's *Characters, or Witty Descriptions of the Properties of Sundry Persons*.

p. 83 ll. 1–2 *fields . . . yields*. Abbott's *Shakesperian Grammar* gives a large number of instances of third persons plural of verbs in -*s*. This inflection probably arose from the northern Early English third person plural in -*s*.

l. 4 *fall*. Autumn.

l. 28 *I married a Wife*. These stanzas come from two different songs among the Roxburghe collection of broadsides in the British Museum. Both are signed M. P., probably Martin Parker (d. 1656 ?), according to Dryden the best ballad writer of his time, and author of 'When the King enjoyes his owne again.'

The first stanza is the first five lines of 'Keep a good tongue in your head' to the tune of 'The Milkmaids'. The second is the last eight lines of stanza 6 of 'The Milke-Maid's Life' to a curious new tune called 'The Milke-maid's Dumps'. See J. P. Collier's *Book of Roxburghe Ballads* (1847).

p. 84 l. 1 *the green-sickness*. 'Chlorosis,' an anaemic disease which affects growing girls and gives a greenish tinge to the complexion.

l. 11 *let Maudlin alone*. Editors have feared that Venator tried to reward her with a kiss.

l. 28 *daping*. To dap, dape, dib, or dibble is to fish by letting the bait dip and bob lightly on the water.

p. 86 l. 33 *'Tis merry in Hall*. See *The Oxford Dictionary of English Proverbs*.

p. 87 l. 1 *Mr. William Basse* (d. 1653 ?), published three volumes of poetry in his lifetime. 'The Angler's Song' is given below, 'The Hunter in his cariere' is 'Maister Basse, his careere, or the new huntsman'. His *Poetical Works* were edited by R. Warwick Bond, 1893. Sir Harris Nicolas identifies 'Tom of Bedlam' with a song of that name in Percy's *Reliques*, II. iii, 19, but many other ballads bear that name.

l. 21 *draw cuts*. To draw lots, by each person drawing a stick or straw from a bundle held with only one end exposed, the shortest or longest being the decisive 'cut'.

l. 26 *Coridon's Song*. John Chalkhill was identified by P. J. Croft in an article in *T.L.S.* 27 June 1958. He went up to Trinity College, Cambridge in 1610 and was presumably born *c.* 1595; he died in 1642 and was buried at St. Margaret's, Westminster. A sister, Martha, was stepmother to Walton's second wife, Ann Ken, and no doubt was the source of Walton's knowledge of his poetry, though he did not marry Ann Ken until more than five years after Chalkhill's death. In 1683 Walton published Chalkhill's 'Pastoral History', *Thealma and Clearchus*, with a preface dated five years earlier. (See George Saintsbury: *Minor Poets of the Caroline Period*, ii. 367–443.) For another song by Chalkhill, see p. 185.

p. 88 l. 14 *russet*. A coarse country-made cloth, originally so called from the russet or reddish-brown colour of much cloth of this quality.

l. 34 *roundelaies*. Songs in which an idea or line or refrain is continually repeated.

p. 89 l. 27 *The Angler's Song*. See note to p. 87, l. 1.

p. 90 l. 34 *fishers of men*. Matthew iv. 18, 19; Mark i. 16, 17.

p. 91 ll. 3–4 *fish the last Food was*. Luke xxiv. 42–3.
l. 14 *prevent*. Anticipate.

p. 92 l. 13 *Excrements*. See note to p. 26, l. 12.
l. 33 *the bark of the Tanners*. The bark of the oak, willow, chestnut, etc., contains tannin or tannic acid, which is used for turning skins into leather.

p. 94 l. 18 *a running line*. 'The running-line, so called because it runs along the ground, is made of strong silk . . . and is thus fitted up. About ten inches from the end, fasten a small cleft shot: then make a hole through a pistol, or musket, bullet according to the swiftness of the stream you fish in: and put the line through it, and draw the bullet down to the shot: to the end of your line fasten an Indian grass, or silk-worm gut, with a large hook.' – Sir John

Hawkins, 1808.

l. 29 *arming*. The barb.

p. 95 l. 13 *distempered*: i.e. not temperate, excessive.

l. 26 *beard*. The barb of the hook.

p. 96 l. 8 *Sticklebag*. Corruption of 'stickle-back'.

l. 12 *bay-salt*. Salt obtained in large crystals, by slow evaporation from sea-water by the sun's heat.

l. 22 *sad*: dark or deep.

p. 97 l. 20 *the Palmer-flie or worm*. A name for various hairy caterpillars of migratory habits, like the pilgrims, who were called palmers because they bore palm-branches or palm-leaves as a sign that they had visited Palestine.

l. 29 *Pliny holds*. *Nat. Hist.* xi. 112. Topsell, in his *History of Serpents* (1608), p. 107, where he refers to this passage, gives the correct story of the caterpillar as the opinion of 'othersome', 'but I am of opinion, that not only this, but by divers other wayes and meanes, they may proceede and increase.'

l. 33 *Coleworts*. Any plants of the cabbage kind.

p. 98 l. 7 *Topsel*. *History of Serpents* (1608), p. 103.

l. 18 *a green Caterpillar*. 'The caterpillar of the privet hawk moth (*Sphinx ligustri*), which is not, as Walton suspects, a "fly of prey", or dragonfly.' – Rennie.

l. 19 *Peascod*. The pod of the pea.

p. 99 l. 6 *Aldrovandus*. *De Insectis* (1602), Lib. ii, p. 275. Ulysses Aldrovandus (1524 ?–1607), a famous naturalist of Bologna. His *Natural History* is in thirteen volumes.

l. 7 *Topsel*. *History of Serpents* (1608), p. 105.

l. 22 *one of them*. Walton takes this description (as indeed most of his dissertation on caterpillars) almost word for word from Topsell. 'From the description, this would seem to be the caterpillar of the Puss Moth.' – Harting. Walton refers the reader to Experiments 728 and 90 of Bacon's *Natural History*. Exp. 728, 'Touching Caterpillars', asserts that caterpillars are bred from dew and leaves, but see note to p. 97, l. 29. Exp. 90, 'Touching

Induration of Bodies', how the body turns its food into bone, though none of its food is so hard as bone, does not seem to illustrate this paragraph.

l. 24 *punctually*. To the point, exactly.

p. 100 l. 2 *Aurelia*. Chrysalis.

l. 14 *Du Bartas*. See note to p. 44, l. 23. This is the ending of the sixth Day of the first Week.

l. 19 *So the cold humor*. Moisture. Though not the offspring of cold mists, the salamander, which is nearly allied to the newt, is only found in damp places.

l. 24 *The fly Perausta*. A misprint in the fifth edition for 'Pyrausta', a fabulous insect; cf. Pliny, *Nat. Hist.* xi. 36, where he talks of a four-legged winged creature, called *pyrallis* or *pyrota*, with the same qualities.

l. 27 *So slow Boôtes*. Walton's note refers the reader to Camden's *Britannia* and to Gerarde's *Herbal* (1597), Bk. iii, ch. 167: 'Of the Goose tree, Barnakle tree, or the tree bearing Geese.' 'There are founde in the north parts of Scotland, and the Ilands adjacent, called Orchades, certaine trees, whereon doe growe certaine shell fishes, of a white colour tending to russet; wherein are conteined little living creatures: which shels in time of maturitie doe open, and out of them grow those little living things; which falling into water, doe become foules, whom we call Barnakles, in the North of England Brant Geese, and in Lancashire tree Geese: but the other that do fall upon the land, perish and come to nothing.'

slow Boôtes. A northern constellation, the Wagoner, situated at the tail of the Great Bear.

p. 101 l. 11 *powder'd Beef*. Salted or pickled beef.

p. 102 l. 13 *their Lecturer*. One of a class of preachers in the Church of England, usually chosen by the parish and supported by voluntary contributions, whose duty consists mainly in delivering afternoon or evening 'lectures'.

p. 103 l. 16 *devout Lessius* (1554–1623). Flemish Jesuit. An English translation of his *Hygiasticon, or, The right course of preserving Life and Health unto extream old Age,* appeared at Cambridge in 1634: it demonstrates the physical, moral, and intellectual benefits of a moderate diet.

p. 104 l. 1 *an ingenuous brother of the Angle*. Whoever gave Walton these directions, had read very carefully 'A Treatyse of Fysshynge' by Dame Juliana Berners, in the *Book of St. Albans* printed at Westminster by Wynkyn de Worde in 1496. Both the names of the twelve flies and the directions for making them correspond almost word for word with her list.

l. 10 *in March*. N.B. – Throughout this book the months are given in the old style, and so during Walton's life were ten or eleven days earlier than ours.

l. 24 *hackle*. The long shining feathers on the neck of certain birds, as the domestic cock, peacock, pigeon.

l. 26 *herl*. A fibre of the shaft of a feather, especially of the peacock or ostrich, used in making artificial flies.

l. 30 *list*. Border.

l. 31 *braked hemp*. Hemp beaten and crushed.

l. 33 *mail*. The breast-feathers.

p. 105 l. 2 *the wings made contrary one against the other*. Dame Juliana has 'the wynges contrary eyther ayenst other', which seems to mean on opposite sides of the body.

l. 17 *Mr. Thomas Barker*. Author of *The Art of Angling* (1651). He came from Bracemeol in Shropshire, and lived at Westminster. Walton makes very free use of Barker's pamphlet, both here and in other passages.

l. 29 *cast*. Contrive.

p. 106 l. 13 *in your own reason*. In your own judgement.

l. 22 *a Plover's top*. His crest.

l. 24 *Crewel*. A thin worsted yarn.

p. 108 l. 2 *in Lapland*. 'They tye three knottes on a strynge hangyng at a whyp. When they lose one of these they rayse tollerable wynds. When they lose an other the wynde is more vehement; but by losing the thyrd they rayse playne tempestes as in old tyme they were accustomed to rayse thunder and lyghtnyng.' (Richard Eden, *Hist. of Travayle*, 1577.)

l. 8 *a smoaking showre*. Walton perhaps means a short shower which would be followed by sunshine, causing the earth to steam.

l. 15 *When the wind is South*. This is to be found in J. S. Halliwell's *Popular Rhymes*, where it is said to be derived from Oxfordshire, but it is known throughout Great Britain in a variety of forms.

l. 20 *as Solomon observes*. Ecclesiastes xi. 4.

l. 25 *there is no good horse*. Given in John Ray's *Collection of Proverbs* (1742) as, 'A good horse cannot be of a bad colour.'

p. 109 l. 3 *May-butter*. 'If during the month of May before you salt your butter you save a lump thereof and put it into a vessell, and so set it into the sunne the space of that moneth, you shall find it exceeding medicinable for wounds.' *Eng. Housew.* (1615), II. iv. 113. Walton probably means that the rain was as thick as this popular medicine.

l. 21 *Mr. Barker*. In his *Art of Angling*. See note to p. 105, l. 17.

l. 31 *Magazine-bag*. Cf. Chetham's *Angler's Vade-mecum* (1681), 'The Angler must always have in readiness a large Magazine Bag or Budget plentifully furnished with the following materials.'

p. 110 l. 19 *dape or dop*. See note to p. 84, l. 28.

l. 30 *holy Mr. Herbert*. See note to p. 43, l. 29. This poem, entitled 'Vertue', is No. 61 of *The Temple*. There are three unimportant errors in the transcript.

p. 111 l. 11 *closes*. The conclusions of musical phrases, themes, or movements: cadences.

l. 30 *a reverend and learned divine*. Christopher Harvie (1595–1663), author of *The Synagogue*, a series of devotional poems appended anonymously to the 1640 edition of Herbert's *Temple*. Walton wrote some commendatory verses for the fourth edition of *The Synagogue*, and Harvie for the 1655 edition of *The Compleat Angler* (see above, p. 10).

p. 113 l. 3 *bears the bell*. Takes the first place.

l. 8 *an even lay*. Bet.

l. 11 *to Use*. At usury: i.e. lend it at interest.

l. 15 *Virgils Tityrus and his Melibœus*. The scene of the first eclogue, a pastoral dialogue between Tityrus and Meliboeus, is *patulae sub tegmine fagi*, 'under cover of a broad beech-tree'.

l. 24 *Dr. Boteler*. 'The person here mentioned I take to be Dr. William Butler, an eminent physician of our author's time, styled by Fuller in his *Worthies* (Suffolk, 67) the Aesculapius of the age: he invented a medical drink called "Dr. Butler's Ale", which, if not now, was a very few years ago sold at certain houses in London, that had his head for sign.' – Sir John Hawkins (1808).

l. 31 *as Charles the Emperor did*. Presumably the Emperor Charles V, who took Florence by siege in 1530; but I cannot find any reference.

p. 114 l. 14 *my Kenna*. His second wife, Anne Ken, whom he married in 1646. She was half-sister to the famous bishop.

Like Hermit poor. The words of this song appear in the *Phoenix' Nest* (1593). Nicholas Lanier (1588–1666), the buyer of pictures, etc., for Charles I's fine collection, set it to music, which he published in *Select Musical Ayres and Dialogues* (1653). The music is given in Sir John Hawkins's edition of the *Comp. Ang*.

l. 22 *my Bryan*. Presumably his dog, named perhaps after Brian Duppa (1588–1662), Bishop of Winchester, or after Brian Walton (1600 ?–1661), Bishop of Chester, apparently no relation of our author.

l. 23 *Shawford-brook*. 'The name of that part of the river Sow that runs through the land which Walton bequeathed to the Corporation of Stafford to find coals for the poor: the right of fishery attaches to this little estate. Shawford, or Shallow-ford, is a liberty in the parish of St.

Mary, Stafford, though five miles distant from the town.'–
Sir Henry Ellis (1815).

l. 30 *composure*. Composition.

p. 115 l. 7 *Legerdemain*. Conjuring tricks.

l. 30 *so very a Gypsie*. So clever a man of business.

p. 116 l. 16 *these last twenty years*. A reference to the
quarrels between Charles I and his Parliament and his
subjects about ship-money, impositions, etc., which re-
sulted in the Great Rebellion.

l. 20 *our late English Gusman*. The English Gusman; or
the History of that unparalleled Thief, James Hind, written by
G[eorge] F[idge], was published in 1652. Hind had been
arrested by order of Parliament in 1651. The original
Gusman was the hero of *The Life of Guzman d'Alfarache*,
which had been translated from the Spanish of Mateo
Aleman into most European tongues, and into English in
1630.

l. 26 *to rip a Cloak, or to unrip*. 'Rip' and 'unrip' have
exactly the same meaning.

p. 117 l. 3 *Schismatick*. One who separates from an
existing church on account of a difference of opinion.
Walton is having another fling at Presbyterians, Inde-
pendents, etc.; cf. note to p. 34, l. 10.

l. 9 *Father Clause*. See *The Beggars' Bush*, not by Ben
Jonson, but by John Fletcher (1576–1625). Gerrard, the
father of Florez, the rightful Earl of Flanders, disguises
himself as a beggar with the name of Clause, and is
elected King of the Beggars at the Beggars' Bush near
Bruges.

l. 16 *draw cuts*. See note to p. 87, l. 21.

l. 20 *Frank Davison* (1575–1619 ?). He published in 1602
A Poetical Rhapsody, a collection of poems partly by him-
self. This 'Song in Praise of a Beggar's Life' was by one
A. W., whose identity is unknown.

l. 22 *burthen*. Burden = refrain.

l. 27 *clappers*. Rattles used by beggars to attract
attention.

p. 118 l. 7 *A hundred herds of black and white.* Sc. 'cattle': metaphorical here for insects.

l. 1 *within the bent of my Rod*: i.e. I would not have let him get away so far that the rod was pulled down into a straight line with the fishing-line.

l. 3 *an ell long.* The English ell is 45 inches.

l. 7 *casting it to him.* A fisherman, finding an obstacle on the bank after he had hooked his fish, has sometimes flung his rod into the river and waded in for it below the obstacle; this seems to have been the device habitually adopted by Piscator with big fish, though it did not meet with Cotton's approval; see below, p. 314, l. 10.

l. 17 *Hares change Sexes every year.* Topsell, *Hist. of Foure-footed Beastes* (1607), p. 266, states this theory as held by 'the common sort of people' and some learned men (Blondus, Aelian, etc.), but dismisses it.

l. 21 *Dr. Mer. Casaubon.* See note to p. 43, l. 2. Casaubon (*Of Credulity and Incredulity*, p. 252) rejects Peucerus's statement, and points out that Herodotus (iv. 105) also rejected similar stories, though many swore to them. Gaspar Peucer (1525–1602) – 'Peuseus' – wrote much on geometry, theology, and medicine.

p. 120 l. 5 *leaves a false quarter.* In farriery a quarter is one side of a horse's hoof. A false quarter is a rift in the hoof.

l. 29 *some swift.* Johnson defines this 'the current of a stream' (*Walton*).

p. 121 l. 7 *form.* The lair in which a hare crouches.

l. 15 *at the snap*: i.e. (strike) at the first touch of the fish.

l. 33 *Gesner observes.* See p. 58, l. 32, and note.

p. 122 l. 1 *Sir Francis Bacon. Nat. Hist.*, Exper. 792.

l. 8 *He also offers. Ibid.*

l. 26 *Doctor Hackwell.* George Hakewill (1578–1649) D.D., Rector of Exeter College, Oxford. He wrote numerous works of a religious nature, which Boswell mentions as having helped to form Dr. Johnson's style. Both the reference to Pliny (*Nat. Hist.* x. 193) and the quotation of a translation from Martial appear on p. 434 of his *Apologie of the power and providence of God in the Government of the World* (1635), IV, vii. § 6.

l. 31 *St. James tells us.* James iii. 7.

l. 32 *Pliny tells us. Nat. Hist.* ix. 172. The reference in the text is probably a misprint for 55, that being the number of the chapter; the references given here are throughout to the sections.

p. 123 l. 5 *Martial.* Bk. IV, Epig. 30. The sovereign was the Emperor Domitian, the fishes lampreys, and the scene his fish-ponds at Baiae.

p. 124 l. 3 *with Solomon.* Ecclesiastes iii. 11.

l. 15 *differ as the Herring and Pilcher.* The Pilchard is closely allied to the Herring, but smaller and rounder in form.

l. 18 *Aldrovandus.* See note to p. 99, l. 6. *De Piscibus* (1613), Bk. V, ch. xiv, p. 593.

Gesner says. See *Hist. Anim.* iv, p. 1234, where it is given as the opinion of Bellonius.

l. 24 *Un Umble Chevalier.* Rondeletius, *Univ. Aquat. Hist. pars alt.* (1555), p. 160. See note to p. 44, l. 15.

p. 125 l. 14 *Salvian.* Ippolito Salviani (1514–72), physician to Pope Julius III and author of *Aquatilium Animalium Historia* (1554). The reference is p. 115 of that work, quoted by Aldrovandus, *De Piscibus*, i, p. 79.

l. 18 *St. Ambrose* (340 ?–397). Bishop of Milan, one of the four Doctors of the Church. Walton refers to his *Hexameron*, v. 2.

p. 126 l. 11 *river Dove.* See Cotton's account (in Pt. II, ch. ii, pp. 250–1) of this river, which he has taken for the scene of his instructions. It appears that Walton often visited him to fish in it.

l. 13 *which runs by Salisbury.* The Wiltshire Avon, the Bourne, the Wylye, and the Nadder meet at Salisbury: the combined stream is called the Avon.

p. 127 l. 10 *kipper*. At the approach of the breeding season, the lower jaw of the male salmon becomes hooked upwards with a sharp cartilaginous beak, which is used as a weapon by the fish when two or more fight for the same female. In this state he is known as a kipper.

l. 24 *to cast his bill*. The eagle does not shed his bill.

l. 32 *Sir Francis Bacon*. See note to p. 75, l. 14. But Bacon says this only of the Carp, Bream, Tench, and Eel, not of the Salmon.

l. 34 *it is to be observed*. The Salmon grows fat in the sea and deteriorates rapidly in fresh water.

p. 128 l. 11 *Gesner speaks*. He says 'eight cubits'. *Hist. Anim.* iv, p. 974, l. 52, to p. 975, l. 16.

l. 13 *Cambden*. *Britannia*. The Teifi separates Pembrokeshire from Cardiganshire.

l. 22 *Michael Drayton* (1563–1631). His *Poly-Olbion* is a long topographical description of England. This passage, with a few unimportant alterations by Walton, is Bk. vi, ll. 39–55.

l. 32 *His tail takes in his mouth*. A myth.

p. 129 l. 4 *yerking*. Akin to 'jerking'.
leaves. Leaves off.

l. 9 *Gesner and others*. In *Hist. Anim.* iv, p. 971 B, he gives it as the opinion of Bellonius that the salmon of the Seine and Loire are large, but less than those of the Thames. For himself he commends those of the Rhine and the Rhône (*Ib.*, p. 973 B).

p. 130 l. 11 *as Cambden observes*. See p. 6, l. 23, and notes.

p. 131 l. 14 *Oliver Henly*. Nothing appears to be known of him.

l. 30 *by expression or infusion*. By pressing the oil out of the berries, or soaking the berries in some liquid.

l. 32 *incorporated*. Taken into their bodies.

p. 132 l. 2 *Sir Francis Bacon*. See note to p. 122, l. 1.

l. 5 *Gesner says*. See note to p. 58, l. 32.

l. 15 *Polypody of the Oak*. The common fern of the

genus *Polypodium*, which grows on oaks and other trees, and on moist rocks and old walls.

l. 19 *Vulnera hederae*. Wounds made in a large branch of ivy exude an oleaginous and whitish balsam, of a most pleasant odour.

l. 22 *Asafœtida*. A concreted resinous gum with a horrible smell.

l. 26 *Sir George Hastings*. See note to p. 73, l. 10.

l. 31 *Tecon*. 'In the south they call him "samlet", but if you step to the west, he is better known there by the name of "skegger"; when in the east they avow him "penk", but to the northward "brood" and "cocksper"; so from thence to a "tecon", then to a "salmon".' – Richard Franck's *Northern Memoirs*, 1694 (ap. J. E. Haring's edition of the *Compleat Angler*, 1893).

p. 133 l. 12 *Artificial Paint or Patches*. The fashion of sticking black patches on the face was introduced in the last years of Charles I, survived the austerities of the Commonwealth, and continued far into the eighteenth century. The original object was to simulate moles, such as Venus had, but these were soon varied by stars and moons and crosses, and even by coaches and horses. According to Addison, ladies indicated their political sympathies by the part of the face to which they affixed their patches. *Spectator*, No. 81.

l. 23 *learned Gesner*. I cannot find these statements in Gesner, but in *Hist. Anim.* iv, p. 594, l. 44, he quotes Cardanus that pikes 'absque semine et ex semine generantur'.

l. 31 *Sir Francis Bacon*. Spedding's edition, vol. ii, p. 127, § 45.

p. 134 l. 4 *Gesner mentions*. On the fifth page of his Letter to the Emperor Ferdinand, prefatory to his *Historia Animalium*, Bk. iv, De Piscium . . . natura. Hakewill refers to it in his *Apologie*, II. vii. § 2, p. 145. Both Gesner and Hakewill give the dates as 1497 and 1230. Hakewill, however, does not say that the inscription was in

Greek, nor that it was interpreted by the Bishop of Worms (Johannes Dalburgus), as does Gesner: so that it is probable that Walton, however little Latin he knew, did have Gesner's book before him.

l. 22 *Gesner relates*. *Hist. Anim.* iv, p. 594, ll. 1 sqq.

l. 28 *the same Gesner*. *Hist. Anim.* iv, p. 594, l. 7.

l. 31 *Killingworth*. Kenilworth.

l. 32 *Mr. Seagrave*. See p. 60, l. 5, and note.

p. 135 l. 6 *It is a hard thing*, etc. The English proverb is, A hungry belly has no ears.

l. 28 *put over*. Properly a term of falconry, used of the hawk passing food from its crop to its stomach.

l. 30 *the venomous frog*. All amphibians have glands in their skin which secrete a milk-like fluid; this is exuded during excitement and possesses more or less poisonous properties. Walton probably believed the stories of frogs spitting venom.

p. 136 l. 2 *Gesner affirms*. *Hist. Anim.* iv, p. 594, l. 6.

l. 16 *Gesner*. *Hist. Anim.* iv, p. 596, ll. 30–5, and p. 592, l. 9.

p. 137 l. 4 *curiosity*. Unduly minute treatment.

l. 11 *Dubravius*. Johann Dubraw (d. 1553), Bishop of Olmütz in Moravia. His *De Piscinis, et Piscium qui in eis aluntur naturis* appeared in 1559, and was translated into English in 1599 under the title, *A New Booke of good Husbandry*. The story is given in *De Piscinis*, Bk. I, ch. vi, pp. 20–2.

p. 138 l. 8 *fishing Frogs*. Known to Aristotle, Pliny, and all the ancient naturalists. See Gesner, *Hist. Anim.* iv, pp. 956–62, 'De Rana Piscatrice.' The inhabitants of Epidaurus call it the Sea-Devil. It was probably the *Lophius piscatorius* or *barbatus*. See note to p. 45, l. 14.

l. 16 *secures the frog*. The reed sticking out on either side of the frog's mouth prevents the snake swallowing him.

l. 19 *Water and Land-frogs*. All frogs are amphibious:

though some species of frogs live less in the water than others, there is no species which does not resort to the water during the breeding season.

l. 20 *Land and Water-Snakes*. There are no English water-snakes, but the grass snake will make long journeys by water, as from the mainland to the Isle of Wight. The female does not, however, produce her young alive.

p. 139 l. 15 *a ledger or a walking-bait*. Both are explained below. *Ledger-bait* = a bait intended to remain in one place.

p. 140 l. 26 *a flesh, and a fish-frog*. See note to p. 138, l. 19. Walton's information is from Topsell, *Historie of Serpents* (1608), pp. 185–7.

l. 32 *paddock*. Still = 'frog' in Scottish and northern dialects. The other sense of 'toad' is now obsolete.

p. 141 l. 7 *Pliny. Nat. Hist.* ix. 159.

Cardanus (1501–76). A physician of Pavia, whose contributions to algebra were his greatest work. In *De Subtilitate* (1550), Bk. xvi, p. 262 B, he says that frogs and fishes are carried off by the wind from the heights and fall on the plains as rain.

l. 24 *mouth grows up*. See note to p. 74, l. 21. I cannot find any foundation for this belief; the frog does, however, hibernate and remain some months without food.

l. 32 *as though you loved him*. Cf. Byron on Walton:
    The quaint, old, cruel coxcomb, in his gullet
    Should have a hook, and a small trout to pull it.
                            Don Juan, XIII, cvi. 7, 8.

p. 142 l. 12 *ravelling*. 'Ravel' and 'unravel' are generally used as synonymous.

l. 20 *pouch the bait*. Swallow it.

p. 143 l. 21 *Dissolve Gum of Ivy*. John Dennys, at the end of his *Secrets of Angling* (see note to p. 38, l. 8), gives this recipe.

Gum of Ivy is the thickened juice of the stem of the ivy.

Oyl of Spike is an inferior oil from lavender.

l. 31 *pretended to do*. Claimed that he was doing.

p. 144 l. 8 *Winter-savoury*. The winter, or mountain, savory is a plant resembling hyssop, used as a flavouring.

l. 24 *Filleting*. A fillet was originally a 'head-band', and hence 'filleting' is any material out of which such a band could be made.

p. 145 l. 7 *hogo*. French *haut goût*, a high flavour.

l. 10 *M.B.* Unknown.

l. 14 *Gesner. Hist. Anim*. iv, p. 593, l. 15.

l. 16 *Thrasymene*. Lake Trasimene, in Central Italy, where Hannibal defeated Flaminius in 217 B.C.

l. 20 *Shelsey*. Selsey.

l. 21 *Amerly*. Amberley.

p. 146 l. 2 *Mr. Mascal*. Leonard Mascall (d. 1589) was clerk of the kitchen to Archbishop Parker. He wrote *A Booke of Fishing with Hooke and Line* (1590). In his paragraph on Carp, he says 'the first bringer of them into England (as I have beene credibly enformed) was Maister Mascott of Plumsted in Sussex'. But the carp is mentioned in 1496 in Dame Juliana Berners's 'Treatyse of Fysshynge wyth an Angle', p. 16.

l. 5 *I told you, Gesner says*. See p. 145, l. 14.

l. 9 *Sir Richard Baker* (1568–1645). Of Hart Hall, Oxford, where he shared rooms with Sir Henry Wotton. He lost his money by going surety for his wife's relations and in 1635 took refuge in the Fleet Prison, where he began to write. His chief work is the *Chronicle of the Kings of England* (1643). These verses, which are in the first edition (Henry VIII, p. 66), refer to the fifteenth year of Henry VIII, 1524.

p. 147 l. 3 *Aristotle. Hist. Anim*. vi. 14, 568[a], l. 18, says five or six times.

l. 4 *Pliny. Nat. Hist*. ix. 162.

l. 7 *be enlivened*. Receive life.

l. 11 *Jovius*. Paolo Giovio the Elder (1483–1552),

Bishop of Nocera, author of many historical works, of an
account of Lake Como, on which he had a villa, and of a
short treatise *De Romanis Piscibus* (1531). I cannot find
the reference. The Lyrian Lake is the Lake of Como.

l. 14 *conceiv'd and born suddenly*. The period of gestation of bears is affected by delayed implantation, and is not
very brief. Aristotle, who gives (*Hist. Anim.* vi. 30, 579ᵃ,
l. 21) thirty days as the period for bears, is probably
responsible for this belief of Walton's.

l. 16 *the Elephant*. The gestation period is twenty-two
months. An elephant is full grown at twenty-five, and
specimens have lived over a century in captivity.

p. 148 l. 28 *a person of honour*. The 'Mr. Fr. Ru.' of the
note is said to be a Mr. Francis Rufford, of Sapey, Wor-
cestershire, who died about 1678, aged 82.

p. 149 l. 1 *considerable*. Worthy of consideration.

l. 5 *Sir Francis Bacon*. Spedding's edition, vol. ii,
p. 128, § 46.

l. 7 *Gesner*. *Hist. Anim.* iv, p. 372, l. 10.

l. 8 *the Palatinate*. A state of the Holy Roman Empire
under a Count-Palatine, which has now been absorbed in
Bavaria and its adjacent states.

l. 13 *Gesner saies*. *Hist. Anim.* iv, p. 369, l. 14.

l. 22 *Janus Dubravius*. *De Piscinis*, Bk. III, ch. ix,
p. 75. See note to p. 137, l. 11.

l. 25 *he says also*. These statements are not to be found
in *De Piscinis*.

p. 150 l. 13 *their King*. Bees have a queen, not a king.

l. 17 *the galls and stones*. Gesner, *Hist. Anim.* iv, p. 373,
ll. 11. sqq. 'Galls' = (1) the gall-bladder and its contents,
or (2) gall-stones, which form in the gall-bladder. I do
not know what these stones in the heads of fishes are; but
see below, p. 162, l. 7, and p. 165, l. 2.

l. 18 *'tis not to be doubted*. So Gesner, *Hist. Anim.* iv,
p. 370, l. 18.

l. 24 *in Leviticus 11*. Verses 9–12.

p. 153 l. 2 *Virgin wax*. Pure, unadulterated wax.

l. 8 *Oyl of Peter*. Rock-oil: petroleum.

l. 27 *curious . . . curious*. (1) = requiring care. (2) = delicate.

p. 154 l. 16 *Dr. T*. I cannot trace him.

l. 23 *Gesner*. 'Suavior est quam salubrior.' *Hist. Anim.* iv, p. 376, l. 20.

l. 31 *to help his grinding*. Fish do not grind their food, but swallow it whole.

p. 155 l. 3 *Gesner. Hist. Anim.* iv, p. 377, ll. 22 sqq.

l. 16 *Sir Francis Bacon*. Spedding's edition, vol. ii, p. 112, § 13.

l. 21 *this Proverb*. 'Qui ha brasme, peut bien brasmer ses amys', quoted by Gesner, *Hist. Anim.* iv, p. 377, l. 41.

p. 156 l. 2 *Tench*. An error for 'bream'.

l. 9 *a most honest and excellent Angler*. Nothing is known of him except his initials; see p. 161.

p. 157 l. 23 *skuls*. Obsolete form of 'schools'.

p. 158 l. 21 *one or two warms*. Presumably when it has once boiled it should be taken off the fire, and then put on again to bring it up to boiling-point.

p. 161 l. 3 *St. James Tide until Bartholomew Tide*. July 25 to August 24.

l. 28 *the Physician of Fishes*. See p. 163, l. 5, and note.

l. 30 *Cambden*. 'The famous river Stoure, abounding with tench and eels'.

p. 162 l. 7 *two little stones*. Gesner, *Hist. Anim.* iv, p. 1179, l. 14.

l. 8 *he is not commended*. Lovell, *History of Animals*, p. 227, quotes Dr. Caius (1510–73) as calling tenches 'good plasters, but bad nourishment'.

l. 11 *Rondelitius*. See note to p. 44, l. 20. The reference is to his *Univ. Aquat. Hist. pars alt.*, p. 157 *bis*.

p. 163 l. 5 *Physician of fishes*. This belief in the healing power of tenches is said to have originated in a fact, which is vouched for by Holinshed, that Tench will crowd round a wounded Pike and nibble at the sore. Rondeletius (*l.c.*, p. 197) says there is a friendship between Pike and Tench, because the Pike uses the slime with which the Tench is covered to heal his wounds.

p. 164 l. 18 *invade*. Attack (a person).

l. 21 *Aldrovandus*. See note to p. 99, l. 6. The present reference is to the *De Piscibus*, v, p. 627, § 1.

l. 23 *Gesner. Hist. Anim.* iv, p. 824, l. 45. The proverb is *ibid.*, l. 56, and the story of the physicians l. 57.

p. 165 l. 1 *Rondelitius*. I cannot find that he says so.

l. 2 *have in their brain a stone*. Gesner, *Hist. Anim.* iv, p. 826, l. 26. See note to p. 150, l. 17.

l. 4 *reins*. Kidneys.

l. 14 *Sir Abraham Williams*. I cannot find any information about him.

p. 166 l. 17 *rove*. Aim, especially in archery.

p. 167 l. 16 *Doctor Donne*. John Donne (1573–1631), D.D., Dean of St. Paul's. *Poems* were first published in 1633. Walton wrote a Life of him. This poem which parodies Marlowe's poem (pp. 81–2) appeared' in 1635 under the title of 'The Baite'. Walton has altered in l. 7 'inamour'd' to 'enamel'd'; l. 15, 'my selfe' to 'mine eyes'.

p. 168 l. 7 *Let course bold hands*. A reference, apparently, to 'tickling' for fish, especially for trout.

l. 9 *sleave*. Divide into threads.

l. 30 *Helena*. I cannot find his authority for this.

p. 169 l. 15 *Rondelitius. Univ. Aquat. Hist. pars alt.*, p. 200, l. 2, 'Like dew-worms' (= common earth-worms) is an addition of Walton's own.

l. 19 *Sir Francis Bacon*. Spedding's edition, vol. ii, p. 128, § 46.

l. 26 *some of the Ancients*. 'Anguillas ex Iove natas Matron Parodus apud Athenaeum fabulatur, nimirum quod eorum generatio incerta sit: qua ratione et fungos et tubera aliqui deorum filios dixerunt.' – Gesner, *Hist*.

Anim. iv, p. 50, l. 27. Matron, a famous parodist of Homer, is quoted by Athenaeus, *Deipnosophistae*, iv. 135.

p. 170 l. 6 Bede's *Hist. Eccles.* iv. 19, quoted by Gesner, *Hist. Anim.* iv, p. 49, l. 14. His derivation of Ely from A.S. *æl*, 'eel', = *ig*, 'isle', is apparently correct.

l. 12 *Barnacles.* See p. 100, ll. 27 sqq.

l. 15 *Lobel.* Mathieu L'Obel (1538–1616), the French physician and botanist after whom the *Lobelia* was named. He passed most of his life in England and became physician to James I. He gives a picture of 'Britannicae Conchae anatiferae' in vol. ii, p. 259, of his *Icones Stirpium* (1581), which contains figures of about 2,000 plants. For Du Bartas on goose-bearing trees and barnacles, see p. 100, ll. 27 sqq.; for Gerard and Camden on the same, see the note to that passage.

l. 17 *Rondelitius.* I cannot find this.

l. 24 *Sir Francis Bacon.* See note to p. 169, l. 19.

l. 25 *in his History.* Spedding's edition, vol. ii, p. 127, § 44: the story is found in Aelian, *Hist. Anim.* viii. 4. Crassus the orator was L. Licinius Crassus (140–91 B.C.). Cn. Domitius Ahenobarbus, who shared the censorship with him in 92 B.C., disliked the luxury in which he lived, and started this story of the Lamprey. Crassus, in a public speech, replied that if he had wept for his lamprey it was more than Domitius had done for any of his three wives. Walton appears to have mixed up Domitius with the Emperor Domitian (A.D. 51–96): the Lamprey was Crassus's own.

l. 31 *Doctor Hackwel.* See p. 122, l. 26 and note. This incident is in *Apologie*, IV. vii, § 6, p. 434, taken from Pliny, *Nat. Hist.* ix. 172.

p. 171 l. 10 *Gesner quotes Albertus. Hist. Anim.* iv, p. 51, l. 17, but the reference given is *Annales Augustae Vindelicae* and not Albertus.

l. 15 *Cambden.* 'Near Altmouth is Ferneby, in whose marshes they dig turf. . . . Below the turf they find a stagnant blackish water, on whose surface swims an oily substance, and in the water are little fishes, which the diggers take up.' *Britannia*.

p. 174 l. 11 *S. F.* I cannot trace this person.

l. 22 *Solomon says*. Proverbs xxv. 16 and 27.

p. 175 l. 15 *as the Jews do*. See p. 150, l. 24 and note.

l. 30 *Winander Mere*. Windermere: *Britannia*.

p. 176 l. 7 *Guiniad*. *Britannia*: Camden says the Gwyniad is peculiar to lake Bala. It is a fish of the salmon or trout kind, with white flesh.

l. 19 *Gesner*. *Hist. Anim.* iv, p. 143, l. 30. The barb is a slender fleshy appendage hanging from the corner of the mouth of some fishes, such as the barbel and the fishing frog.

p. 177 l. 27 *Rondiletius*. See Gesner, *Hist. Anim.* iv, p. 145, l. 24, who gives not Rondeletius, but Albertus (see note to p. 74, l. 21), as his authority.

p. 178 l. 2 *Gesner*. *Hist. Anim.* iv, p. 145, ll. 48 sqq.

Gasius. Antonio Gazi (*c.* 1450–1530), an Italian physician. This passage occurs in his *De conservatione Sanitatis* (Venice, 1491), ch. cxxxvii, reg. 8, which is quoted by Gesner.

l. 17 *Plutarch*. See *De Sollertia Animalium*, ch. xxiv.

p. 179 l. 12 *store*. Archaic without the indefinite article. Cf. Milton, *L'Allegro*, l. 121, 'With store of ladies, whose bright eyes', etc.

l. 24 *tries conclusions*. Tries experiments.

l. 26 *the long shower*. It began on p. 108.

l. 34 *Doctor Sheldon*. Gilbert Sheldon (1598–1677), Warden of All Souls and Archbishop of Canterbury, prominent adviser of Charles II. His benefactions to Oxford University include the Sheldonian Theatre.

p. 180 l. 12 *a leash*. A set of three. Originally used of greyhounds, three being the number fastened to one leash.

l. 31 *Hunting in Chevy Chase*. See p. 81, l. 2 and note.

p. 181 l. 17 *Groundling*. In the Elbe districts *Gründling*, elsewhere *Grundele*. See Gesner, *Hist. Anim*. iv, p. 474, ll. 42 sqq.

p. 182 l. 7 *a Pope*. A small thick-bodied freshwater fish of the Perch family, seldom more than six inches long.

l. 15 *reserved*. Secluded.

l. 27 *Ausonius*. See note to p. 44, l. 20.

l. 33 *Allamot salt*. The American editor suggests that Allamot is a corruption of Alto Monte in Calabria, where there was formerly a salt mine of great value. But even that could hardly turn a bleak into an anchovy. The word is unknown to the *N.E.D*.

p. 183 l. 1 *a Pater-noster line*. So called from its resemblance to a rosary, in which the Paternoster, a special bead indicating that the Lord's Prayer is to be said, occurs at regular intervals. The whole rosary also is called a paternoster.

l. 8 *answerable*. Capable of answering requirements.

l. 12 *Sir Henry Wotton*. See note to p. 4, l. 10.

p. 184 l. 21 *Shovel-board*. The players shove or drive by blows of the hand pieces of money or counters towards certain marks, compartments, or lines, marked on a table: also called 'shovelpenny', or 'shove-halfpenny'.

l. 28 *dogged*. Surly.

l. 30 *my Song*. For Jo. Chalkhill, see note to p. 87, l. 26. This song appears only in *The Compleat Angler*, and apparently (see p. 187, l. 10) here in an altered form.

p. 186 l. 10 *fray*. Frighten.

p. 187 l. 15 *without replications*. Without answers or protests.

p. 188 l. 5 *Culverkeyes*. See note to p. 55, l. 16.

l. 9 *that Field in Sicily*. The field whence Persephone was carried off to Hades by Pluto; see Diodorus Siculus, *Bibliotheca Historica*, V, iii, § 2.

l. 16 *my Saviour said*. Matthew v. 5.

l. 23 *the Poet*. I cannot trace these verses.

l. 31 *Phineas Fletcher* (1582–1650). Rector of Hilgay in Norfolk. These lines are in *The Purple Island, or The Isle of Man*, Canto XII, sts. 3, 5, 6. Walton has, as usual, made various alterations in the text.

p. 189 l. 6 *certain*. Unvarying.

l. 22 *piece of an old Catch*. This is found on p. 62 of *Select Ayres and Dialogues composed by . . . Henry Lawes*, etc., London, 1659.

l. 28 *Hodg-poch*. 'Hotchpot', refers to shaking (Fr. *hocher*) in a pot, but whether originally a term of cookery or not, is uncertain.

p. 192 l. 5 *Musick! miraculous*. From the last page of Playford's *Select Ayres*. They are there signed 'W. D. Knight'. It is suggested that they were written by Sir William Davenant (1606–68), the poet and dramatist, though they are not included in the most recent edition (1972) by A. M. Gibbs.

l. 12 *Waller*. Edmund Waller (1606–87), poet and politician. These verses first appeared in his *Poems*, 1645.

l. 30 *the tother cup*. 'Tother' arose from a misdivision of Middle English 'thet (that) other' into 'the tother'.

p. 193 l. 29 *Some say*. The Latin name is *Leuciscus rutilus*, but 'Roach' came into English from the Old French *Roche*, which is of unknown origin.

p. 194 l. 22 *London-bridge*. The only bridge over the Thames at London in Walton's day. It was a stone bridge, built between 1176–1209, of twenty arches, with a draw-bridge and a chapel and crypt in the centre. Houses were afterwards built along both its sides (cf. the Ponte Vecchio at Florence) and seriously impaired its strength. It was finally pulled down in 1832 after the erection of a new bridge (1825–31) sixty yards higher up the river.

p. 195 l. 9 *Henly Bridg*. The present stone bridge replaced the old wooden one in 1786.

l. 13 *Manchet*. The finest kind of wheaten bread.

l. 34 *pottle*. Two quarts.

p. 196 l. 16 *not less than a handful*. A linear measure = 4 inches. The same as the 'hand' used in measuring horses.

l. 18 *All-hallantide*. All-Hallowtide: the season of All Saints. All Saints' or All-Hallows' Day is November 1.

l. 34 *firkin*. A small cask, originally one containing a fourth part of a barrel.

p. 197 l. 16 *Michaelmas*. The feast of St. Michael, 29 September.

p. 198 l. 28 *Sir George Hastings*. See note to p. 73, l. 10.

l. 29 *Sir Henry Wotton*. See note to p. 4, l. 10.

p. 199 l. 4 *Philosophers Stone*. A reputed stone supposed by the alchemists to possess the property of changing other metals into gold and silver, the discovery of which was the supreme object of alchemy.

l. 7 *the Rosi-crucians*. Members of a supposed society or order of the Rosy Cross, said to have been founded by one Christian Rosenkreuz in 1484, who were reputed to claim various forms of secret and magic knowledge, such as how to transmute metals, to prolong life, and to command the elements.

l. 14 *float Fish*. Presumably fish of a kind that can be taken by a baited line supported by a float.

l. 18 *out of an old Fish-book*. I cannot trace it.

l. 24 *green*. See p. 216.

l. 30 *Mr. Margrave*, etc. On the last page of Part II of the fifth edition (1676) is this notice: '*Courteous Reader*, You may be pleased to take notice that at the sign of the Three Trouts in St. Paul's Church-Yard, on the North Side, you may be fitted with all sorts of the best fishing tackle by *John Margrave*.' Nothing else is known of Mr John Stubs.

amongst the booksellers. Before the Great Fire of 1666 the irregular area surrounding St. Paul's Cathedral was chiefly inhabited by stationers (publishers and booksellers were not yet differentiated).

p. 200 l. 22 *Frumity*. 'Frumenty', a dish made of wheat boiled in milk and seasoned with cinnamon, sugar, etc.

p. 201 l. 10 *a Piper*. So called because it forms a pipe or tube.

l. 12 *a twopence*. A small silver coin, called also a half-groat, issued till 1662.

l. 28 *to be so ordered*. Does this mean 'should be so classified'?

p. 203 l. 30 *all without scales*. The minnow has scales, but very minute. So also the eel, which is popularly supposed to lack them.

p. 204 l. 24 *Tansie*. Lit. 'immortality' (Gk. ἀθανασία); the *Tanacetum vulgare*, a perennial herb whose leaves were formerly used as a seasoning.

p. 205 l. 2 *Gesner*. *Hist. Anim*. iv, p. 481, l. 52.

l. 10 *Gesner*. *Hist. Anim*. iv, p. 475, l. 58.

p. 206 l. 11 *Matthiolus*. Pietro Andrea Mattioli (1500–77), a Sienese physician and botanist. I cannot find the reference.

p. 208 l. 7 *Dr. Heylins Geography*. Peter Heylin (1600–62), sub-dean of Westminster and chaplain to Charles I, in 1621 published a Geography, of which a much augmented edition appeared in 1652 as *Cosmographie*. From p. 208, l. 10, to p. 210, l. 4, is a quotation from Heylin, pp. 259–60, almost word for word.

l. 10 *Thamisis*. The derivation from 'Thame' and 'Isis' is erroneous: the river is known as the Thames from its source (Ullen Farm, in the parish of Coates, 3 miles WSW of Cirencester) to the sea, except in the vicinity of Oxford and poetically.

l. 23 *a German poet*. The poet is unknown, but Heylin gives the Latin original.

p. 209 l. 3 *Trent*. This derivation from Fr. *trente*, 'thirty', is of course fanciful; cf. p. 252.

l. 11 *Estuarium*. For Lat. *aestuarium*, 'estuary'.

l. 12 *namely, Ure, Derwent*. Heylin has 'namely, Your, Derwent, I have adopted the more likely 'Ure' in place of 'Your'.

l. 14 *as the Danow.* The Danube. The Drave, the Save, the Theiss (or Tisza) are among its chief tributaries.

l. 15 *changeth his name into Ister.* In the early editions this passage has been mistranscribed, to read 'changeth his name into this of *Humberabus*, as the old Geographers call it'. The whole passage is taken from Heylin (see note to p. 208 l. 7 above) and there seems to be no point in perpetuating a nonsensical mistranscription.

l. 22 *impregnable Town of Barwick.* Berwick is still surrounded by a complete set of ramparts of Elizabethan date and some remains of Edward I's fortifications. It was anything but impregnable, being frequently taken by English or Scottish.

l. 25 *Mr. Drayton.* See note to p. 128, l. 22. These lines are from Amour 24 in *Idea's Mirrour*, London, 1594.

l. 31 *Carlegion Chester.* The British name was Caer Leon ar Dyfr Dwy, 'the fortress of the legion on the Dee water'.

holy. Cf. Milton's 'Wizard Stream' and Spenser's 'Dee, which Britons long ygone Did call divine'.

p. 210 l. 1 *Cotswool.* The hills of Gloucestershire in which the Isis (Thames) rises. See note to p. 208, l. 10.

l. 3 *their Willies.* The Wylye, a Wiltshire river, which rises near Kingston Deverill and joins the Nadder near Wilton.

l. 4 *the old Lea.* In 896 the Danes towed their ships up the Lea and erected fortifications within twenty miles of London. Alfred the Great had the river obstructed lower down and drove out the Danes with the loss of their ships.

l. 15 *Dr. Wharton.* See note to p. 34, l. 34. Jesse says this fish is 'no doubt meant for the Sea-frog or Sea-angler' (*Lophius piscatorius*).

p. 211 l. 11 *Grotius.* Hugo de Groot (1583–1645) wrote numerous poems and three tragedies, of which *Sophomphaneas*, or *Joseph*, was issued in an English translation by Francis Goldsmith, 1652. It includes a chorus in praise of the Nile.

l. 25 *Dr. Lebault*. Walton's authority is *Maison Rustique, or, the Countrey Farme, translated into English by Richard Surflet. Now newly Reviewed, Corrected and Augmented ... By Gervase Markham* (London, 1616). This chapter is founded on Bk. IV, chaps. xi–xvii, pp. 505–16, which deal with 'The Poole, Fishpond, and Ditch for fish'.

p. 212 l. 6 *Bavins*. Bundles of brushwood or light underwood bound with only one withe or band. Faggots are bound with two.

l. 15 *Owlers*. A dialect form of 'alders'.

l. 23 *Dubravius*. See note to p. 137, l. 11. The reference is to Bk. II, chap. i, pp. 28, 29.

p. 213 l. 14 *Candocks*. The yellow water-lilies.

 Reate. A species of water-crowfoot (*Ranunculus fluitans*).

p. 214 l. 26 *marle-pits*. Marl was used as a fertilizer.

p. 215 l. 17 *top*. The end-piece of a jointed fishing-rod is called the 'top'.

p. 217 l. 2 *small Ale*. Ale weak in malt and probably without hops or other bitter ingredient; cheaper than ordinary ale.

l. 12 *Copperas*. 'Green vitriol' or 'proto-sulphate of iron', which is a salt formed by sulphuric acid with ferrous oxide.

l. 26 *a Lie-colour*. Lye is alkalized water made by pouring water over the ashes of wood or other vegetable matter, whereupon the salts in the ashes are dissolved in the water. The lye is almost colourless.

p. 218 l. 31 *his preventing grace*. See note to p. 21, l. 6. By the theologians the grace of God is said to 'prevent' or 'go before' human action or need with spiritual guidance and help.

p. 219 l. 12 *Solomon says*. Proverbs x. 4.

l. 15 *a man of great observation*. I cannot trace him.

l. 30 *unconscionably*. Unconscientiously.

l. 33 *Diogenes* (d. 323 ? aet. 90). It was Socrates (see Diogenes Laertius, *Vitae Philosophorum*, II, v. 25) who used frequently to say Πόσων ἐγὼ χρείαν οὐκ ἔχω; when he saw the multitude of things that are sold. There may be a similar tradition about Diogenes the Cynic, but I cannot find it.

p. 220 l. 4 *finnimbruns*. Trifles; a word of purely arbitrary formation.

p. 221 l. 15 *in St. Matthew's Gospel*. Ch. v, verses 7, 8, 3, and 5. In each case A.V. has 'are', not 'be'.

p. 222 l. 3 *a man after God's own heart*. 1 Samuel xiii. 14.

p. 223 l. 1 *Tottenham High-Cross*. An ancient wooden cross stood on the east side of the high road in the centre of Tottenham. An octagonal brick column, erected in 1600, much restored, still marks its site.

l. 12 *Caussin*. Nicholas Caussin (1582 ?–1651), confessor to Louis XIII of France, and author of *The Holy Court* (5 vols.) and other devotional works.

l. 25 *a grave Divine*. Said by Sir John Hawkins to be Dr. Donne (see note to p. 167, l. 16) in his sermons.

p. 224 l. 6 *Sack*. Probably from Fr. *vin sec* = dry wine, but in the seventeenth century a general name for a class of white wines formerly imported from Spain and the Canaries.

l. 7 *Nectar*. In classical mythology, the drink of the gods.

l. 10 *the Verses*. They appear in *Reliquiae Wottonianae*, edited by Walton, under 'Poems found among the Papers of S. H. Wotton', and they are headed 'A Description of the Countrey's Recreations', and signed 'Ignoto'.

l. 22 *glozing*. To gloze or gloss = to veil with specious comments or glosses, hence to fawn or wheedle.

p. 225 l. 9 *Mask*. A masque.

l. 32 *Ceres*. In Latin mythology, the Goddess of Corn.

p. 226 l. 9 *another very good Copy*. In the first and second edition, Walton has 'some say, written by Dr. D.', i.e.

Dr. Donne. It is clear that Walton, who edited Wotton's poems and did not include this one, is very doubtful about it. They are attributed to Sir Kenelm Digby in some MSS.

l. 20 *damask'd*. 'Having the colours of the damask rose,' which is supposed to have been brought originally from Damascus. The flowers 'be neither redde nor white, but of a mixt colour between red and white, almost carnation colour'. – Lyte, *Dodoens* (1578), VI, i. 654.

l. 24 *alone*. Professor Grierson conjectures 'a loane', Donne's *Poetical Works* (1912) I. 466.

l. 33 *mind*. This makes no sense. The one manuscript which has 'mine' is probably right. If 'mine' is correct, 'richest mine' is a metaphorical term for 'a very rich man'.

p. 227 l. 11 *vie Angels with India*. Rival India for wealth. An angel was an English gold coin, bearing a figure of the Archangel Michael defeating the dragon. It was first struck in 1465 by Edward IV and last in 1634 by Charles I.

p. 228 l. 2 *St. Austin*. St. Augustine of Hippo (354–436), the greatest Father of the Latin Church. His *Confessions* describe his conversion from an immoral life, partly by the sermons of St. Ambrose. The passage is ix. [iii.] 5.

l. 24 *Socrates* (470 ?–399). The famous Greek philosopher, whom the Athenians put to death for impiety: his philosophy survives in the works of his disciple Plato. I cannot find the reference.

p. 229 l. 5 *Lillies that take no care*. Cf. Matthew vi. 28 and Luke xii. 27.

l. 9 *Let everything*. Psalm cl. 6.

PART II

p. 239 l. 3 *Father*. See p. 245, l. 9.

l. 7 *Being*. An absolute use of the pres. part., 'it being the case that', i.e. since. Cotton is very partial to the phrase, which is not to be found in Walton and is now obsolete.

l. 19 *a suddain new Edition*. 'The Universal Angler,

made so, by three Books of Fishing, The first by Mr. Izaac Walton, the Second by Charles Cotton Esqre, the Third by Col. Robert Venables. All which may be bound together, or sold each of them severally. London, printed for Richard Marriott, and sold by most Booksellers. MDCLXXVI.' The first part was the fifth edition, much corrected and enlarged, of *The Compleat Angler*; and the third part the fourth edition of a pamphlet, *The Experienced Angler, or Angling Improved*.

p. 240 l. 7 *the Cypher*. See title, p. 237, and p. 247, l. 27. It was a monogram composed of Walton's and Cotton's initials. Walton, who saw to the details of publication, had this cipher engraved for the title-page of Cotton's part.

l. 14 *Berisford*. Beresford Dale, a continuation of Dove Dale to the north, forms the grounds of Beresford Hall, which passed from the Beresfords early in the seventeenth century to the Stanhopes of Elvaston, whose heiress eloped with Cotton's father. In Cotton's time it was a picturesque gabled building of the sixteenth and seventeenth centuries, but it was pulled down in 1856.

p. 241 l. 15 *Ashborn*. Ashbourne. The village of Brailsford (Brelsford) is 7 miles along the road. Neither Viator nor Piscator is very accurate in his distances.

p. 242 l. 13 *There is good land*. A proverb, cf. Donne, *Elegie II*. 36.

p. 244 l. 27 *by Mr. Izaak Walton's good leave*. See p. 121, l. 22.

p. 246 l. 4 *nicer*: i.e. more intimate or familiar.

l. 13 *when you, and he*. See p. 103, l. 12, and p. 120, l. 13.

l. 29 *dispense with such a divertisement*. Allow such a diversion.

p. 248 l. 18 *the Talbot*. 'Stood in the market-place and was the first hostelry in the town. It sank to a pot-house in the eighteenth century, and was demolished in 1786.' – Hawkins.

l. 21 *Henmore.* Or Scholebrooke, a very small stream which flows through Ashbourne and joins the Dove about two miles lower. It forms the boundary between the two teams (Up'ards and Down'ards) in the Shrove Tuesday football match. (See note to p. 54 l. 23.)

p. 250 l. 19 *Bently Brook.* A tributary of the Dove. Our travellers would cross it at Fenny Bentley, 2 miles N. of Ashbourne.

l. 31 *Dove.* The Dove rises near Axe Edge, 4 miles SSW of Buxton (see note to p. 253, l. 3), and flows S. for 40 miles between Staffordshire and Derbyshire until it joins the Trent near Egginton, 4 miles below Burton. The most famous part of its course is the 3 miles from Ilam to Mill Dale, known as Dovedale, of which Dr. Johnson said, 'He that has seen Dovedale has no need to visit the Highlands.'

l. 33 *so called from the swiftness.* From Celtic *du* (black).

p. 251 l. 11 *Wires.* Weirs.

l. 26 *not far from . . . Trentham.* The Trent rises from New Pool, near Biddulph in north Staffordshire, and flows for more than 15 miles before it reaches Trentham.

l. 29 *Forrest of Needwood.* An ancient royal forest in Staffordshire, disforested in 1801 and now mostly under cultivation.

l. 31 *Dunnington.* Donnington Park, 2 miles from Castle Donnington.

l. 32 *Wildon.* Wilne, 2 miles above the junction.

p. 252 l. 3 *Trent derives its name.* See note to p. 209, l. 3. Trentham is, of course, a derivative of Trent.

l. 29 *two lesser.* The Lathkill and the Bradford unite with the Dakin and run into the Wye just below Haddon Hall.

p. 253 l. 3 *Buxtons.* Buxton, a spa with both hot and cold springs. They were known to the Romans; and in mediaeval times were famous for the miracles performed by St. Anne, to whom a chalybeate spring is dedicated.

They became fashionable in Elizabeth's reign, when Mary Queen of Scots, as a prisoner, paid four visits to Buxton.

l. 21 *Awberson*. Probably Alvaston.

l. 24 *Awber*. So the first edition: a misprint for the Amber, a river of NE Derbyshire, 4 miles long, which flows into the Derwent, 3½ miles N. of Belper.

l. 25 *Eroways*. The Erwash or Erewash, which rises in west Nottinghamshire and joins the Trent near Attenborough. It forms the boundary between Nottinghamshire and Derbyshire.

p. 254 l. 26 *lay my heels in my neck*. Curl myself up and roll down the hill.

l. 32 *the sign of a Bridg*: i.e. 'the mere semblance of a bridge'. This bridge at Mill Dale, 9 miles from Ashbourne, is still standing.

p. 256 l. 6 *Tom Coriate*. Thomas Coryate (1577 ?–1617) started his career as a kind of privileged buffoon in the Court of James I; inheriting some money, he travelled mostly on foot to Venice and back, and wrote *Coryats Crudities*. It is the first handbook to Continental travel, and is for the most part faithful and instructive. He solicited testimonials from every eminent contemporary, and in 1611 the work was published with an abundance of mock commendatory verses by Donne, Jonson, Campion, Drayton, Inigo Jones, and others. In 1612 Coryate set out overland to India, where he died at Surat in 1617. (See Michael Strachan, *The Life and Adventures of Thomas Coryate*, 1962.)

l. 16 *a Church*. The church of Alstonefield, a parish 7 miles from Ashbourne. It contains a carved pew belonging to Beresford Hall.

l. 34 *Penmen-Maure*. Viator thinks Hanson Toot as terrifying as Penmaenmawr, on the coast of Carnarvonshire, which rises to 1,553 feet.

p. 257 l. 34 *More-Land's*. The Moorlands of Derbyshire, which extend from just north of Ashbourne up to the Peak.

p. 258 l. 22 *resolve me*: i.e. answer the question I put you.

p. 259 l. 19 *dinner*. Luckily about midday; see end of Chap. VI.

p. 260 l. 25 *Piscatoribus sacrum*. 'Dedicated to fishermen.'
l. 31 *Mr. Cotton's Father*. Charles Cotton the elder was a distinguished man, of whom Clarendon gives a lively portrait.

p. 262 l. 31 *in his Compleat Angler*. See pp. 103–7.
l. 33 *your Steel*: i.e. for striking sparks from flints.

p. 263 l. 17 *Ground-bait*. See Part I, chap. x,
l. 25 *By hand*. 'That is, the bait running on the ground with several shot or a small bullet, without a float.' – Browne. See below, Chap. XI.

p. 264 l. 28 *daping*. See note to p. 84, l. 28.

p. 265 l. 7 *presently*. Immediately.

p. 266 l. 31 *your Master Waltons direction*. See p. 217, l. 23.

p. 267 l. 4 *to fish fine*: i.e. delicately.

p. 268 l. 23 *arming*. Fastening the hook to the line.

p. 269 l. 7 *dubbing*. The materials used in the dressing of an artificial fly.
l. 9 *a Hackle*. The making of a hackle-fly is given in Part I, p. 106.
l. 24 *Towght*. A length or section of an angler's hair-line, a link.

p. 270 l. 27 *warp*. Twist.

p. 271 l. 10 *Captain Henry Jackson*. I cannot trace him.

p. 273 l. 18 *They who go to Rome*. This proverb originated with St. Ambrose, who in his thirty-sixth Letter to Casulanus says, 'Quando hic sum [i.e. at Milan] non jejuno Sabbato; quando Romae sum, jejuno Sabbato,' it being the custom to keep Saturday as a fast in Rome and not in Milan.

l. 31 *New-River*. An artificial river formed (1606–13) by Sir Hugh Myddelton to supply London with water. It rises from several springs near Ware, and draws further supplies from the Lea at Broxbourne. Piscator naturally despises it as a sluggish stream.

p. 275 l. 34 *strike*: i.e. by a turn of the wrist to hook a fish which has failed to hook itself.

p. 277 l. 11 *calver*. 'Part in flakes.' – Browne. A calver fish is probably 'a fish freshly taken, when its substance appears interspersed with white flakes like curd'. To calver is to behave, when cooked, like a calver fish.

l. 16 *skip-jack*. A name given to a large number of small fishes which dart through and sometimes skip out of the water. Here applied jocularly to the small grayling.

p. 278 l. 1 *as Dametas says*. Sir Philip Sidney, *Arcadia* (1590), Bk. i, p. 83, where Dametas sings:

> For if my man must praises have,
> What then must I that keepe the knave ?

l. 8 *Pike*. A northern English word for a pointed or peaked summit, or a mountain with a pointed summit; cf. Langdale Pikes. This rock is still to be seen standing in the river.

l. 11 *young Mr. Izaak Walton* (1651–1719). Walton's only surviving son, who became a prebendary of Salisbury Cathedral and died unmarried.

l. 32 *cobling stones*. 'Cobbles', water-worn rounded stones, especially of a size suitable for paving.

p. 280 l. 20 *my father Walton*. See Part I, p. 104, l. 4.

p. 282 l. 8 *Martin*. An animal of the weasel family which yields a valuable fur.

l. 33 *the whirl*. I do not know what part of the feather this is: cf. p. 288, l. 27.

Estridg. Ostrich.

p. 283 l. 15 *barb*. Clip.

l. 32 *Camlet*. A light stuff, made of the hair of the Angora goat.

p. 284 l. 1 *brended*. Brindled.

l. 17 *my father Walton*. See Part I, p. 107.

p. 285 l. 3 *Isabella coloured Mohair*. Isabella is greyish yellow. Queen Isabella of Spain, wife of King Ferdinand, vowed not to change her linen until the Moors had been driven from Spain, but since this took longer than she had expected her linen became of this colour.

l. 24 *a Skinners Lime-pits*. Pits in which tanners dress skins with lime to remove the hair, etc.

p. 286 l. 31 *Tammy*. Or 'tamin', a thin woollen or worsted stuff highly glazed.

p. 288 l. 27 *whirl*. See note to p. 282, l. 33.

p. 289 l. 1 *Cow-Lady*. Lady-bird, also called Lady-cow.

p. 290 l. 12 *turning into those two Flies*. Only the stone-fly comes from the caddis-worm. The green-drake is from a gnat which feeds under water in a hole dug in a bank, or under the shelter of loose weeds. – Rennie.

l. 23 *discloses*: i.e. discloses itself.

l. 34 *a Ship at Hull*: i.e. being driven by the force of the wind or current on the hull alone with sails furled.

p. 291 l. 25 *cross*. Across.

p. 292 l. 14 *the whisks of the tail*. A few long projecting hairs.

l. 15 *fitchet*. Polecat.

l. 18 *a Barbary Tree*. The barberry bush. Its bark yields a bright yellow dye.

l. 19 *Woody viss*. Or 'wiss', the moisture that exudes from bark in preparing it for tanning.

l. 25 *after he was absolutely gone*: i.e. after the last living fly of the species had disappeared.

p. 295 l. 19 *stream and still*: i.e. flowing and still water.

p. 296 l. 21 *diapred, or water-wings*. *Diapered* = adorned with a diaper or small uniform pattern, such as is found on the linen so called. *Water wings* are those of a fine transparent matter with no down on them – as a dragon-fly's, for example.

p. 297 l. 6 *yesty colour*: i.e. yellowish.

p. 298 l. 18 *Jersey Wool*. R. Holme, *Armoury* (1688), iii. 286, says, 'Jersey is the finest Wool taken out of other sorts of Wool by Combing it with a Jersey Comb.'

p. 299 l. 11 *Harry-long-leggs*. Now 'daddy-long-legs'.

l. 20 *dubbing pulld out of the lime of a Wall*. Hairs mixed in the mortar tend to make it stronger.

l. 25 *a sanded Hog*: i.e. of the colour of sand.

p. 300 l. 8 *snow-broth*. Melted snow. The word is in *Measure for Measure*, i. iv. 58, 'A man whose blood Is very snow-broth'.

l. 30 *hit of a day*. So first edition; but ? misprint for 'off' or 'on'.

p. 301 l. 12 *damming*. For all these poaching methods see Richard Jefferies, *Amateur Gamekeeper*, chap. viii.

p. 303 l. 3 *prevented*. Anticipated.

p. 304 l. 24 *hard stale Beer*. Beer becomes 'hard' or acid and also 'dead' or flat from being stale. For this purpose it is not to be so stale as to be quite flat.

l. 29 *Winter-Savoury*. See note to p. 144, l. 8.

p. 305 l. 26 *a good holding way*. I do not know why bottom fishing is more likely to retain the fish.

l. 31 *more, or less*: i.e. some days more, some days fewer.

p. 307 l. 7 *of two, or three handfuls long*. A handful or handbreadth or hand was a lineal measure of 4 inches; used now only in measuring the height of horses.

p. 308 l. 25 *the tail of a . . . stream*. A quiet part, where smooth water succeeds a swift or turbulent flow.

p. 309 l. 19 *lyes alwaies loose*: i.e. not among weeds, or in holes.

p. 310 l. 7 *the Ash-grub*. This and the dock-grub are both beetle-grubs.

p. 311 l. 34 *Oyl of Ospray*. Oil obtained from the *Pandion haliaetus*, a large bird of prey which preys on fish.

p. 312 l. 6 *artificially*. Skilfully.

l. 28 *those baits*. See Part I, p. 96.

p. 314 l. 10 *throwing in his Rod*. See note to p. 119, l. 7.

p. 317 l. 16 *a part of your Margin*. The marginal notes on pp. 260 and 278 are by Walton.

p. 320 l. 4 *intend*. Observe.

l. 29 *The Mause*. The Meuse.

p. 321 l. 15 *Caves*. There was a small natural cave in Beresford Dale in which Cotton used to hide from his creditors.

dog-star. Sirius, in the constellation of the Greater Dog, the brightest of the fixed stars. When rising nearly with the sun, it was supposed to cause excessive heat.

l. 32 *disgrace*. Disparage.

p. 322 l. 5 *Try, to live out to sixty*. He failed: he died in 1687, aged fifty-seven.

The Oxford World's Classics Website

www.worldsclassics.co.uk

- Information about new titles
- Explore the full range of Oxford World's Classics
- Links to other literary sites and the main OUP webpage
- Imaginative competitions, with bookish prizes
- Peruse *Compass*, the Oxford World's Classics magazine
- Articles by editors
- Extracts from Introductions
- A forum for discussion and feedback on the series
- Special information for teachers and lecturers

www.worldsclassics.co.uk

American Literature

British and Irish Literature

Children's Literature

Classics and Ancient Literature

Colonial Literature

Eastern Literature

European Literature

History

Medieval Literature

Oxford English Drama

Poetry

Philosophy

Politics

Religion

The Oxford Shakespeare
